Justin (Byung Uk) Lee (byunguk@gmail.com)

He got his BA and Master's degree of computer science at KAIST(Korea Advanced Institute of Science and Technology). He as a finance expert who majored in computer science got many 'first' in his life. While he was working for LG electronics, he went on a long business trip to Microsoft, Redmond, WA, USA to build the first Korean Windows CE version 1.0 and 2.0. He was the first to start service of real time auto insurance quotation comparison of all non-life insurers through online in 1999 when he established his own company. Later he worked for several life and non-life insurers which includes Samsung Life as a Chief Marketing Officer and as a Chief Sales & Marketing Officer. He was the first to launch a saving product which uses Equity-Linked-Security as its underlying. Later, he developed daily averaging savings product also for the first time in the world.

He got outstanding knowledge on blockchain and machine learning and is doing heavy activities in research area. He also does lecture on blockchain at various places such as Ministry of National Defense, universities and so on.

| Acknowledgement |

I thank my wife and two lovely sons who always supported me. Family always has been a major source of energy in everything.

I give special thanks to Byungsoo Kang of Carnegie Mellon University for his contribution in translating this book. He did great support in such a short period of time.

.

INTRODUCTION

Bitcoin has become the one of the hottest potato recently. Currently, its market price is over 240 billion USD and on a rollercoaster as I am writing this book. While Chinese government completely banned cryptocurrency exchange(a broker) and Korean government also announced they might will, Zug, a city in Switzerland, announced that they will accept bitcoin for their utility bills. What makes bitcoin such a focus of attention? Some say it is a revolution of modern technology, while others argue that it is a huge bubble and fraud often comparing it to the Tulip mania. Who is right in this debate? In short, both arguments are right. However, both arguments talk about completely different things. The speculation involving cryptocurrency looks pretty much like the Tulip mania. Nevertheless, the decentralization application area pioneered by blockchain, which was the base technology used for the first decentralized cryptocurrency, is a huge innovation and proposes many interesting questions on direction for a future system. The reason why those two arguments are in sharp contrast to each other is that the terms "Bitcoin" and "Blockchain" have been used intermingled without distinguishing between technology and application.

Bitcoin is far from legal tender nor would become in the future. As we will analyze in the second part of the book, let alone financial or economic functional aspects, bitcoin is too much inconvenient and defective to be a currency even from a technical point of view. This is because its original design was more concerned with robust implementation of the technology rather than convenience as a currency and this is quite natural considering the fact that inventor is scientist, not an economist. If someone claims that people should invest in bitcoin with the argument that it would become a future currency or describes government regulations on the speculation around cryptocurrency as suppression on future technology, he or she is either confused about the terminology or a totally unreliable scammer. Bitcoin is already like a critical patient in an intensive care with a respirator and an artificial heart, barely prolongs its life.

Although bitcoin is in a desperate need of an urgent surgery because of a design defect, the surgery is far out of the question due to conflicts of interest of stake holders, and all it can do is to get only an emergency medicine. In addition, those who believe they are heavily using cryptocurrency through so called exchange(from now on this book will refer to so called 'cryptocurrency exchange' as 'cryptocurrency broker' or simply broker and reason will be explained in coming chapter) actually have never been used the cryptocurrency at all. They are only busy internet banking through a virtual account between brokers and banks with USD![1]

Meanwhile, the blockchain technology, which is the base technology of bitcoin, has suggested a new way of constructing a computer system configuration more safely and efficiently without requiring too much individual cost, which used to require tremendous amount of investment. Also blockchain targets to remove unnecessary intermediary by using decentralized application concept. Blockchain resembles the concept of Collaborative Community of Sharing Economy. A considerable number of people voluntarily take over a distributed jobs and do the work that used to be done by a central server alone. Now, there is no need to invest an astronomical amount in a central server for security protection and maintenance, etc. The money saved would be distributed among the voluntary participants for their efforts. While the overall cost would be decreased significantly, the stability would improve dramatically. A win-win relationship has formed for everyone. If the industry, including the financial sector, doesn't fully understand the concept and benefit of blockchain properly and thus fails to adopt it, it might not be able to keep up with the competition in system implementation and effectiveness of maintenance as well as stability. Also, blockchain is expected to solve some problem of information asymmetry and unequal distribution of financial power between individual and big financial institute at the same time. It is anticipated that this will fundamentally help fix the problem of big institute alone endlessly accumulating private information without proper consent.

---

[1]Please refer to *5. Security and privacy*

As of 17th, Dec, 2017, there are already 1,376 known cryptocurrencies in the market, and in 2017 alone, nearly 600 new cryptocurrencies were launched. It is like there are 2 new cryptocurrencies every day. 8 years have passed since blockchain first appeared, and now it offers a convenient environment for every programmer to easily develop a cryptocurrency. All of the related technologies are free to use under the open source license policy. It is rather surprising to find out that there are only about 1,400 cryptocurrencies known to the market considering the easiness of making a new cryptocurrency.

I wrote this book to help people understand blockchain properly. In order to do so, a comprehensive analysis equipped with knowledge in both computer related technology and finance is required. However, the market is only filled with those monotone books such as a technical programming books about decentralized application programming, books that are madly praised by those who have a direct stake in cryptocurrency, or books that incite readers to trade bitcoin without having any technical or financial background. Even books with dozens of recommendations quoted often failed to distinguish between the general concept of blockchain and the specific concept of bitcoin blockchain or even made a wrong claims with an incorrect understanding of the technical part.

This book provides an in-depth analysis of cryptocurrency and blockchain, from both knowledge of technology and financial aspect. Through this, we will be able to view the future of cryptocurrency and blockchain as an unbiased, integrated opinion based on objective facts. It is never an easy job to clearly explain cryptocurrency and blockchain. On the technical side, it is necessary to discuss its data structure, algorithm, secure hash function and asymmetric cryptography behind it, as well as its general concepts. On the financial side, the concept of currency and investment, basic theory of economics, and game theory must be explained also. However, you should not worry too much about the contents that are unfamiliar to you because understanding new concepts is always fun, but not easy. This book is designed to approach the answers by repeatedly explaining story in chapter by chapter. For this, instead of explaining all of the challenging concepts in one place, the big picture is presented and individual concepts are explained little by little repeatedly. The key concepts will be constantly commented through a reference to the footnotes.

This book consists of 9 chapters in 2 parts and 5 appendices that include detailed technical descriptions. It is best to read the book in its natural order, but if a reader has a good understanding of the structure and fundamentals of bitcoin, then he or she may skip directly to Part 2 immediately. If the reader ever needs an understanding of the details while reading Part 2, the reader can go back to Part 1 on demand at any time and could find related materials.

Part 1 introduces bitcoin and blockchain in general then explain the technical side of bitcoin blockchain in detail.

Chapter 1 of Part 1 is an easy introduction which explains the general features of blockchain and bitcoin with illustrations. Chapter 2 defines terms related to blockchain and draws the big picture while explaining all of the operational principles of bitcoin and blockchain with ease. Chapter 3 introduces structure of a block and transaction which are key components of blockchain. In addition, Chapter 3 explains decentralized consensus and Proof-of-Work(PoW), which are also key concepts of blockchain. After reading up to Chapter 3, the readers will have a complete understanding of the superordinate concepts of blockchain and bitcoin.

Chapter 4 explores how the concepts introduced in Chapter 3 are actually implemented and therefore has the most technical descriptions. Chapters 3 and 4 can be seen as quite challenging by some readers. However, all of the particularly complicated technical parts will be explained separately in the appendices at the end of the book, and Chapter 4 will mostly focus on explaining the concepts. Chapter 4 explains the details of the hash puzzles of block known as a mathematical problem required to be solved to obtain bitcoin currency. Chapter 5 discusses the security and privacy issues of bitcoin and blockchain. We will define each element and learn more about what security issues can occur regarding each element.

Part 2 is the core of this book, which describes the economic and financial aspects of bitcoin and blockchain as well as their future.

Chapter 6 explains why it is impossible for bitcoin to be a currency, explore the design defects of bitcoin, and find out what kinds of discussions are ongoing to overcome those defects. Also, it will examine bitcoin as a currency and explain the greed of the evil circles involving cryptocurrency. In light of the definition of investment explained by Benjamin Graham, Warren Buffett's mentor, it will be explained why the mania surrounding cryptocurrency cannot be an investment. Chapter 7 investigates those who maximize their profits through cryptocurrency and focuses on the dark side of cryptocurrency including money laundering of black money.

Chapter 8 will discuss the future of bitcoin and cryptocurrency. As a result of analysis, we conclude that experiment of bitcoin as a currency is a total failure. In addition, the distinction between public cryptocurrency and commercial cryptocurrency will be introduced when we look into the future of cryptocurrency market. Chapter 9 spotlights potential of blockchain and its countless usages, irrelevant to the cryptocurrency mania. Also, it summarizes in detail the general consideration points required when designing a blockchain.

Target reader of this book

This book is written for everyone. I tried to incorporate the concept and functionality of bitcoin and blockchain and as well as their socioeconomic significance into this book. Therefore, I separated comprehensive analysis from in-depth technical dissection so that the readers can choose on their own. I organized the book in such a way that developers, the media, policymakers as well as the general public could have a clear understanding of cryptocurrency and blockchain. Through this, the general public will understand why bitcoin speculation can never be an investment, the media can use the book as a basis for more accurate reporting, and the government can refer to it as the base data for improving relative regulations.

A little bit of knowledge in computer terminology is required to read this book efficiently. The more knowledge you have about this field, the more you could get out of this book, but it is not mandatory for understanding the whole context. There will be parts that require some more knowledge for comprehension, but they have been marked separately and completely isolated from the context of the other parts. Thus, you should be able to understand the whole context even if you skip them. All of the technical contents related to blockchain itself were based on Satoshi Nakamoto's original online white paper, and all of the detailed technical contents about the implementation of bitcoin system were based on the technical documents of bitcoin.org, which currently operates and does the maintenance of bitcoin system.

This book was written in late 2017 and thus many of figures such as bitcoin USD price, number of cryptocurrencies might be different from the latest information. Due to high fluctuation of the bitcoin price, some value might not be accurate due to the market situation of the time of release of the book.

Conventions
All reference documents will be referred using alphabet from A to z.

Part 1explains the concept of bitcoin and blockchain as well as its base technology.

Chapter 1 covers the birth of bitcoin and blockchain and the basic terminologies about bitcoin blockchain. Chapter 2 gives the definition of blockchain and explains its operational principles in plain English. The material covered in Chapters 1 and 2 will be further analyzed in detail from Chapter 3.

Chapter 3, as a technical part, will clearly explain the concept and core technologies of bitcoin system.

Chapter 4 examines the underlying technologies of each concept. All technologies that constitute bitcoin system such as cryptographic hash function, asymmetric cryptography or public-key cryptography, block hash puzzle, block difficulty control, transaction, and merkle tree are explained in detail.

Chapter 5 explores the security, stability, and privacy issues of bitcoin and blockchain.

1. Birth of bitcoin and its Status

Chapter 1 outlines the background and current state of bitcoin and blockchain. Chapter 1 can be thought of as drawing a big picture for understanding bitcoin and blockchain. There you may face some unfamiliar terms or concepts, but you don't need to worry too much, for they will be repeatedly discussed in depth in the following chapters.

Chapter 1 will particularly touch on the following topics.

- Birth of bitcoin
- Unit of bitcoin and financial transaction
- Types of bitcoin unit
- Types of bitcoin face value
- Maximum reserves of bitcoin – 21 million bitcoins
- Why Satoshi developed bitcoin
- A currency not under the control of any country or institution
- Financial transaction which doesn't require a confidential intermediary
- Is issuing cryptocurrency legal?
- Appropriateness of the name of cryptocurrency
- The number of issued cryptocurrencies

1.1. Birth of bitcoin

On the evening of January 3rd, 2009 at 19:05, tension was apparent on Satoshi Nakamoto's face. The room was already quite dark, but street was still bright and clear. His eyes were sparkling more than ever. All coding and testing have already been done, but the launch was repeatedly being delayed due to minor problems happening at once. He had been awfully busy trying to fix several problems after posting his white paper online in the previous year, but anyhow he was finally finishing the project. The bottom of the empty coffee mug was covered with coffee powder like sand in the beach. Finally one press on the enter key would mean the creation of something that hadn't been known to the world ever before. Would Hephaestus have felt the same when he created Pandora, the very first woman, from soil? After moistening his throat with a sip of water, Satoshi Nakamoto calmly pressed the Enter key. 07:15:05 PM, January 3rd, 2009, Nakamoto's old computer generated the very first block after making mechanic noises for nearly 10 minutes to solve the hash puzzle. Genesis block, the very first block and blockchain, was born in the world at last! The name of the cryptocurrency that genesis block gave birth was bitcoin! Genesis block was only 285 bytes big, and the amount of bitcoin issued from mining the first block was 50 bitcoins. Bitcoin became the world's first blockchain based cryptocurrency, created through so called blockchain technology.

i Blockchain was implemented in 2009 by applying the concept explained in the white paper 'Bit coin: A Peer-to-Peer Electronic Cash System' published in 2008.[j] Because the author used the pseudonym 'Satoshi Nakamoto' when he (or possibly a group of people) published his paper, his real identity is still hidden in a veil of mystery until now. Recently, an Australian computer scientist named Craig Wright identified himself as Satoshi Nakamoto, and assuming from his private encryption key, it is almost certain that he is really Satoshi Nakamoto. Anyway, since a lot of people still use the name Satoshi Nakamoto and it could be a group of persons, we continue to refer to a real identity as Satoshi Nakamoto in this book.

Although genesis block was created on January 3rd, the actual operation of bitcoin started 5 days later from block 1, which was created at 12:54:25 PM (EST) on January 8th. Since then, new blocks have been created continuously every 10 minutes on average. Meanwhile creation time of genesis block was actually 02:15 AM (EST), January 3rd, but here I describe as 07:15 PM (AEST) for reality purposes since Craig Wright is from Australia. However, all the other times described in this book would be according to EST, i.e, GMT-5.

Up until December 18th, 2017, which marks 3,271 days since the creation of genesis block, over 500,000 blocks have been created. Also, unlike genesis block which has only one transaction recorded, recent blocks have over 2,000 transactions. Table 1-1 compares genesis block with the # 500,000 block. When genesis block was created, the subsidy was 50 bitcoins, while subsidy of # 500,000 block has now been reduced to 12.5 bitcoins only, which is about 25% of the initial subsidy. There are 2,701 transactions stored in the block 500,000. Also, regarding block difficulty, which tells how hard it is to create a block, it has been increased from 1 being genesis block's difficulty to 1,873,105,475,221.61 with the block # 500,000. To put it simply, it has become about 1.87 trillion times more difficult to make a block compared to making genesis block.

	Genesis block	# 500,000 Block
Block Number (Height)	0	500,000
Creation Time	2009-01-03	2017-12-18
Size (byte)	285	981,404
Total number of transactions in a block	1	2,701
Block Subsidy	50 Bitcoins	12.5 Bitcoins
Transaction Fee	0 Bitcoin	3.39351625 Bitcoins
Block Difficulty	1	1,873,105,475,221.61

Table 1-1 Comparison between Genesis block and block 500,000

Bitcoin is to be given in reward for generating a block. The reward is composed of subsidy, which is fixed, and transaction fee, which is variable. Genesis block gave out 50 bitcoins in subsidy and 0 bitcoin in fee. The block 500,000 gave out 12.5 bitcoins in subsidy and 3.39351625 bitcoins in fee, which amount to 15.89351625 bitcoins in total. Applying the current market price of bitcoin, which is roughly at 20,000 USD, Satoshi Nakamoto made 1M USD with genesis block, and the person who made the block # 500,000 got 300,000 USD for just 1 block. Satoshi Nakamoto is said to have mined over 1 million bitcoins so far, and it is worth about 20 billion USD. Satoshi Nakamoto would be among world wealthiest 30 people in the world. The content on subsidy is introduced in *1.3 Maximum reserves – 21 million bitcoins*, and commission, which is variable, is explained more in detail in *3.2.4 Transaction Fee*
3.2.4. Transaction Fee

Generally in computer science, block usually refers to a logical unit of data storage. Blocks in bitcoin act like storage for transaction history record. Anyone can attempt to create a new block, but not everyone is able to actually succeed in creating a block because one has to solve an attached quiz called hash puzzle to make a new block and that hash puzzle is extremely costly to solve. Blocks in bitcoin are chained together in the chronological order of creation and then stored. Because these blocks looked like they were chained up all together in a straight line when they are logically aligned and stored, people began to describe it as a blockchain, and soon the name settled as a proper noun. Figure 1-1 shows a depiction of blockchain. It will be explained in detail later that blocks are continuously being made every 10 minutes on average.

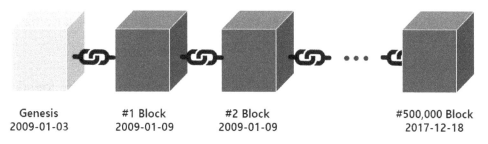

| Genesis | #1 Block | #2 Block | #500,000 Block |
| 2009-01-03 | 2009-01-09 | 2009-01-09 | 2017-12-18 |

Figure 1-1 Blocks standing in line in a blockchain

1.2. Bitcoin unit and transaction

US dollar system uses two units, the cent and the dollar, and there exists 13 different face values. There are 7 kinds of bills: 1, 2, 5, 10, 20, 50, and 100 dollars and 6 kinds of coins: 1, 5, 10, 25, 50, and 100 cents. All expenditures are made up of a combination of these face values. For example, you can pay someone 30 dollars with a 50 dollar bill then accept 20 dollars in change or simply with three 10 dollar bills. Now, let's find out how many units and face values bitcoin has.

1.2.1. Types of bitcoin unit

Similar to US dollar system, bitcoin uses two units. One is bitcoin and the other is satoshi. As USD is the abbreviation of US dollar, BTC is a usual abbreviation of bitcoin. Satoshi is often abbreviated as sat or s. 10 BTC is the same as 10 bitcoins, and 1000 s or 1000 sat is the same as 1000 satoshis.

While 100 cents make up a dollar in USD, in bitcoin, it takes 100 million satoshis to make a bitcoin. In other words, 1 satoshi is only equivalent to 0.00000001 bitcoin. For this reason, in some cases, intermediate units such as micro-bitcoin and milli-bitcoin are also used for convenience. Then, there are four units to bitcoin now. 1 satoshi becomes 0.00000001 BTC, 1 micro-bitcoin becomes 0.00001 BTC or 1000 sat, and 1 milli-bitcoin becomes 0.001 BTC or 100,000 sat.

From the fact that 1 million satoshis make 1 bitcoin, someone has even argued that 1BTC will eventually become equivalent to 100 million dollars. The somewhat weird logic behind this is that, if 1 satoshi become equivalent to 1 cent (why? Nobody knows) and thus at that moment, 1 bitcoin will automatically become 1 million dollars.

Also, John McAfee who is famous for his antivirus software and the founder of McAfee Associates, said on twitter the following:

"When I predicted bitcoin at $500,000 by the end of 2020, it used a model that predicted $5,000 at the end of 2017. BTC accelerated much faster than my model assumptions. I now predict bitcoin at $1 million by the end of 2020. I will eat my dick if wrong."

As of the end of 2017, total market capitalization of bitcoin has already reached 317B USD and surpassed that of Samsung. I don't know what model John McAfee used to predict this trend, but if 1BTC really become 1 million USD in 2020, then market capitalization of bitcoin will exceed the combined GDPs of France, Japan, and China and will tie to USA's GDP. Someday some bluffer's prediction might exceed entire sum of legal tenders on globe.

> *i* US dollar is a legal tender. A legal tender is a legally designated currency of a country whose circulation is enforced by law. American stores have the right not to accept euros but cannot refuse USD because the circulation of USD is forced by law. Normally, a country has its own legal tender and usually has only one unique legal tender, but there are countries that have more than one legal tender in the world. Among the 28 European countries that are often referred to as the Eurozone, 19 countries including Germany and France recognize the euro as a common legal tender. However, Zimbabwe announced to recognize legal tenders of 8 other countries which include the USD, Botswana Pula, British Pound, the euro, Australian dollar, Chinese yuan, Indian rupee, and Japanese yen as their legal tenders in 2014.

1.2.2. Types of bitcoin face value

Bitcoin does not have predetermined fixed set of face values. In other words, there could be infinite number of face values. As bitcoin number of transactions grow more diverse face value types are made by the size of the change.

As will be described in the next section, the total issue amount of bitcoin is fixed. Thus actual number of possible face values is not infinite but also is fixed. As the total amount of bitcoin is 21Million, the theoretical total possible number of face values is combinations of total BTC and satoshi, which is 21,000,000 × 100,000,000 + 1. Yes, it is practically no different from infinite but still is mathematically finite.

There are two interesting points to note in bitcoin transaction. One is that you cannot split the current bitcoin face value. For instance, if you have a face value of 5 BTC and you are supposed to pay only 3 BTC, you can't split the 5 BTC and pay only 3 BTC. You would have to pay the whole 5 BTC and need to get 2 BTC back as a change. This is conceptually completely in line with the fact that we can't pay a portion of bill by tearing a paper bill down in small pieces. Therefore, payment should always be done in its full just as a normal paper money, and the remaining amount is to be returned as a change. Another interesting fact about bitcoin transaction is that you don't receive your change from recipient. Interestingly, your recipient will always get the exact amount requested. Thus, he doesn't have to give you the change. Then, who is giving you the change? Let's look at the following figure.

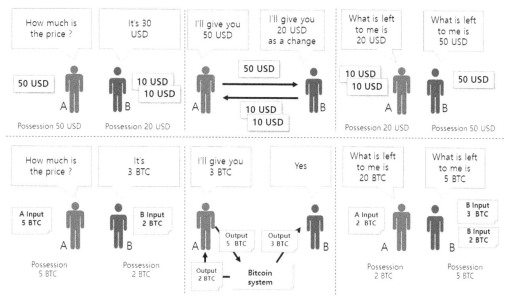

Figure 1-2 Comparison between normal transaction (above) and bitcoin transaction (below)

Figure 1-2 compares normal USD cash transaction with bitcoin transaction. In normal transaction illustrated above, one pays for the value of a product with a combination of banknotes and coins that have predetermined fixed face values and receives the change from the recipient with the same method. In this case, if the recipient is incapable of coming up with the exact precise combination of the change with his money, things may become awkward. Anyway, even if the transactions are repeated infinitely, the number of face value types, which is fixed at 13, never changes.

On the other hand, bitcoin transaction method is a little bit different. At the beginning, A has 5 BTC and B has 2 BTC. The number written inside the green box that says "input" is the amount of bitcoin each has possessed. A is trying to pay B 3 BTC for the price of a product. In this case 3 BTC does not directly go to B, but goes through the bitcoin network system and the following procedures.

- Step 1: Among all inputs which A has, bitcoin bitcoin wallet(wallet is a software and will be explained later) searches proper combination that can pay 3 BTC. In the illustration above, there is only 1 input, and its size

21

is 5 BTC. Since, it happens to be big enough to pay 3 BTC, this input is chosen.

- Step 2: A cannot split the chosen bitcoin, so A transfers the whole 5 BTC to bitcoin network system as shown in the yellow box. Bitcoin network recognizes that this sum is big enough to pay 3 BTC and that it truly belongs to A, so bitcoin system pays B exactly 3 BTC. Then, it gives A 2 BTC in change. In this process, B receives exactly 3 BTC, so B doesn't need to take care of the change.

- Step 3: As a result of the transaction, A is left with an input of 2 BTC, and B has 2 inputs, 3 BTC (received from A) and 2 BTC (initially belongs to B), which amount to 5 BTC.

In actual bitcoin transaction, the change A receives will always be less than the example above because all transactions must pay a fee. This part will be explained further in *3.2.4 Transaction fee*, but to summarize, all transactions in bitcoin system are considered valid only when they are recorded in a new block and then added to the blockchain data. At this point, you must pay a fee to the person who recorded your transaction history by making a block. The current minimum transaction fee is 1000 sat. Therefore, the actual change that A receives would be the amount left after the transaction minus that fee. If A pays 1000 sat as a fee in the example above, the actual change would be 1.99999(=2 − 0.00001). 1000 sat is about 20 cents if we apply current bitcoin price. You may think the transaction fee is not so much, but it's actually not that in reality. As of now, a transaction with the minimum fee of 1000 sat will hardly be processed. On average, people are paying 30 USD, 150 times more than the minimum. This fact will be very important in Part 2 of this book, so let's try to keep this in mind.

Looking at the bitcoin transaction in Figure 1-2, we can see that the transaction takes place through the bitcoin network rather than directly between A and B. The transaction happens indirectly through the bitcoin network without needing A and B directly communicate with each other.

1.3 Maximum reserves – 21 million bitcoins

Bitcoin is not issued by any institution, country, nor private company. Bitcoin system is not owned by anyone. Every member of the bitcoin system is deemed to be the owner. Satoshi Nakamoto, developer of bitcoin, has already left the project (forever) in 2010 for the independence of an operation, and now the system is being operated and maintained by a voluntary, non-profit developer group called bitcoin community.

i Bitcoins issued by system got owners, but the system itself does not. It is operated by a voluntary, non-profit group. The system evolves through decisions that have been agreed by the majority to be reasonable and objective rather than to benefit certain people. Meanwhile, cryptocurrency systems that appeared recently have owners, which means that they are developed and maintained by private companies. Of those cryptocurrencies, some don't even have a system of competition like mining. Moreover, there exists a cryptocurrency that is entirely owned by its owner from the birth. I strictly distinguish between public and commercial cryptocurrencies in that public cryptocurrency is operated voluntarily by a non-profit group, while commercial cryptocurrency is issued by a private enterprise. These two types of cryptocurrency have very different design directions, purposes, development and maintenance procedures as well as development backgrounds. This is one of the key topics of Part 2 and will be discussed more in *7.3 Commercial cryptocurrency* and *8.2. Future of Cryptocurrency*

Bitcoins are issued only when a new block is created, and the person who created the block receives those bitcoins. Creating a block or more commonly is referred to as a mining is an act of trying to get the subsidy and fee through issuing bitcoin as if mining gold in a gold mine. In this book, 'mining' and 'making block' are used interchangeably.

In order to make a new block, it is mandatory to complete an intentionally designed extremely costly steps which consume enormous computational resources over a certain period of time, and this is the basic mechanism of bitcoin blockchain for preventing manipulation and keep integrity. This is called Proof-Of-Work(PoW). You will soon be able to understand fully why PoW was referred to as an act of 'consuming computational resources over a certain period of time' as you read over *3.6 Proof-of-work – finding nonce*. A significant investment of resources including mass computing hardware, manpower, and a lot of electricity is required for proof-of-work. Therefore, in order to expect someone to make a block through PoW, which requires vast amounts of resources, one needs proper motivation, and that is the reward for mining.

One of the reason why we call the act of making block as 'mining' is that bitcoin is a finite resource. Earlier, I explained that the subsidy for making the first block was 50 BTC, but block subsidy in fact is designed to halve every 210,000 blocks. Let's take a look at the Figure 1-3.

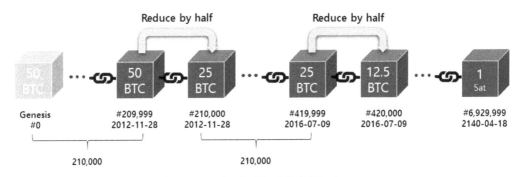

Figure 1-3 Bitcoin block Subsidy change

Figure 1-3 shows how the block subsidy halves every 210,000 blocks. For the first 210,000 blocks, the subsidy was 50 BTC, but the subsidy reduced in half with block #210,000, which is the 210,001st block (block number starts at 0). Likewise, from 02:36:13, July 9th, 2016, when block #420,000 was created, the subsidy once again reduced in half to 12.5 BTC. The reason why the block subsidy for block #500,000 (in Table 1-1) was 12.5 BTC is because the subsidy had already been reduced in half twice.

i Where do newly issued bitcoins get stored? It was already mentioned that blocks store transactions. If you look at the very first transaction of each block, you always find that its block subsidy is recorded there. For example, if you look at the first transaction of block #500,000, it is stated that 15.89351625 BTC has been paid. As it was explained in Table 1-1, it is the sum of the block subsidy 12.5 BTC and the fee 3.39351625 from the transactions.

Earlier, I explained that block difficulty is a measure of how difficult it is to create a new block. Bitcoin system automatically adjusts the difficulty periodically for every 2016 blocks so that it would always take 10 minutes on average to create a block. Block #420,000 was created on July 9th, 2016. Assuming that the system will continue to adjust the difficulty precisely and exactly, then we are able to come up with a graph in Figure 1-4 after some calculations. Because the subsidy will reduce in half every time 210,000 blocks are created, and there will be a newly created block every 10 minutes, we can easily calculate the total cumulative production of bitcoin. Bitcoin subsidy will no longer exist once the 6,930,000th block is created. Of course, miners will still be able to receive transaction fee even if the subsidy disappears.

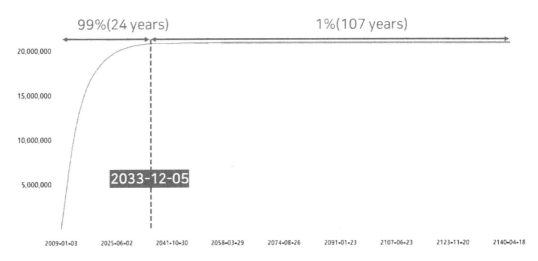

Figure 1-4 Total cumulative production of bitcoin

Figure 1-4 is a graph that shows the total cumulative production of bitcoin. Theoretically, the very last subsidy will be given with the creation of #6,929,999 block on April 18th, 2140, and subsidy will be only 1 satoshi. If you add up all of the bitcoins that will be issued until then, it would be exactly 21 million BTC. Theoretically, bitcoin is supposed to be issued over 131 years, but as you can see from the graph, 99% of the total issuance is to be done within the first 24 years, then only 1% of amount is to be issued over the remaining 107 years. Therefore, the actual depletion of bitcoin could be regarded as in 2033 instead of 2140. As the block subsidy reduces, bitcoin system environment will face a significant changes. This is because the motivation to create a block strongly weakens as the subsidy for proof-of-work reduces. Let's examine this more in depth in Part 2.

i The next subsidy half-life time is estimated to be on July 6th, 2020. From this point, the subsidy reduces to 6.25 BTC. Whether or not to continue mining even if the block subsidy is reduced by half once again is directly related to stability of bitcoin blockchain and sustainability. Stability of system will seriously and drastically decrease if the number of miners or block difficulty sharply decreases and could stop operating completely!

This is also related to 51% attack, which is one of intrinsic weakness of blockchain. I will explain about this more detail in ***3.6.2 51% attack***.

1.4 Why Satoshi developed bitcoin?

Satoshi Nakamto seemed to have followed cypherpunk spirit of David Chaum who firstly developed so called E-cash concept in 1981, which had something to do with protecting privacy of financial transaction. Later, Wei-Dai in 1998 and Hal finney in 2005 also followed similar spirit and proposed brand new concepts such as decentralized consensus and Proof-of-Work with computational puzzle respectively, which all became important building blocks of bitcoin system. In this sense the biggest target of Satoshi was simply to remove intermediaries in financial transaction for anonymity without so much as improving nor providing convenience in existing transaction system.

In this section, we will discuss on what values Satoshi was trying to bring through bitcoin in the sense of cypherpunk.

i The biggest value Satoshi Nakamoto explained throughout his paper is the removal of unnecessary fees. He pointed out that role of financial institutions as an active intermediary rather than a simple broker is the background of high fee. It seems that he probably disliked the fact that mediation could affect the transaction itself. What he ultimately suggested as a solution was a kind of transaction that could never be modified once written, and he called it completely irreversible. Currently, the core principle that allows bitcoin to keep its integrity is prohibitively irreversible property. Simply put, although it can't be completely irreversible, theoretically it can be somewhat completely irreversible stochastically. The expression 'prohibitively' not only implies its difficulty but also the fact that it is too difficult to manipulate so that it 'prohibit' someone from fraud and make them give up themselves.

Cypherpunk is a compound word of 'cryptography' and 'punk'. Cypherpunk refers to any activist who advocates cryptography as a tool to protect privacy. Normally David chaum is said to be the technical root of this activity and this can be guessed from title of his paper "Security without identification: Transaction System to Make Big Brother Obsolete". This movement is the result of resistance to reckless surveillance and serious invasion to privacy from government.

1.4.1. An independent currency not under the control of any country or institution

Bitcoin is issued by its own hard coded software logic within system. It is issued according to predefined set of rules, it is impossible to control the amount of issuance (unless some day community decides to change source code to expand an amount of issuance). Since its closed ecosystem is built on its own, it hoped to be an independent financial ecosystem from the external forces(actually this had never been the case for the reasons which will be explained in coming chapters). Also, bitcoin advocators insist that once the whole world adopts the bitcoin to commercial transaction, people won't have to worry about unnecessary fee nor foreign exchange rates and that bitcoin will become a perfect, defect-free currency no interest group can ever influence.

Controlling the amount of currency in circulation is directly connected to price stabilization. This used to be a purpose and mission of Central bank of each country. The Central bank controls the issue amount of currency and stabilizes prices through interest rate policies. The fact that bitcoin is free from external forces and independent may sound wonderful, but has no clear clue at all if that independence itself could truly bring values.

Though it will be examined more deeply in Part 2, arguing that a cryptocurrency is completely independent if it is being issued without any intervention is too naïve. Bitcoin can be purchased with a legal tender at any time. Therefore, it is strongly subordinate and linked to legal tenders. As long as cryptocurrency is traded with legal tenders (and yes, it will be forever) it can never truly be independent. Rich guys around the world have enough legal tender to purchase bitcoin at any time and also fully aware of how to sell bitcoin back to the public with enough margin. Value of bitcoin in legal tender is completely controlled by supply and demand. If you have the power to control the circulation, you can control the price at any time because bitcoin doesn't have any intrinsic value at all by itself. If all the legal tenders on earth have disappeared and bitcoin has replaced their position (of course this will absolutely never happen), then it would be after all the rich people have already exchanged enough of their legal tender wealth to bitcoin.

Bitcoin cannot be in circulation without being closely tied to price against legal tender. All the stores would frequently change the prices of their products according to price of bitcoin linked to legal tenders. If the menu of the store is a booklet rather than a tablet, then the store wouldn't display the prices because they can change anytime.

1.4.2. Financial transaction without trusted third party

Alex met with Diana at a restaurant to buy a used laptop directly from her.

Alex and Diana will be meeting again in *2.2 Basic principles of Bitcoin blockchain* for the same reason, so let's keep the situation in mind for later. As it turns out, Alex was a bad guy. We will find out why later.

The laptop was in good condition, and Alex decided to pay Diana 400 USD, so on the spot, he used his smartphone to transfer 400 USD to Diana. Even though Alex and Diana used different banks, but the transfer didn't even take 30 seconds. Soon, the two left the restaurant, Diana withdrew 400 USD from the ATM machine installed in front of the restaurant, and the two went their separate ways happily. This account transfer may seem like nothing, but there actually were at least 4 institutions involved and 3 steps to be taken. Let's look at the next illustration.

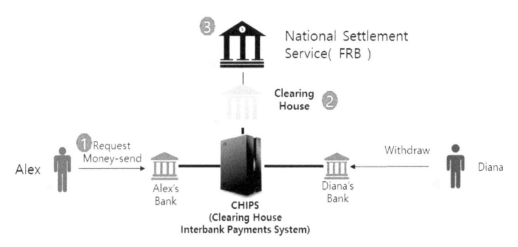

Figure 1-5 Payment through CHIPS

Figure 1-5 shows how the transfer is made between Alex and Diana. For this transaction to take place, 4 institutions, Alex's bank, Diana's bank, Clearing House, and National Settlement Service(NSS), are involved. Now, Alex, Diana, and the 4 institutions carry out the following 3 steps.

①　Payment: Alex requests his bank to pay 400 USD to Diana's account at her bank. Alex's bank checks if there is anything wrong with this request. If everything is OK with Alex's balance, Alex's bank requests Diana's bank to pay Diana 400 USD. Upon receiving the request, Diana's bank immediately pays 400 USD to her. This task is called 'payment'. Even though the transaction between Alex and Diana is over after this payment, but in fact, it is not over between Alex's bank and Diana's bank. Diana's bank still needs to receive the 400 USD from Alex's bank which it paid to Diana on behalf of Alex's bank. These remaining processes are called clearing and settlement.

② Clearing: Clearing House calculates the total amount of money that should be exchanged between Alex's bank and Diana's bank. This task is called clearing.

③ Settlement: NSS has an accounts opened by each bank. NSS transfers the amount calculated by the Clearing House from Alex's bank to Diana's bank.

A system that handles both the payment and settlement of monetary values is commonly referred to as payment system. Payment system is a key part of the basic infrastructure of financial transaction of one country, and the efficiency and reliability of the payment system is one of the most important key indicators for measuring the financial development level of the country. Construction of payment system requires billions of dollars and it requires a lot of manpower and cost for maintenance and operation.

Bitcoin system is a payment system, but there is no intervention of any institutes as in figure above. This is because it has eliminated the need for it. Each person directly performs payment, clearing, and settlement. Also, it's been implemented in a way that clearing itself becomes settlement. Satoshi Nakamoto believed that it is possible to eliminate all the unnecessary transaction fees through this innovation. In 2016, US banks collected 34.6 billion USD as fee income.

i Ironically, bitcoin transaction fee of today is never cheap at all. Rather, it is on average tens of times expensive than bank, and it's constantly increasing to 100 times of that of bank. Satoshi Nakamoto strongly argued that small transactions are being critically impeded by expensive transaction fee of bank, but actually, bitcoin transaction fee is unfavorable to small transactions. Bitcoin charges for the size of the transaction data in bytes instead of the transaction amount. Whether you trade 1M USD or just 1 USD, the transaction fee would be the same as long as it has same bytes size in transaction description. Bitcoin system favors large amounts and is against small amounts. For now, there is no need to trade less than 10 ~ 20 USD at all because the transaction fee cost is higher than that! This is also highly related to sustainability issue of bitcoin and will be discussed more detail in *8.1.2. The fee strikes back*

Most people introduce blockchain only as a distributed ledger, but I always emphasize about its payment system aspect. This is not only because ledger is only a small part of the payment system but also because it gives a passive impression that all it does is just recording. The early version of blockchain, which is used by bitcoin, doesn't support a complete smart contract, so it may seem passive. However, the latest blockchain supports smart contract by default, so it is no longer just a passive ledger but an active and self-executing payment system. Significance and functionality of smart contract will be discussed more in *4.3.2.2. Smart Contract.* Another point to note is that distributed ledger cannot reflect big difference between distributed system and decentralized system. Currently, there are many systems which use distributed ledger but not a blockchain at all in strict terms.

The reason for an intervention of a reliable institution in financial transactions is for the complete trust of given transactions. We don't need to worry about using credit cards and doing account transfers in real life because we (normally) strongly believe that financial transactions are always recorded honestly as long as a trustworthy financial institutions are involved in the middle. Though it has been a long belief that financial transactions could not be done without the involvement of trustworthy financial institutions, Satoshi Nakamoto showed that reliable financial transaction could actually be possible without financial institutions with the help of blockchain. He described this as 'proof has replaced trust'. With blockchain technology, individuals keep copy of every transactions on their ledgers directly instead of banks, and the technology is designed to enforce only true records to be kept and detect and reject manipulations immediately. This is possible because blockchain is capable of proving if a given record is true or not at all times.

> *i* Strictly speaking, it is more proper to say that proof creates trust rather than saying proof replaces trust. In any cases a transaction without trust cannot be possible. Thus, the claim that proof replaces trust could be regarded that we trust that proof. We will revisit this topic in ***3.3 Trust vs. Proof.***

Like the terms payment, clearing and settlement were not so quite trivial to comprehend, the terms mediation, brokerage and relay is not so straightforward. The role of relay could be seen as it is included in the role of mediation, but the two concepts can also be seen completely separately. Mediation basically means a third party's active intervention and this concept is closest to what is meant as a third party by Satoshi Nakamoto. Satoshi Nakamoto believed irreversible transactions that are impossible to be mediated to be ideal. But this belief is a little bit impractical. There are lots of situations that requires mediation in financial activities. There are times when someone's mediation is necessary. For example, if you lost your credit card and have to suspend the use of the credit card, or you sent money to a wrong bank account number, someone has to intervene. Also, there should be ways to find or reset your forgotten passwords. Bitcoin system never allows individual's mistakes. If a mistake happens, then that's it. If you forget your password, then that's it. You can never recover your lost bitcoins. There is no going back. Of course, there aren't any institutions to intervene. One click of a button, and that is the end. What is done is done. You cannot revert what has been done in any cases. It's completely irreversible. Is this irreversibility with no intermediary is really ideal?

1.5. Is issuing cryptocurrency legal?

Who makes cryptocurrency? Can someone issue a cryptocurrency simply because he or she wants to? Whether it is legal or not to issue a new cryptocurrency may vary from one country to another. Most countries don't have clear legal provisions regarding this matter. Since criminal laws regarding currency in most countries only deal with the forgery of legal tenders or checks issued by financial institutions and possession or circulation of forged banknotes and checks, issuing a new currency won't be restricted by law as long as it doesn't counterfeit any legal tenders or checks. However, some countries do punish manufacturing of anything similar to a currency even if it's not a forgery, but this is also only confined to manufacturing of things that are similar to banknotes circulated within a country or abroad, so it can be interpreted that issuing a cryptocurrency is not restricted as long as there is no similarity between the cryptocurrency and the legal tender.

But the fact that issuing cryptocurrency is OK just because it has no relation to legal tender means that we are now confusedly saying currency to something that is completely not related to currency at all!

1.5.1. Appropriateness of the Name 'Cryptocurrency'

It is clear that the term, cryptocurrency, surely cause a lot of confusions to the general public. Terms like cryptocurrency and bitcoin implicitly appeal to people as legal tenders due to its name. In fact, the question on legality of issuing a cryptocurrency itself could be a nonsense. When people talk of currency in real life, they always mean the legal tender. Since cryptocurrencies are not legal tenders, above question does not make sense at all. Such a question only exists because its name includes word 'currency'. Whether cryptocurrency or bitcoin is a currency or not will be more fully discussed in *Chapter 6 Currency and Bitcoin*.

According to the true concept of blockchain, cryptocurrency just exists only for the sake of sustainability of blockchain. In this sense, a term such as token or other similar one must be used instead of cryptocurrency. However, in case of bitcoin, things are complete opposite. Bitcoin blockchain exists only for the sake of a cryptocurrency. Blockchain which exists only for the purpose of cryptocurrency is useless and need to be removed for the reasons explained in chapter 8 unless someone really finds a good reason to override my argument in chapter 8.

Blockchain can serve various purposes which include financial transaction, proof of identity or event, legal presentation, or anything which script can describe. In this case, blockchain exists for some specific mission (of course never include a purpose of cryptocurrency) and token is given to participants. Token is a compensation to be given to those who put their efforts into operation of blockchain. Participants can use their tokens to receive something that has been predetermined beforehand such as legal tender or its equivalent.

i There is a cocktail called Long Island Iced Tea. It's basically a strong, cold drink made of liquors that are over 40% ALC / 80 Proof such as rum, vodka, or tequila. Long Island Iced Tea Corporation [2] located in New York borrowed its name from the popular cocktail. The company is famous for its black tea and lemonade and is listed on NASDAQ. The closing price of the company on December 20th, 2017, was 2.44 USD. However, on the next day, stock price increase by 271%, and the closing price was at 6.61 USD. The reason behind such a sharp rise was unexpected. It was all only because the company announced to change the name of the company to Long Blockchain Corporation. By putting the word 'blockchain' in the name of the company, its stock price increased by 271% over one day. The company continues to maintain its stock price in the 5 USD range since then. Later NASDAQ gave the company warning to make unlisted unless they stop deluding investors by using unrelated name. In many situations people are never reasonable.

1.6. The number of Cryptocurrencies

---

[2] Ticker symbol in Nasdaq is LTEA

8 years have been passed since the advent of bitcoin which is the first blockchain based cryptocurrency. Then how many cryptocurrencies are there in the market since the creation of bitcoin?

As of December 28th, 2017, 1,376 cryptocurrencies are registered on CoinMarketCap[3], and about 600 new cryptocurrencies emerged in 2017 alone. Also, there are 7,716[4] cryptocurrency brokers that are commonly referred to as cryptocurrency exchanges. The biggest reason that there are so many cryptocurrencies on the market is that the implementation technology is relatively simple and the development environment is well constructed. Also, source codes can be used for free for most of the technologies. Some of the cryptocurrencies may be well-designed based on their own philosophies, but most of them are just useless another clones which are made only for economic gains from speculation and scam.

Let alone the question of whether we can use the word 'asset' when we estimate an economic value of cryptocurrency, which will be discussed separately in Part 2, it is quite surprising to know the total amount of assets of all 1,376 cryptocurrencies. As of December 28th, 2017, the total amount of asset of all of the cryptocurrencies in the market is 617 bn USD, and bitcoin alone accounts for 46.2%, which is 285 bn USD. If there is a person who is trying to make money by mining, I would rather recommend him to make a new cryptocurrency (We will learn more in *2.3.3.3 The league of their own – Mining*, it is almost impossible for an individual to succeed in mining).

Because market price of a cryptocurrency varies from country to country, the total amount of asset varies depending on which price one bases for one's calculation. For example, total amount of asset of bitcoin calculated according to the U.S. market price was 285bn USD, but if it were calculated in Korea, it would be 325bn USD instead. Market price of bitcoin is around 20 ~ 30% higher in Korea

---

[3] http://www.coinmarketcap.com
[4] As of 7th May, 2018, there are 1,614 cryptocurrencies and 10,776 brokers.

than in U.S. Even within the same country, market prices of cryptocurrencies vary from broker to broker. Because of this, a term cryptocurrency exchange is wrong, and thus, cryptocurrency broker would be more proper term. This is because, instead of gathering all the supplies and demands in one unified trading rate, each broker has its own supplies and demands and acts as an individual broker. It is easier to understand if you think about the listed stock market and over-the-counter stock brokerage. Like the word 'cryptocurrency' gives a wrong impression that it is an actual currency, it is a kind of sales gimmick in which they use the term 'exchange' and appeal to people as a feeling of stock exchange market. These brokers even use the term 'blockchain exchange' and further intensify the confusion. From now on, only the term 'cryptocurrency broker' will be used instead of 'cryptocurrency exchange' throughout the book.

Meanwhile, these differences in the market prices of cryptocurrencies quite well shows the pitfall of using unrealized gain as a measure of asset value. Alex, who retails cranberry, is worried because he bought 1,000 pound cranberries for 20 dollars per pound but sales are not so good. People won't even buy his cranberry for even 20 dollars per pound. However, thanksgiving is next week. As thanksgiving is around the corner, the price of cranberry skyrocketed, and people are now willing to pay 100 dollars for a pound of cranberry. Alex is now very excited. Alex now generates a profit of around 80 USD for every pound he sells, so he can make about 80,000 USD if he could sell all his cranberry. But, as the price of his cranberry was too high, he was able to sell only 200 pounds of cranberry. The thanksgiving holidays ended, the demand for cranberry dropped again, and now nobody would pay even 15 USD for a pound of cranberry.

People are always bound to make the most of their limited resources because money isn't infinite. Those who would normally buy a certain pounds of cranberries are forced to control their consumption by reducing a purchase amount within an appropriate range of total expenditure according to the increased prices. Discussion on realized gain and unrealized gain will be further detailed in **6.3.4 realized gain and unrealized gain**.

Deceiving consumers with unrealized (market) price is the most frequently used technique by pyramid selling companies. The critical mathematical error behind this scam used by pyramid selling companies is that they always assume the resources and demand are infinite. Of course, this fact is completely concealed from the victims. People tend to go wild over unrealized (market) prices because the prices are too tempting to have them stay reasonable and look for the deception behind it. The previously mentioned argument that 1 bitcoin will eventually be equivalent to 1 million USD is in a similar context. The argument only anticipated the future of 1 bitcoin price but overlooked the fact that asset of bitcoin will exceed the GDP of US. GDP of United States is 18.6 trillion USD. If money were infinite, it may be possible scenario but there even can be situation in which expectation for bitcoin asset continue to be overblown to the point where its asset exceeds entire legal tenders on earth. We will discuss this more in Part 2.

Following table shows the top 10 cryptocurrencies according to their total assets as of December 28th, 2017.

	Name	Total Asset (USD)	Unit Price (USD)	Total # issued so far
1	Bitcoin	284,869,003,650	16,989	16,767,850 BTC
2	Ethereum	70,327,460,695	727.86	96,622,236 ETH
3	Ripple	52,685,236,992	1.36	38,739,144,847 XRP
4	Bitcoin Cash	44,813,071,540	2654.73	16,880,463 BCH
5	Litecoin	13,723,940,654	251.77	54,509,833 LTC
6	Cardano	10,094,108,591	0.389327	25,927,070,538 ADA
7	IOTA	9,561,584,174	3.44	2,779,530,283 MIOTA
8	Dash	8,592,819,310	1104.44	7,780,250 DASH
9	NEM	7,947,116,999	0.883013	8,999,999,999 XEM
10	Monero	5,834,796,461	375.73	15,529,227 XMR

Table 1-2 Top 10 cryptocurrencies due to total asset

Each cryptocurrency has slightly different properties. For the most part, they have the same basic concepts such as mining reward and mining difficulty, but their compensation systems and difficulty systems are different from one another. For example, the total amount of bitcoin available for mining until 2140 is only 21 million BTC while ethereum issues 18 million ethers every year. As a result, as of the end of December, 2017, the amount of ethers mined so far has already reached 96.67 million, which is nearly 6 times of bitcoins mined over the past 8 years. On the other hand, ripple doesn't have the mining system at all. Rather, the company issued 100 billion coins(XPR) all of which were owned by themselves from the beginning. Also, although bitcoin is designed to create a block every 10 minutes, ethereum creates its block every 15 seconds, ripple does so every 4 seconds, and 'dash' argues that they process their transactions in real time. While bitcoin blockchain is based on Proof-of-Work, ethereum is in the process of developing a new algorithm called Casper which is based on Proof-of-Stake. Bitcoin Cash set the size of the initial block to 8M and allowed it to be modified later in order to remove the limit on bitcoin block size of 1M. Also, Z-cash and bitcoin gold are designed in such a way that mining by using ASIC machines is impossible.

It is quite interesting to know that despite the fact that bitcoin is the very first blockchain cryptocurrency and thus got lots of design defects and also is comparatively unstable which is still somewhat in its experimental stage, but it is the most beloved in the market. Cryptocurrencies that came about after bitcoin were created by improving many defects of bitcoin and by newly defining various characteristics. Thus, we can say these cryptocurrencies normally are functionally better, but they haven't attracted enough public attention compared to bitcoin. There will be even more new types of cryptocurrencies in the future, but none of them will be able to stand against bitcoin for long. Although this is of course a result of the preemption effect, it could also be interpreted that the public's selection criteria doesn't really care about functionality or usability. This is because a lot of people think of cryptocurrency as a speculation object and don't plan to actually use in real life. Therefore, for the purpose of speculation, preemption effect of bitcoin is a far more useful value than its functionality as a currency.

By the way, then who made all these 1,376 cryptocurrencies? Do cryptocurrencies have owners? If so, would the owners be individuals or corporations? If corporations owned cryptocurrencies, who own those corporations?

If you were a wealthy man, how would you make money regarding cryptocurrency? There are several ways. First, you can expect to make future gains from buying several cryptocurrencies including bitcoin. Another way is to personally establish a company and issue a cryptocurrency on your own. The last method of increasing your wealth regarding cryptocurrency is to acquire shares of an already established cryptocurrency-issuing company. Which method would be the best? The wealthy don't hesitate about the best choice. They can implement all these methods at the same time, and they are already doing so. This is the very reason why cryptocurrency can never be independent nor an ideal currency. Contrary to Satoshi Nakamoto's naive wish, cryptocurrency is a perfect tool for greedy shark to exploit other's pocket. Whenever their avarice is exposed, they utilize blockchain as a shield arguing that attack against them is a persecution to emerging technology called blockchain. This tactics work fabulously because people can hardly tell cryptocurrency from blockchain. The shark always misleads people to believe that cryptocurrency is identical to blockchain itself and cannot be separated, which is a complete nonsense. We will look more into this point later in Part 2 alongside concepts such as public cryptocurrency and commercial cryptocurrency.

Summary

- Bitcoin is the cryptocurrency which uses blockchain technology and was created on January 3rd, 2009.

- If you compare between the genesis block and # 500,000 block, the number of transaction recorded in the block increased from 1 to 2,701, and the difficulty of making a block increased by 1.837 trillion times.
- Bitcoin doesn't have a fixed set number of face values, so a new face value is created every time there is a change.
- Bitcoin uses two units, bitcoin(BTC) and satoshi(sat). 100 million sat is equivalent to 1 BTC.
- Bitcoin is only issued when a new block is created, and the subsidy of bitcoin issued periodically halves so that no more bitcoin will be issued after the 6.93 millionth block is created. Thus the sum of a total number of bitcoins issued and will be issued in the future is limited to 21 million.
- The person who created the block receives a block reward, and the block reward consists of a fixed amount of subsidy and a variable amount of transaction fee.
- Bitcoin was created to serve the following two purposes.
    - Independent of any country or institution
    - Financial transaction that doesn't require trusted third party
- The term cryptocurrency is confusing and misleading for the word currency within the term causes confusion with legal tender.
- As of December 28th, 2017, 1,376 cryptocurrencies are registered on CoinMarketCap and traded on 7,717 cryptocurrency brokers.

2. Definition of blockchain and its operating principle

In Chapter 1, we learned about the birth of bitcoin and discussed its current status. In Chapter 2, we will review various terms surrounding bitcoin and blockchain in order to minimize the confusion on terminology and examine the basic operating principle of bitcoin. Chapter 2 will cover the following topics.

- Terminology – Bitcoin and Blockchain
  - Centralized System vs. Distributed(Decentralized) System
  - Definition of Blockchain and Bitcoin
  - other terminology
- Basic Operating Principle of Bitcoin Blockchain
- Using bitcoin
  - Bitcoin Wallet
  - Full node and Simple Payment Verification(SPV) node
- Creating a block – Mining

2.1. Defining terminology – Blockchain and Bitcoin

In 2.1, we give definitions to the terms that will be used throughout the book. It is never easy to clearly define what blockchain is. Blockchain is a technology, a data structure, and an algorithm at the same time. It would be too broad and comprehensive if we define blockchain using all these aspects, and if we focus only on a specific aspect, then the definition would become too narrow. Actually, Satoshi Nakamoto never used the proper noun blockchain at all. All he ever used were a common noun block and chain. The word 'blockchain' transitioned from a common to a proper noun later as people started using it as they read and interpreted the paper. Therefore, the definition of blockchain is the process of collecting what people commonly interpret that paper and make it a formal sentence.

Blockchain will be defined twice in the book. The first definition will be from the perspective of finance and a little bit biased to cryptocurrency for the convenience of explanation, while the second definition will be the closest to its true nature. The first definition, which is more frequently used one from the perspective of finance, will be given in this chapter, then I will give the substantive definition of it later at the end of the book.

This books is to explain about blockchain, and we've only finished Chapter 1 so far. Therefore, definition of blockchain given in this chapter is more likely meant to minimize the confusion from the terminology for later explanations. So, it is totally fine even if you don't understand it immediately. The definition in this chapter is only supposed to help the reader avoid confusion from unfamiliar terms and suggest reader areas to read more carefully.

To begin with let's first consider the difference between centralized system and distributed system. We can't explain blockchain without distinguishing between centralized system and distributed system.

2.1.1. Centralized vs. Decentralized System

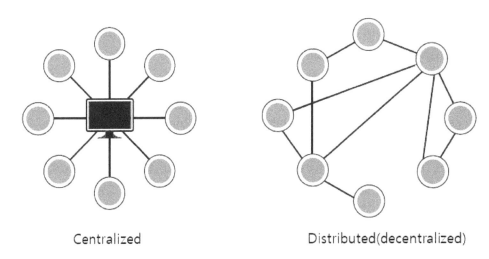

Centralized   Distributed(decentralized)

Figure 2-1 Centralized System and distributed (Decentralized) System

Figure 2-1 compares typical centralized system and distributed system. The circles refer to nodes (individual computers) connected to the network. One difference that's quite obvious to notice after just looking at the figure is that in centralized system, all nodes are directly connected to a central server, whereas in distributed system, there isn't no central server and thus there is no one node that is directly connected to all of the other nodes. However, all nodes are connected to one another indirectly. Distributed system is sometimes also known as a decentralized system.[5]

In a centralized system, its central control system, which serves as a server, provides all of the services. Each node requests the server for a service and waits

---

[5] Actually distributed and decentralized system is a quite different and will be detailed later in this section.

for a result. All data is to be recorded in the centralized system. However, if there happens a failure in centralized system then all service gets stopped. Internet banking is a typical example of a centralized system. Users log on to the centralized system of the bank, request for services, and wait for results. All of the transactions are recorded securely in the database of a bank.

A distributed system does not have a centralized control unit. Every node is basically equal. Services are usually processed individually on a per-node basis. Generally, the nodes don't know about each other. Although services are well distributed and processed properly within the system, it is normally impossible to know how the services are distributed. One extreme example of a distributed system would be the Peer-to-Peer system, commonly known as P2P system. Napster, or file sharing that uses torrent are typical examples. Users download specific files but do know whose computers they are downloading their files from. Ultimately, you may be downloading your requested music or files onto your computer, but those files may come from the next door or from down under. Of course, someone is downloading the file shared from your computer as you are downloading it onto yours. The most fundamental characteristic of a P2P system like this is that every node is a consumer and provider at the same time and has equal rights and responsibilities.

i Blockchain is similar to the spirits of sharing economy and collaborative community. Blockchain can be compared to a small ecosystem. What used to be done by a central server alone is now distributed among and done by lots of voluntary participants. Therefore, there is no more need to invest an astronomical amount to construct, maintain, and operate a central server. The money saved is distributed among those who voluntarily participate in the system according to established rules. This method not only greatly reduces the total cost but also improves security and stability dramatically. Also, the distribution of the saved money forms a Win-Win relationship among all the participants in the ecosystem. We will learn more about this in *Chapter 9 The future of blockchain.*

2.1.2. Definition of Blockchain and Bitcoin

Now, we are ready to define what blockchain is. Previously, I mentioned that blockchain is a concept that includes technology, data structure, and algorithm. Though there are numerous definitions of blockchain in the market already, if we digest the most common one and combine formerly defined several definition then we can reach our first and concise definition of blockchain as follows.

"Blockchain is the base technology of a decentralized ledger which can be safely used in an anonymous system."

Blockchain refers to a technology. Sometimes it is explained in the point of decentralized ledger or a technology of decentralized ledger. In this book, we will refer to a technology of decentralized ledger. Thus, it is a holistic concept and not limited to a specific application.

i Bitcoin is the name of the first cryptocurrency implemented using blockchain technology. From now on, a term bitcoin alone only means the name of the cryptocurrency. In other cases, terms like 'bitcoin blockchain' and 'bitcoin system' will be used instead. As briefly explained earlier, there are currently 1,376 different cryptocurrencies. All of them use blockchain, but the methods of implementation are all different. Thus, bitcoin blockchain and ethereum blockchain are totally different from each other and are separately classified.

All the terms used in the book from now will generally follow below rules.
- o Blockchain refers to a technology. Thus, blockchain and blockchain technology are the same.
- o Other than that, we'll add a corresponding term after blockchain. For example, blockchain data or blockchain algorithm will be used.
- o When referring to programs and methods of implementation for which blockchain is used in a specific application area, we will use the word

system. Bitcoin system refers to programs and their methods of implementation for which blockchain is applied to the field of bitcoin cryptocurrency.

○ Bitcoin is the name of a specific cryptocurrency. In other cases, we will add a corresponding term at the end like the case of blockchain.

Distributed ledger and decentralized ledger is a way different concept. If we don't discriminate terms between distributed and decentralized then there is overlap between traditional distributed network and blockchain network. Actually many blockchains in the market is actually not a blockchain but more close to traditional distributed network in strict term. As I go further to the topic in coming chapters you will more clearly see the difference of distributed and decentralized.

2.1.3. Explanation of additional terminology

In this section, we will clarify and organize additional terms that used to be intermixed and confused. Just like language itself evolves, technical terms also evolve to reflect more practical aspects of properties. Here, we try to uniquely pin point one representative term among several confusing similar words in order to help people better understand the context of the book.

2.1.3.1. Cryptocurrency vs. Virtual Currency – Cryptocurrency

Cryptocurrency, digital currency, virtual currency, cyber currency, and e-currency are extensively used in the market. Generally these terms usually mean similar things, but they are different from each other, strictly speaking. Virtual currency emphasizes the aspect that the currency exists without substance, and digital currency emphasizes that value display and storage is digitalized. Cryptocurrency emphasizes that issuance, transaction, and storage of the currency is protected by an encryption technique. Since normally digitalized currencies use encryption techniques, digital currency is basically cryptocurrency.

Bitcoin is a digital currency and a cryptocurrency at the same time. Recently there is real material for bitcoin such as coin shaped bitcoin or plastic card with some real bitcoin amount attached as a face value. Then now bitcoin is no longer a virtual? Also, if a legal tender is digitalized, then it becomes a digital legal tender and this is exactly the way we use through internet or smart phone banking. Therefore, a digital currency is not necessarily a virtual currency. Thus not a single term can depict bitcoin. However following the trend where the people recently heavily use a term cryptocurrency to refer to a blockchain based currency, we follows that trend and will use cryptocurrency to refer to bitcoin like blockchain based digital cash. However please note that this is not because cryptocurrency is a proper term but because we just choose one that majority people prefer to use.

Conceptually, there isn't one specific term that seems better than the others, but I will only use the term cryptocurrency throughout the book unless there is a special reason. It is because the term cryptocurrency is used for most of the time in the industry that is leading the blockchain technology.

> *i* European Central Bank defined virtual currency as "a digital representation of value that is neither issued by a central bank or a public authority, nor necessarily attached to a fiat currency, but is accepted by natural or legal persons as a means of payment and can be transferred, stored or traded electronically" However this definition cannot explain government triggered one such as Venezuela petroleum based cryptocurrency. And on top of that, bitcoin is never a generally accepted payment tool at all. This loose and a bit coarse definition shows one aspect of the chaos and misunderstanding on cryptocurrency seen to authoritative institution.

2.1.3.2. Distributed vs. Decentralized – Decentralized

The term decentralized has begun to be used heavily recently. This is because the term 'distributed' is a very wide and extensive concept, and thus, cannot fairly represent key feature of blockchain. Therefore, the term decentralized has completely replaced the term distributed and has been rapidly spreading among cryptocurrency developers. The key distinction between these two concepts can be explained as follows.

The essence of a distributed system is the distribution of work. It is not so discrepant from the definition of a distributed system in a broad sense even if a certain node intervenes unilaterally in order to control either the distribution or synthesis of work as long as work is distributed. However, it cannot be a decentralized system. No nodes can ever intervene in the distribution or synthesis of work in a decentralized system. In other words, a distributed system is a broad concept only observed from the perspective of distributing work, whereas a system can be considered to be decentralized only when it is a distributed system and also doesn't allow any node to intervene in the distribution and synthesis of work at all times. If there is a node that serves a particular role, then a hacker's target becomes obvious. Thus, it could be understood that the concept of blockchain becomes more blurred as the parity of all the nodes in the system gets disrupted.

i Most technology become stronger when it is combined with other one. Technology hardly can survive alone in its isolation. Distributed and centralized systems were also the case. In many situations a hybrid of the two systems were much more efficient and useful. Therefore, whether blockchain as perfect isolated decentralized system is right or not remains to be seen. Actually, some of the cryptocurrencies that were introduced recently assign each nodes different tasks. This trend is expected to be intensified as blockchain begins to be used commercially. Since blockchain is originally designed to be completely public and this feature of blockchain conflicts with commercial needs in many cases.

The reason why blockchain is much safer from hacking is that hackers cannot pick a clear target to attack. Under a centralized system, there exists a clear target to attack which is the central server that presumably has most valuable information and control power at single place. However, a blockchain-based system where all the nodes are basically equal doesn't have a clear target to attack. Even though hackers successfully intrude a couple of nodes, that's it. It will never affect the rest of universe.

Hereafter in this book, I will use the term decentralized instead of distributed. Therefore, distributed consensus, distributed system, and distributed application are all replaced by decentralized consensus, decentralized system, and decentralized application.

2.1.3.3. Node, Peer, and Computer

When discussing a network, the terms node, peer, computer, and user are often intermixed and used in wrong contexts. Although these terms are not so clearly distinguished from each other, generally we refers to all the computers or users participating in a network as nodes. Among these many nodes, those that are directly connected with you are called peers. In this sense, a term 'computer' was looked at from a computing resource's viewpoint, and a term 'user' was looked at from an actual user's viewpoint. Meanwhile, if you look at the decentralized system in Figure 2-1, the node at the top has two peers because it is connected to two nodes, one to the left and the other to the right, while the node on the bottom is only connected to one node to the left, so it has one peer. There are 8 nodes in total in the network, but each node is connected to a different number of peers. This book also distinguishes between a node and a peer in the same manner.

2.2. Operating Principle of Bitcoin Blockchain

Earlier, it was briefly explained that the name blockchain originated from the description of the logical data structure in which blocks are lined up in chains. In an analogy to everyday life, if we compare blockchain data to a financial ledger book, it would look like the following figure.

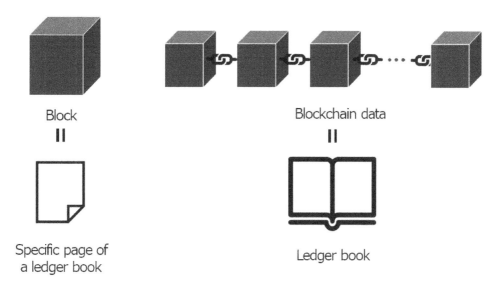

Figure 2-2 Comparison between blockchain data and traditional ledger book

Figure 2-2 shows comparison between blockchain data and traditional ledger book. Each block in blockchain data can be compared to a specific page in a ledger book. As all these pages make up a ledger book, the blocks come together make a whole blockchain data. If you look into every block, you can see all the transactions that took place since genesis block was generated. As of the end of December, 2017, over 500,000 blocks have been created. Observing all the blocks starting from the genesis block will let you examine all the transactions that have ever taken place for the past 8 years since bitcoin was created! Another interesting fact is that the blockchain data contains over 500,000 blocks are stored not in one specific server. Previously, I explained that a decentralized system does not have a central server. Therefore, this blockchain data is duplicated and stored in every participant's computer individually in the system. Let's look at the next figure.

💡 As mentioned several times, each block got 2,000 ~ 3,000 transactions stored in it. Let's not be confused that a block has just one transaction only because a block was compared to a page of a ledger.

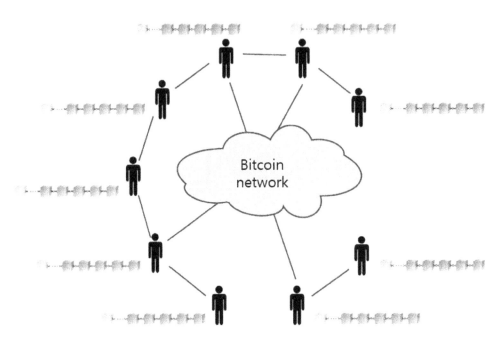

Figure 2-3 Every participants of the system stores blockchain data individually

Figure 2-3 shows how everyone stores the entire blockchain data individually. Yellow block in front of the blockchain data stored in each one symbolize the genesis block. You can see that all the blocks and transactions stored in blockchain data since 2009 since genesis block was created.[6] Thus, a particular node examining a transaction means that it examines a data stored in its own local computer not asking to some server or something.

---

[6] There are around 290,000,000 transactions happened during the period.

The transaction method itself is also quite different from the conventional centralized system. Let's look at the following figure.

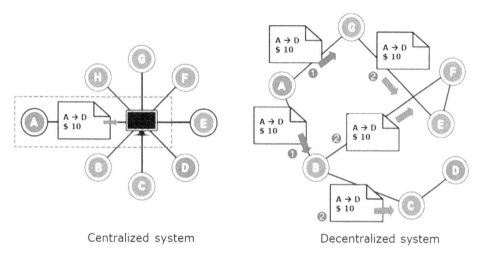

Centralized system   Decentralized system

Figure 2-4 Method of dealing a transaction

Figure 2-4 shows how a centralized system and a decentralized system each deals with a transaction where node A tries to transfer money to node D. In the centralized system on the left of the figure, node A connects to his bank and fills out his account transfer request form. Filled out request form is processed by the central server of bank safely, and the result gets stored in the database of a central server as well. Later, when D connects to bank and checks an account balance, he can verify that A has properly wired the money. Nevertheless, all the processes for the account transfer happens only within the dotted lines in the left figure. All the other nodes including D doesn't participate in this account transfer.

On the other hand, under the bitcoin system where the concept of central server is not existent, node A broadcasts the information to all the other nodes after compiling the transfer request. Let's look at the right side of Figure. ① Node A broadcasts the transaction form, which he filled out, to nodes B and G who are directly connected to him. ② B and G then relay the transaction that they received to their respective peers F, C and E. This process is repeated until all nodes in the system receive the transaction. For D to actually receive the bitcoin, someone (of course possibly including A and D themselves) must make a block and record that transaction into newly made block.

Each node is to verify if the requested transaction well comply the given rules. If the transaction violated the rules, then it would be immediately discarded. Transaction that have been well constructed complying the rules will be queued in the waiting room of every node until it gets stored to newly made block.

> *i*   Both in centralized and decentralized system, it is an only one node which records a transaction at a given moment. The difference is that in centralized system, recording node is predetermined and is fixed while in decentralized system, node which records transaction is to be selected every round. The right to record a transaction at a given round is given to the node which gets the hash puzzle answer first. Thus, one secret of every distributed nodes could have an identical data at all times is from the fact that the data is in fact written only by (chosen) one and not by every node.

All nodes participate in a block making competition in order to get a block reward. The reason why making a block is a competition is because only the very first node which succeeded in making a block wins, and all the other losing nodes' work will be discarded in vain. In order to make a block, a node has to solve a very difficult puzzle called hash puzzle. After putting all transactions that are to be processed into a block template, which is a template for a new block, all nodes start to find an answer to hash puzzle. This block template will only become a valid block once the answer to hash puzzle is found. We call the answer to a hash puzzle a 'nonce'. A node which succeeded in finding the nonce immediately broadcasts the completed block to the other nodes just like the way a node broadcasts a transaction. This is to make other node add a newly created block to the existing blockchain data of each node. After receiving the new block, nodes will investigate the block if it is valid by the verification rule and check if all the transactions stored in the block are ok. If the block passes all the tests, then it gets added to the blockchain data, and the length of blockchain data increases by 1.

i After one node broadcasts newly made block, the role of all other nodes is either to agree on or to abandon that block. If all nodes agree on that block then consensus is made. Agreement should be unanimity. Agreement is not an arbitrary discretion but a result of sanity check. Once the sanity check is passed, all node must agree, but if there is a bleach of rule in block then node must abandon the block. Thus the process of synchronizing status of all node is simply, firstly to elect someone who records a transactions and then agree on that record. If everything is OK in the process of electing (=solving hash puzzle), recording and agreeing, then distributed consensus is achieved!

Once the winner of the block making competition is settled and block is added to existing blockchain data, then all other nodes immediately discard what they were doing and start a new competition for the next block. This competition is usually repeated every 10 minutes. This is because the system is constantly adjusting the difficulty of the hash puzzles so that it would take 10 minutes on average to solve a hash puzzle. A block can roughly contain 2,000 ~ 3,000 transactions. Since 144 block are created daily (because a block is created every 10 minutes) the daily processing capacity is around 300,000 transactions. Sometimes the capacity of bitcoin system is said to be around 7 TPS(transaction per seconds) but actually it hardly can process 2,000 ~ 2,500 transactions per 10 minute, which results in only around 3 ~ 4 TPS.[7]

i It is one of the fatal problems of bitcoin that only 144 blocks are created per day and the maximum capacity of a block is limited to 1 megabyte in size. Because of this limitation, no matter how much the number of

---

[7] 7 TPS is only theoretical maximum and would hardly happen in real time scenario

transactions grows, the processing capacity cannot be increased. This is will be discussed again in detail *3.7.3 Segwit and Segwit 2x* and *8.1.2 The fee strikes back.*

All transactions in the bitcoin system should be written according to given set of rules. Someone may try to violate the rules through manipulation, but the system is designed to immediately detect any bleach that doesn't abide by the rules using the secure hash technique that will be explained in *4.1. Hash function*. It could be possible to try to manipulate system by complying with secure hash function logic, but the system is designed to require a prohibitively expensive cost to do so. Thus, no one will even dare to attempt such an idea.

Meanwhile, as it can be guessed from Figure 2-4, the time it takes a transaction to be broadcasted to all the nodes would be all different from node to node. This is because the network capacity and response time of the computer is different for every node, and some nodes can even be asleep with their computers shut down due to the geographical time difference on earth. If the node is asleep and is disconnected from bitcoin system, then it is unable to receive the transactions that happened while it was disconnected. But when the computer is turned on the next day and connects to the network, it receives all the late transactions and blocks that have been created at once, verifies them according to the rules, and then add them to the blockchain data in order to catch up its data with that of the rest of the nodes. Like this, all the transactions and blockchain data that are stored individually may not necessarily be exactly the same among all nodes at some given point. However, the status of all the nodes will 'eventually' synchronize with each other as time goes by through an algorithm called decentralized consensus.

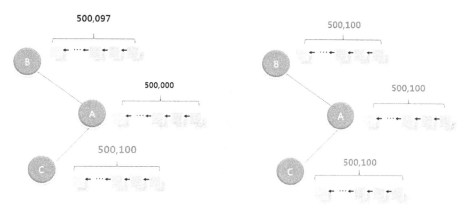

Figure 2-5 Conceptual diagram which briefly explains decentralized consensus

Figure 2-5 is a conceptual diagram which briefly explain the concept of decentralized consensus. Node A which was asleep over the night then connected again to the system will notice that its data is different from data of its peer as it connects to the bitcoin system. While it has 500,000 blocks, node B has 500,097, and node C has 500,100 blocks. C has the most blocks, which is 3 more than B's. The rule is very simple. Choose the blockchain data which required the greatest efforts in construction. If all the individual block requires the same amount of effort or energy, then the longest blockchain data would be selected, but if the required effort is different for each block, then weighted sum should be calculated in order to help choose the heaviest blockchain data and then copy the contents. It is shown in the figure that A and B adds blocks according to C's blockchain data, which is the longest, and ultimately A, B, and C's blockchain data would reach a consensus.

i When two blockchain data conflicts each other, the one that has more accumulated energy invested in making always win the game. This concept exactly coincides with the longest blockchain data in most of cases. Seldom, this may not be the case because difficulty of block changes periodically. However, since "the blockchain data that has the biggest accumulated energy invested in making" is too lengthy and unclear, thus we will refer to it as 'the heaviest blockchain data' instead from now on.

Ironically Satoshi Nakamoto only used the term 'the longest chain' in his paper.

Proof-of-Work(PoW) in bitcoin system can be summarized as a process of finding a nonce, an answer to a hash puzzle. Previously, it was mentioned that one must pay a prohibitively expensive cost in order to manipulate blockchain data and cover up the traces. This prohibitively expensive cost is directly related to PoW and nonce. When a transaction in a block or any item in block is manipulated, the nonce value changes, so one has to find a new nonce value again. Even though one managed to find new nonce for manipulated block that's not enough. He or she not only needs to find a new nonce but also needs to make a heaviest blockchain data. Otherwise newly manipulated blockchain data will be lost a battle against heavier blockchain data and will be discarded. Thus some other blockchain data that is heavier will eventually replace manipulated data. As a result, one must be continuously creating blocks and manipulating at the same time until one catches up with all of the blockchain data in the system and outrun them.

Not only the probability of winning this competition is extremely low, but also there aren't enough reasons to do so anyway. The fact that one is capable of manipulating the blockchain data means that one has significant hash power capacity to be able to make a new block by winning a block making competition. Then theoretically, it is much more profitable to produce new blocks and get block rewards than struggling to manipulate block. That is, not only is blockchain data manipulation very improbable, but also manipulation itself should be done under predefined set of rules! (Otherwise the block which violated a given rule will be discarded immediately no matter heavy it is) This will be explained more in detail in *3.6.2 51% Attack*. Therefore, people naturally give up the idea of manipulating the data and stick to produce blocks, and a virtuous cycle forms as a result.

A virtuous cycle in which people stick to produce honest blocks instead of attempting manipulation due to higher reward can be conversely interpreted that people might cease to produce honest blocks and attempt to manipulate the data once the reward for producing blocks is not enough. Previously, it was said that the reward reduces by half every time 210,000 blocks have been produced (roughly every 4 years). As this will be explained again in Part 2, this problem is one of the critical defects bitcoin has and could even threaten the very existence of bitcoin.

Now, it may seem like all the problems are solved and a safe ledger has been made, but the biggest problem still remains. It is a problem of double spending, which arises from the fact that each node has different condition in receiving broadcasted data due to network bandwidth and computing resources, etc. Double spending refers to the attempt to spend a single bitcoin multiple times. Attempting to spend a bitcoin more than once can be prevented effectively by the rule set of bitcoin blockchain.

Alex and Diana from *1.4.2 Financial transaction without trusted* reappears, but this time, they are conducting a trade using bitcoin. As already mentioned, Alex was a bad guy. Let's look at following situation to find out why.

Alex(node A) and Diana(node D) met each other for a direct transaction. Diana plans to sell her second hand laptop, and Alex is paying 400 dollars for the laptop. After checking the item, Alex agrees to pay Diana 400 USD worth in bitcoin, so Alex gives Diana 0.02 BTC which corresponds to 400 USD according to the market price of bitcoin. Alex transfers 0.02 BTC to Diana using the bitcoin wallet (a program which uses bitcoin that will be explained in the next section) while Diana is watching. After Alex completed his transfer request, Diana goes back home in relief. Should Diana really be in relief? Some of you who are sharp-sighted may have already picked up that Alex only finished the transfer request but didn't quite complete the transfer itself. Because if 10 minutes haven't passed, a block is not even created. Transfer request is only letting the other nodes know of the transaction in which Alex intends to pay Diana 0.02 BTC. Now, let's find out what could happen.

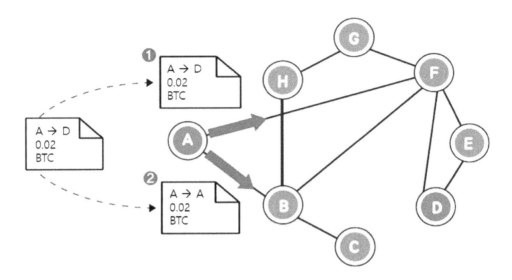

Figure 2-6 Alex attempts double spending

Figure 2-6 shows a situation where Alex is attempting double spending. Immediately after parting with Diana, Alex makes another transaction and also broadcasts it to the system, a request that he pays himself with the same bitcoin which he used to pay Diana just before. Alex is trying to spend the same bitcoin twice. Alex is thinking that if the second transaction gets processed first, he may be able to intercept the bitcoin to be paid to Diana. Now, let's take a closer look at what kinds of scenario could happen.

In this case, we cannot know whether the normal request, ①, will be processed first or ② will be processed first because it depends on the condition of the network. There are two possible outcome of this attempt.

The most probable outcome is that ① and ② both get discarded. When each node gets transaction, it first examine if given transactions follow rules. If both ① and ② have been simultaneously delivered to a node that is currently making a block, the node will immediately know that two different transactions are attempting to use the same bitcoin and would discard both of them. The second situation is that only one of either ① or ② gets processed and recorded. This situation happens when only either of one is delivered to a node which is making a block and the other one is not yet delivered due to network latency. Since neither of them have been confirmed to be spent, both are deemed normal yet. Thus, the block records the transaction that has been delivered first and adds it to the blockchain data. As soon as one of the two transactions get added to the blockchain data, the other transaction becomes an abnormal transaction which has violated the rules. Thus, if ① gets processed first, ② gets discarded and vice versa.

It should be noted here that even though blockchain technically solved the problem of double spending but did not solve it in terms of commerce activity. Although bitcoin system figured a technical way to perfectly prevent bitcoins from being spent twice, it cannot distinguish between well-intentioned and ill-intentioned transactions. Also, it cannot guarantee that transactions that are submitted first will get processed first. We will discuss this problem again in *i* Due to such a problem, bitcoin transaction must be watched for a certain period of time once it is submitted. It has been mentioned that it takes roughly 10 minutes for block to be produced. This means that it takes at least 10 minutes to record a transaction. It would take even much more time to check the double spending problem. Such inconvenience is one of the main reasons why bitcoin is not quite suitable to be used as a currency in real life. We will talk about how long it really takes to be safe about the double spending problem in *3.4 Double spending and Authentication.*

2.3. Using Bitcoin

Steps needed to be taken in order to use bitcoin are actually quite simple. Once you download a bitcoin wallet, you are basically all ready to use bitcoin, and downloading a bitcoin wallet takes less than a minute. However, there is not much that you can do until you actually get some bitcoin from someone even if you have downloaded the bitcoin wallet.

2.3.1. Bitcoin Wallet

The minimum software required to actually use bitcoin is bitcoin wallet. Once you install bitcoin wallet you can connect to bitcoin system and thus start transaction. Bitcoin wallet generates account called bitcoin address for you and also generates private and public keys for secure transaction.

There are a numerous number of wallet programs in the market. Recently released wallets let you trade multiple cryptocurrencies including bitcoin and even support exchanges between different cryptocurrencies. For example, you can exchange bitcoin with ethereum right away. A bitcoin wallet has three main roles.

- Generation and maintenance of private/public key for account management

- Submission of bitcoin transactions to the system
- Management of bitcoin balance

2.3.1.1 Generation and Maintenance of private/public key for account management

Bitcoin transactions take place using bitcoin addresses. Thus bitcoin address is like bank account number. Bitcoin address has information about public key which could verify the owner of an account. Public key is a core safety mechanism for bitcoin transaction. Contents related to keys will be discussed in detail in *4.2. Cryptography*

Once a bitcoin wallet is downloaded, firstly two keys are generated for the user. The generated keys are very important information which will protect all of the transactions in the future. Bitcoin system uses an asymmetric cryptography technique which maintains security by publishing a pair of keys. Between the two keys that make a pair with one another, public key is shared among others and private key(also called secret key) is kept in secret from the others. Since private key is the only way to confirm the owner, there may be no way to recover it once it's lost or exposed to others.

Bitcoin system is decentralized. As a result, it doesn't have anything like a customer center as banks do. If your private key is lost or stolen, there is no way to solve the issue. Therefore, the only solution is to always thoroughly make backups and make sure that your key is not exposed to others. If you forget your bank account password, you may visit a bank or make a call to a customer center, then you can reset the password after identifying yourself, but under bitcoin system, an irrevocable damage can happen if you cannot take care of your own security. This is one aspect that shows bitcoin is never a tool for public but is a tool only for someone who have certain amount of computer knowledge at the moment.

For this and several reasons, bitcoin wallet provides a number of safety mechanisms. It offers various ways to back-up and lets you easily change bitcoin addresses to protect account. As we will discuss more in *5.1.3. Bitcoin wallet – individual security,* bitcoin wallet should be chosen carefully. The market is flooded with various bitcoin wallets, and some of them could be terribly weak in security. There may even be a program that are made by hackers to look like a bitcoin wallet. Because of this problem, there are a number of physical devices on the market that function as wallets as a hardware instead of software. This will be discussed briefly in the next section.

2.3.1.2. Submission of Bitcoin transactions to the system

The main purpose of a bitcoin wallet is to write a bitcoin transaction and submit it to the system. To submit a bitcoin transaction to the system, you must get the bitcoin address of the recipient and then create the transaction according to the rule. Following figure shows how a bitcoin transaction looks like in bitcoin wallet.

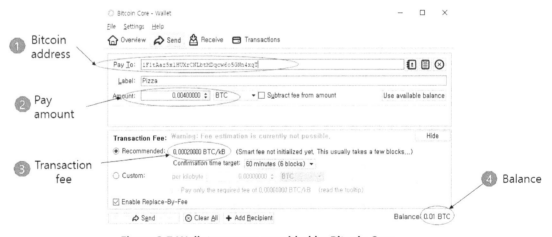

Figure 2-7 Wallet program provided by Bitcoin Core

① shows the bitcoin address of the recipient. The address does not contain anything about the recipient's name or other personal information. This address contains information about the recipient's public key, as described above. ② shows the amount of bitcoin to be transferred. Current displayed unit is BTC, but it can be changed to milli-BTC or Micro-BTC for convenience. ③ shows the transaction fee. In the figure, the transaction fee is 1000 sat, which is the minimum fee. ④ shows the total balance. The amount of coin to be spent in ② cannot exceed the balance of ④.

As mentioned in the previous section, there are many hardware bitcoin wallets in the market. In most cases, all the data is stored in a separate physical device, and you connect it to a computer like you do with a USB device only when you want to use it. Considering the convenience and performance of the latest smartphones, you may not feel the need to use a separate physical device, but if you read through *5.1.3. Bitcoin wallet – individual security* you will understand that the usefulness of a hardware bitcoin wallet is in its safety and security rather than convenience. Following figure shows bitcoin wallets that are actually being sold on Amazon. Cheap ones cost about 75 USD, but expensive ones can go up to 200 USD.

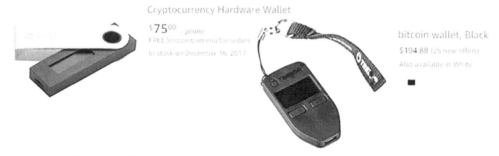

Figure 2-8 Hardware bitcoin wallets which are being sold on Amazon

 Simply memorizing your password is not enough. If your private key is stored on your smart phone and you lost your smart phone you have no way to recover the key and thus will lose everything. If your smart phone is broken then you'll lose all your bitcoin!

2.3.1.3. Management of bitcoin balance

Bitcoins are not stored in single block but stored in several blocks scattered along blockchain data. As explained in Figure 1-2, at the end of the transaction (at the bottom of the figure), after entering into the transaction, the input of B was not combined into single 5 BTC but was drawn separately as 3 BTC and 2 BTC, respectively. These bitcoin balances are always kept scattered over several blocks. In the case of B, the two inputs are stored in different blocks. Depending on the time and sender of a bitcoin, bitcoin transactions are all recorded on different blocks. Therefore, for the purpose of convenience, it is necessary to logically gather bitcoins that are scattered in numerous blocks and display the total amount.

Figure 2-9 shows how a bitcoin wallet calculates the total balance of B, in which the inputs are scattered in two different blocks.

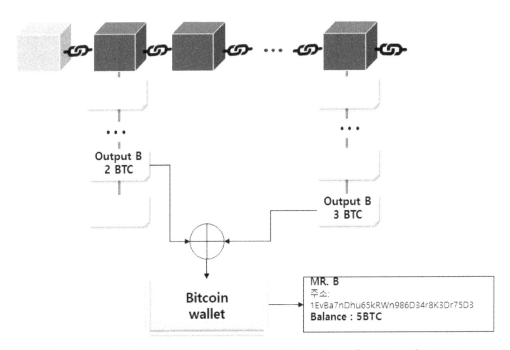

Figure 2-9 Role of wallet to create a combined view of scattered outputs

As bitcoins are scattered around many blocks and each block does not contain any historical global status data at all, bitcoin blockchain is sometimes called a 'blind' blockchain. To understand history on specific bitcoin, one has to look up every blocks by tracing back. A blockchain which came later than bitcoin such as ethereum does not follow this convention but has concept of an account. Ethereum keeps track of status of an account in the form of TRIE[8] data structure and thus has no need to trace back like bitcoin.

It should be noted here that bitcoin wallet simply serves to display the total amount of logically summed up balances in the wallet program for the sake of the user's convenience and cannot affect the contents of actual blockchain data. Therefore, it is displayed in total but the actual balances are still remains to be scattered over different blocks. Meanwhile, bitcoin wallet can also determine which bitcoin fragment (or collection of them) should be used when user needs to spend bitcoin. Thanks to this feature, users can feel as if their bitcoins were combined in one. It is not important to the users which block has which bitcoin or how their bitcoins are scattered. The only important thing is the total balance.

So far, bitcoin transactions have been portrayed as if they were using personal name, but it is only a conceptual explanation for convenience. In practice, only bitcoin address which is made up of complex codes is being used. Figure 2-10 shows a typical bitcoin address used for bitcoin transaction.

---

[8] TRIE is a tree structure which has radix(or prefix) based index. We won't discuss about this structure at this book

Figure 2-10 Bitcoin address and its QR code

Bitcoin address always starts with 1^9 and its length is variable with around 34 characters. This address is not an arbitrary one but a generated one through complex rule. Bitcoin address contains many information regarding the owner of this bitcoin, which is a public key information of an owner. As bitcoin address is quite complex to human eye, normally people uses QR code instead.

2.3.2. Full Node and Simplified Payment Verification Node

2.3.2.1. Full Node

The general philosophy of a decentralized system is that all nodes have the same rights and duties and perform exactly the same role. However, it is somewhat unrealistic that every node has to store blockchain data which could be possibly enormously large. So, Satoshi Nakamoto, from the beginning, designed two different types when implementing the system: one is full node and the other is simple payment verification(SPV) node. The reason for this is that it is never an easy task to receive entire blockchain data. Currently, to download entire blockchain data of more than 500,000 blocks, one must receive data of about 150

---

[9] You can see detailed explanation at **appendix C**. Actually there is a case where bitcoin address starts with 3 and you can see the explanation at **4.3.2.1. PTPKH.**

~ 160 GB. It is obviously impossible for a person using a smartphone to download 150 ~ 160 gigabytes just to use bitcoin. Therefore, all of the nodes constituting the current bitcoin network is differentiated between nodes which has downloaded the entire blockchain data and nodes which only downloaded the necessary minimal information. A node that downloads and stores all the data is called a full node, and a node that downloads only the minimum information is called a simple payment verification(SPV) node. Of course, it is entirely up to users to decide which node they would join as.

Do you remember we discuss earlier that bitcoin has around 4~5 TPS(Transactions Per Second) capacity. The average TPS of VISA credit card is 2,000 and can handle 4,000 in high peak. Theoretically VISA can handle 56,000 TPS. If someday bitcoin is improved to handle 4,000 TPS then it roughly would generate 115G bytes data a day and 42 T bytes an year. This is basically the biggest concern of all blockchain applications. By the way, this is another reason that bitcoin has no chance to be a currency even in the future. No node would effectively copy 115G bytes data every day!

To become a full node, you need to install bitcoin core client software from bitcoin.org or bitcoincore.org. The bitcoin core is a client software that provides an interface that can use all the functions of bitcoin system. As of December 2017, version 0.15.1 is distributed as the latest version. A full node can perform the role of validating a transaction submitted to the system through bitcoin core and also generating a new block. The minimum computer specification required to be a full node recommended by bitcoin.org is as follows:

- Desktop or laptop with an operating system of the latest version (Windows, Mac OS X, or Linux)
- At least 180 GB of disk space
- 2 GB of RAM memory
- Broadband internet access with upload speed at least 400Kb (50K bytes) per second

- Stay connected for at least 6 hours per day

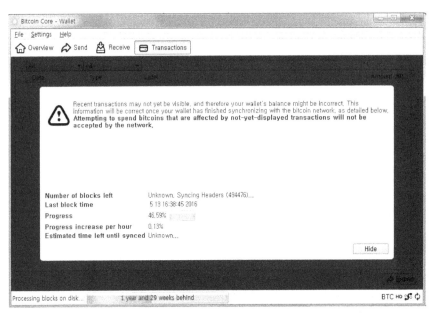

Figure 2-11 Bitcoin core is downloading blockchain data

Figure 2-11 shows what it looks like to download the entire blockchain data using bitcoin core. The process of downloading a whole block is almost similar to the process of receiving a shared file through a P2P tool such as torrent. The download speed varies depending on the status of the peer nodes that are directly connected at the moment of downloading.

When you first connect to bitcoin system, how do you know where the full nodes are and what are their IP addresses? In the normal network service there are name servers that record the IP addresses of each node, usually called the DNS or Domain Name Server. Similarly bitcoin core has a name server called DNS Seed, which tells the IP address of the currently active full nodes. Bitcoin core has a hard-coded function that tells the IP of this DNS seed. Therefore, bitcoin core first finds the DNS seed through the hard-coded function, and the DNS seed informs the IP addresses of currently active full nodes. The DNS seed servers continuously search each

70

node, dynamically updates the IP addresses of the currently active full nodes, and inform the latest information whenever there is a request. The DNS seed is maintained by some of the bitcoin community members.

Debug window

Information | Console | Network Traffic | Peers

NodeId	Node/Service	User Agent	Ping
88	173.9.80.250:8333	/Satoshi:0.15.1/	393 ms
89	75.126.126.220:8333	/Satoshi:0.15.0.1/	350 ms
90	73.246.115.182:8333	/Satoshi:0.15.1/	271 ms
91	155.4.210.149:8333	/Satoshi:0.15.1/	308 ms
92	185.35.139.250:8333	/Satoshi:0.14.0/	618 ms
93	2.227.253.109:8333	/Satoshi:0.15.0.1/	569 ms
94	138.201.151.45:8333	/Satoshi:0.15.1/	556 ms
110	138.68.79.49:8333		N/A

173.9.80.250:8333 (node id: 88)
via 14.63.24.23:30379

Whitelisted	No
Direction	Outbound
Version	70015
User Agent	/Satoshi:0.15.1/
Services	NETWORK & BLOOM & WITNESS
Starting Block	499029
Synced Headers	N/A
Synced Blocks	N/A
Ban Score	N/A
Connection Time	17 m 30 s
Last Send	16 m 11 s
Last Receive	15 m 5 s
Sent	2 KB
Received	8 MB
Ping Time	393 ms
Ping Wait	N/A
Min Ping	393 ms
Time Offset	-47 s

Figure 2-12 Examining peers using bitcoin core software

Figure 2-12 shows peer nodes that are currently connected to the network using bitcoin core software. In the figure, the numbers in the column labeled 'ping' are a measure that tells how stable the communication link are. It measures the time spent exchanging simple messages. The lower the number, the shorter the time to send and receive messages, which means faster communication. In the figure, it is currently trying to connect with 8 peers, 7 of which are in good communication, but we can see that the last node (Node Id 110) is not connected because the ping value is N/A. In addition, the right side of the figure shows the communication history with Node Id 88. Looking at the details of 'Received' shown in the middle, it can be seen that about 8 MB of data was received from this peer.

If bitcoin core is installed, a bitcoin wallet is installed at the same time, making bitcoin transaction easy. But if you are going to use only a bitcoin wallet, there is no reason to install bitcoin core. It is fine to install bitcoin core out of curiosity, but you don't need to install bitcoin core if you don't intend to devote a huge amount of money to equip yourself with professional machines and mine yourself bitcoin by making blocks.

This book aims to explain the basic concepts of bitcoin system and blockchain. Therefore, for the sake of convenience of explanation, in many cases, it is assumed that all nodes are full nodes. Unless otherwise stated, basically all nodes are assumed to be full nodes.

2.3.2.2. Simplified Payment Verification Node

A node that is not a full node and has only downloaded a wallet is called a Simplified Verification Node or SPV. SPV refers to a node that only downloads the header information of the blocks instead of the entire blockchain data.

A size of block is variable and can grow to a maximum of 1MB, but the size of a block header is always fixed and is only 80 bytes in size. Approximately 4.2M (= 80 * 144 * 365 = 4,204,800 bytes) is enough to download a year's worth of the block header data. Even if you try to download 10 years' worth of the block header data, 42M is enough, so there is no burden compared to a full node that needs to download 160G bytes. Most users who use bitcoin on their smartphones are SPVs. The block header only contains information that can track the transaction's information, not the full transactional information. If a SPV needs data for an individual transaction, it requests the data from a full node and receives the data separately.

2.3.3. Mining – making block

The term mining is used to describe the making of a new block. Considering that it was called mining even when price of bitcoin was insignificant, it looks like that people decided to call it mining because the number of bitcoins is limited rather than because making blocks guarantees a fortune. However, considering the current market situation of bitcoin where price is rising significantly, there couldn't be a better name than mining. I mentioned earlier that one must find a nonce, an answer to a hash puzzle, to make a block. To find a nonce, one has to perform a series of operations repeatedly until the specified condition is satisfied. The number of iterations is usually billions of times!

2.3.3.1. Mining using CPU and GPU

The first bitcoin could be mined using the CPU of a home computer. However, as the difficulty of mining gradually increased, mining with CPU became very inefficient considering the electric power used, and mining with personal computers became more difficult due to the appearance of professional miners who use more powerful hardware. People quickly began using GPU that is much more efficient than CPU. GPU is a graphics card chip designed for efficient graphics processing on a computer. Now, mining with CPU is practically impossible.

A graphics card is a chip developed specifically for fast computation processing. Also, the power consumption is much more efficient than a CPU. Therefore, GPU is overwhelmingly superior when it comes to computation throughputs per power consumption. Cryptocurrency mining is not the only field in which GPU is preferred to CPU. Recent machine-learning programs related to artificial intelligence support GPU without exception and rarely use CPU to process big data. There are many differences between a CPU and a GPU, but the biggest difference is in parallel processing capability. CPU is basically composed of several cores for sequential processing, but GPU is designed to enable massive parallel processing in thousands of units. Hash puzzles are perfectly parallelable. Therefore, GPU is much more efficient than CPU in mining. This is also true of artificial intelligence machine learning, and in many areas where parallel processing is possible, GPUs are overwhelmingly used more than CPUs. On the other hand, FPGA or field programmable gate array is used in conjunction with GPU. Unlike general semiconductor chips, in which the circuit and its purpose is fixed, FPGA has a characteristic of reconfiguring the circuit for its purpose through programs. Although FPGAs are expensive, they are generally known to be more cost efficient than GPUs.

2.3.3.2. Mining with Professional Machines

ASIC or Application Specific Integrated Circuits are semiconductor chips designed for specific applications. Most of the recent mining is done by ASIC. Figure 2-13 shows a bitcoin mining dedicated hardware that is actually sold on amazon.

Figure 2-13 ASIC hardware for mining being sold on Amazon

Machines dedicated to mining sold on amazon usually cost well over 1,000 USD. Ant Miner is a company that sells mining hardware and operates the largest mining community in the world called Ant-pool at the same time. It is estimated that Ant Miner takes up 20 ~ 25% of the total bitcoin amount mined over the world. At the moment, trying to succeed in bitcoin mining as an individual is like trying to catch up with a sports car with bicycle. For this reason, a lot of miners have migrated recently to newly introduced cryptocurrencies that are less competitive because the basic principles of mining are similar in most cryptocurrencies.

Meanwhile, some of the recently introduced cryptocurrencies are designed to have inherited the original blockchain concept but with a slight twist, making it virtually impossible for the ASIC to mine in order to prevent the system from being dominated by some forces. EquiHash puzzle, which is used by some cryptocurrencies as their block hash puzzles, is designed to require a colossal memory usage if an ASIC tries to mine. Therefore, it gets more difficult for some forces with professional machines to dominate the system.

2.3.3.3. The league of their own – Mining

Tom Hanks, Gina Davis and Madonna starred in the movie 'The league of their own', a film by director Penny Marshall, released in 1992. The movie is about an American female professional baseball league that actually existed in 1943. During World War II, most of the male athletes joined the army for the war and the operation of male professional baseball league became difficult. So the women's professional baseball league was set to fill the gap. The league had a cold start, but gradually it got attention with the efforts of the athletes and built popularity. However, regardless of their efforts, after the war was over and the male players returned, they lost their standing and were dissolved. Because at that time, professional baseball was only for men. It was not a place for women no matter how hard they tried. After this movie, the term "league of their own" began to be used when a certain group dominated an area exclusively and blocked the approach of the outside world.

There are thousands of professional mining companies around the world, with the top three companies monopolizing nearly 50% of the total blocks, and the top ten together monopolize more than 90% of block mining. Block making has already become the professional miners' own league.

This is because building a block is not just about investing a lot of time and effort. Only the first person to make the block after roughly 10 minutes of fierce competition becomes the winner and the rest becomes the loser, and the game is repeated. In other words, it is like a 100-meter race. Once the winner is determined, everyone returns to the starting point, and all the previous efforts become completely useless. Even the second place has nothing left. Only the first place is meaningful. Ultimately, if an individual is thinking of winning this game against a professional, it is like riding a bicycle and hoping to catch a Lamborghini.

The only mining method available as an individual is to join the mining pools and provide computing resources, and if mining is successful, one is to be given a portion of the compensation. At this time, if you participate in a pool with an ASIC machine, you can increase your chance of getting reward, but it will cost you more electricity, so you should weigh that carefully. The effort for mining is a perfect example of division of labor. Therefore, the speed of work increases proportionally as more people gather. In fact, almost every major vendor is working in the form of distributed and parallel processing. However, as you can imagine, there are very few rewards for tens of thousands of people participating in mining, and usually you can get your reward only if you contribute more than a certain threshold every time, so you might not even get 1 sat.

Bitcoin adjusts the difficulty for every 2016 blocks (theoretically 1,209,000 seconds, about two weeks). The reason for adjusting the difficulty is to keep the time it takes to make a block at roughly 10 minutes. This is a countermeasure against Moore's law that the performance of semiconductors would be continuously improved, so that the block production time would be shortened proportionally. However, bitcoin has formed a vicious loop in which the more difficult mining becomes, the more difficult it is for individuals to approach. When someone begins to make blocks faster than planned by using massive amounts of hardware, the system has to raise the level of difficulty. Then the miner has to use the latest high-end equipment again to cope with raised level of difficulty. In the end, the difficulty must increase exponentially, and individuals can't catch up the difficulty raise. In Table 1-1, it is already explained that the difficulty of # 500,000 block become 1.87 trillion times of genesis block.

As we will see in Part 2 again, this is one of the weaknesses of bitcoin, and because of this a movement to apply methods other than Proof-of-Work to blockchain is in heavy discussion. Bitcoin has now lost its neutrality and has formed a vicious circle that is increasingly dominated by some forces. Currently miners seem to allocate their resources to major currencies. When the market price of a specific cryptocurrency changes suddenly, they will reallocate resources according to the trends. In this case, the generation rate of the block of a specific cryptocurrency temporarily sharply increases while the rate of other cryptocurrencies would be remarkably decreased. All of these vulnerabilities are consequently a challenge for Bitcoin. Making blocks and its difficulty will be explained in detail in *4.1.5. Nonce and block hash puzzle*.

Summary

- A centralized system has a central server connected to all nodes to control and coordinate all nodes.
- A decentralized system does not have a central server and all nodes are identical and have equal rights and obligations.
- The reason why the blockchain operating in a decentralized system is safer from hacking is that a hacker does not have a clear target.
- Our first and widespread definition of blockchain is as follows
    "Blockchain is the base technology of a decentralized ledger which can be safely used in an anonymous system."
- Bitcoin is the name of a cryptocurrency and is the world's first decentralized cryptocurrency implemented using blockchain.
- Each block included in the blockchain data can be thought of as a separate page of the ledger.
- Just as individual pages together form an entire ledger, blockchain data is composed of blocks, which form a decentralized ledger.
- Transactions in bitcoin system is done not through the central server, but by broadcasting transactions to all nodes of the system.
- To make a block, you have to solve a hash puzzle. In other words, creating a block is a process of finding a nonce which is a solution to hash puzzle.

- Through decentralized consensus and proof-of-work, blockchain of each node can maintain the same information and prevent forgery and falsification.
- The double spending problem is to use one bitcoin more than once, which is effectively solved by blockchain. (but may not be in commerce point of view)
- Bitcoin wallet program performs the following functions.
  - Management of bitcoin balance
  - Generation and maintenance of private/public key for account management
  - Submission of bitcoin transactions to the system
- A full node must download more than 150 GB of data and stores the entire blockchain data.
- Simple payment verification node(SPV) is a node that only downloads block headers. Most of nodes that only use wallets are simple payment verification nodes.
- Initially, it was possible to use a CPU for mining, but now it is impossible.
- Recently, bitcoin mining is almost only possible through ASIC, and most of the mining has been dominated by few mining forces.
- Bitcoin block difficulty increases exponentially, and mining leads to a vicious circle in which only some groups monopolize mining, which is a fatal weakness of bitcoin.

3. Bitcoin System

So far, we have examined bitcoin and blockchain in general and clarified a number of terms in order to minimize confusion.

In chapter 3, all of the salient concepts of bitcoin and blockchain will be discussed.

This chapter will explain the structure and formation of a block, which is the standard unit of blockchain data, and give a detailed explanation on how transaction is processed. Also, we will examine 'Trust and Proof', 'Decentralized consensus', and 'Proof of Work', which are the fundamental concepts of bitcoin system. Moreover, we will examine 'hard fork' and 'soft fork' which are technical difficulties related to the maintenance and upgrade of bitcoin system.

The contents covered in chapters 3 and 4 are quite easy to comprehend if the reader has minimal knowledge in computer science. However, some readers may still find the contents difficult. In that case, the readers are recommended to skip chapters 3 and 4 completely and come back on demand. I have repeatedly indicated specific paragraphs for referral.

i   From Chapter 3 on, hexadecimal notation will appear. In decimal system, only numerals 0 through 9 are used for each digit, whereas numerals 0 through 15 are used for each digit under hexadecimal system. In this regard, numerals from 10 to 15 are mapped and represented by alphabets A through F, in sequence. For example, 15 is a 2-digit number in decimal, but it can be represented by a hexadecimal F, which is 1 digit. In order to distinguish hexadecimal numbers from decimal numbers, hexadecimal numbers are always prefixed with '0x' unless it is stated differently. Therefore, 15 is 0xF, 16 is 0x10, and 46 is 0x2E in hexadecimal. Under hexadecimal system, 2 digits or letters make up 1 byte. In the previous example, 0x10 is 1 8 bits. In other words, under hexadecimal system, 1 digit is 4 bits.

Chapter 3 will especially deal with the following topics.

- 3.1. Block
  - ○ Structure of Block
  - ○ Numbers associated with block
  - ○ Collision of blocks
- Transaction
  - ○ 3.2.1. Coinbase Transaction and Normal Transaction
  - ○ Submission of transaction
  - ○ UTXO – Unspent Transaction Output
  - ○ Transaction fee
- Trust vs. Proof
- Double spending and authentication
  - ○ Double spending
  - ○ Authentication
- Decentralized consensus
- Proof of Work – finding nonce
  - ○ Proof of Stake
  - ○ 51% Attack
- Hard Fork and Soft Fork
  - ○ 3.7.1. Validating rules that used to be invalid – Hard Fork
  - ○ 3.7.2. Invalidating rules that used to be valid – Soft Fork
  - ○ SegWit and SegWit2X

3.1. Block

3.1.1. Structure of Block

Previously, it is explained that a block in general refers to a logical unit which stores data, and a block with regard to blockchain data stores transactions. Now, let's analyze block with regard to blockchain data in detail and find out what kind of data is stored in block.

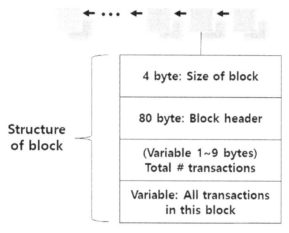

Figure 3-1 Structure of a block

Figure 3-1 shows a detailed description of components of a block. As shown in the figure, a block consists of 4 logical units, that is, 4 fields.

The first field of a block is the size of a block. In bitcoin system, the size of a block is variable. The minimum size is about 215 bytes, and the maximum size is 1 megabyte. In any case, the size cannot exceed 1 megabyte as it is hardcoded that way.

The second field, which is highlighted in yellow, is the block header. It is 80 bytes, and all of the information in the block is stored in these 80 bytes. Even the summarized information of all transactions in the block is stored in the header as well. Surprisingly, 2,000~ 3,000 transactions information which is nearly

1,000,000 bytes, can be compressed into 32 bytes. We will examine more about this in **4.3.1. Merkle Tree**

The third and fourth fields are information related to transactions which are to be stored in the block. The third filed contains the total number of transactions in the block with variable length between 1 and 9 bytes. So, it may be 1 byte or 9 bytes at most, depending on the situation. Generally it can be seen that Satoshi tried to squeeze every bytes and thus wanted to save storage with every means possible. Sometimes even an one byte can affect entire transaction to be successfully included or not.

Let's look at the following figure.

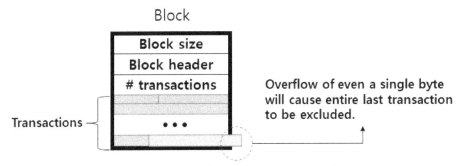

Figure 3-2 Overflow of a last transaction

Figure 3-2 depicts a situation in which the last transaction cannot be stored into the block because of overflow. Since the block size is limited to 1 megabyte, a transaction may not be stored if it exceeds by only 1 byte. This is because a transaction cannot be split. As storing a transaction in the block is directly linked to transaction fee, it is very important to maximize the number of transactions to be stored. For this reason, the total number of transactions is set to be variable instead of fixed in order to store as many transactions as possible.

The fourth field is the actual transactions. There are usually 2000 to 3000 actual transactions stored in a block stacked in a row. The probability of storing one more transactions increases as more bytes are saved in the third component.

We didn't fully discuss the second component, which was highlighted in yellow, because it is quite complicated. However, we must examine it anyway. It might give you a little bit of headache, but it is necessary as this is the core of a block. As has been mentioned several times, the reader may find the explanations difficult because they are unfamiliar rather than challenging. Nevertheless, in order to understand bitcoin system correctly, one should not skip to examine the block header because it is the most important component of all. So, let's cheer up and take a look at it.

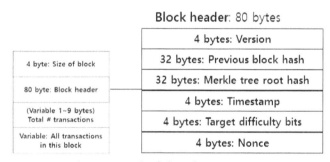

Figure 3-3 Block header structure

Figure 3-3 shows a detailed description of the block header. As shown in the figure, the block header consists of 6 different elements, and its size is fixed at 80 bytes as mentioned previously. Detailed explanation of each element will be given in the appendix, so I will just briefly touch on the concepts only.

The first element is the version. It is the version of bitcoin core system at the time of the block creation. If we compare this version to everyday life, it is like legislative revision information. As laws get revised, bitcoin blockchain can change its rule on demand. Decentralized consensus and other rules about validation of a block may well be changed as well whenever it is necessary.

Therefore, information about the version is very important because it tells the user what rules were applied to validate the block when it was generated.

The second element is hash value of the previous block. We haven't discussed hash yet, so you don't need to know it yet. You may regard the block hash as a particular number unique to that block. People call each other by their names, but blocks don't have names. Instead of names, block has particular unique number called 'block hash value'. Every block has its own unique hash value. I don't mean to scare you, but this is how # 500,000 block hash value actually looks like.

0x00000000000000000024fb37364cbf81fd49cc2d51c09c75c35433c3a1945d04

Yes, the number is quite long and complex. Though it is 32 bytes in size, 32 bytes is not as big as it sounds to a computer. Like we used to refer to the # 500,000 block before, you just can simply consider this just as an ordinary number. What is important here is the fact that the previous block hash value is stored in the current block. In other words, the current block refers to the previous block, and that previous block refers to its previous block, which forms a long chain of blocks. This is the reason why it is called blockchain. Meanwhile, the previous block hash value is also used to generate the hash value of current block. Since the previous block hash value is used in making the hash value of current block, one tiny change to any hash value will lead to a cascaded change in all of the values after the change point. We will discuss this property further in *4.1. Hash function.*

The third element may be unfamiliar. It is called a Merkle tree root. Fortunately, we'll skip this part momentary, so let's put this aside for a while. You may remember that I explained earlier that we can condense the information of all the transactions, which is almost 1,000,000 bytes, into only 32 bytes. Merkle tree is what makes this possible. Merkle tree root contains 32 byte data of the condensed information so that even a tiny change in any of the 2000 to 3000 transactions can be effectively detected. This is the magic of the hash function and a great power of mathematics.

The fourth is the time stamp or the time at which the block was generated. Earlier, I explained that blocks are stored separately on everyone's computer. Therefore, the time recorded in a block follow the time zone where the computer is located.

The fifth and sixth elements are related to the famous mathematical problem. When bitcoin was first introduced it has been known that if someone solves difficult mathematical problem then he or she will be given a bitcoin. Lots of people must have been curious about the math problem. In fact, it is not so correct to call it a 'mathematical problem.' It is more of an 'arithmetic problem.' Anyway, it is true that this arithmetic problem is extremely difficult. What I mentioned earlier as a 'problem that is deliberately designed to make people consume computational resources over a certain period of time' was this very arithmetic problem. The fifth value is the information related to the difficulty of the arithmetic problem, and the sixth is the actual correct answer to the problem. The correct answer to the arithmetic problem is called 'nonce'.

It was difficult, but everything has been explained finally. Readers who want to know more in detail can immediately jump to *Appendix 1 - - Structure of Block* for further details.

3.1.2. Numbers Associated with Block

Blocks in blockchain data have several important numbers associated with them. Each block can be uniquely identified with block hash number rather than a name. Bitcoin programmer always uses block hash number to identify specific block, but as block hash value is 32 byte long and complex, in many cases block height is used instead when human talks about specific block.

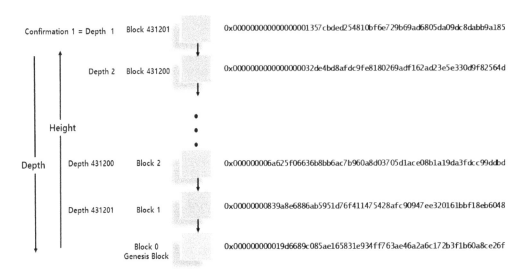

Figure 3-4 Block depth(confirmation) and height

Figure 3-4 shows a stack-looking arrangement of all the blocks, starting from the genesis block. If we stack a block logically from the genesis block then we can create a concept of height(or floor number).

The height of the block increases by 1 just as normal building does. The genesis block is 0, the next block is 1, and so on. Each block has an order added to the blockchain data, and the order never changes, so the height of a specific block will never change. Therefore, # 0 block and # 500,000 block we used to refer earlier was the height of that block. The 32 bytes values shown at the rightmost of the Figure 3-4 are the block hash of each block. This number is unique to each block and has an information related to the proof that the block indeed was created complying with all the given rules.

Meanwhile, there is a concept of block depth which is opposite to block height. Block height is absolute number and therefore does not change, whereas depth of a block is relative and constantly changing. Depth of a block is an indicator of how many more blocks are generated after the creation of a specific block. In contrast to the height of the genesis block being 0, the depth of the most recently created block is always 1. Then, each time another new block is added, the depths of all other blocks are incremented by 1. Therefore, in Figure 3-4, # 431,201 block, which is the most recent block, has the height of 431,201 and the depth of 1. The genesis block has the height of 0 and the depth of 431,202. #431,200 block has the height of 431,200 and the depth of 2.

Depth of a block is directly related to the stability of the block. As we will examine again later, blocks newly added to the blockchain data may also be abandoned. According to decentralized consensus rule, if two separate blockchain data with different size or composition conflict, all the different parts of the lighter blockchain data must be updated to those of heavier blockchain data. This kind of incident is more likely to happen to more recently added block due to network latency. Stability of a specific block will exponentially increases as many more blocks are added following it. Depth of a block is sometimes referred to as "confirmation". If confirmation of block is 3, it means that 2 additional blocks have been added since that block was inserted into the blockchain data. It is usually recommended that you wait for 6 confirmations for a big and important transaction. In other words, it is better to watch your transaction until 5 more blocks are added after your block has been added. It is very unlikely that a block with 6 confirms would be abandoned from the blockchain data. Table 3-1 summarizes the concepts of depth, height, and block hash discussed in this section.

	Variability	Explanation
Block Depth	Always changing and ever increasing	The most recent block has the depth of 1. Adding a block leads to the increment of 1 to the depths of all the other blocks. Also called 'confirmation'.
Block Height	No change. Fixed	Genesis block has the height of 0. Each time a block is created, The height increases by 1. Tells the order of the block.
Block Hash	No change. Fixed	Unique address of the block. A hash value of 32 bytes.

Table 3-1 Depth and height and hash value of a block

3.1.3. Conflict of blocks

A block is a logical unit that contains data. In bitcoin system, the purpose of a block is to record bitcoin transactions. When some node made a new block, it immediately broadcasts newly made block to the system. Broadcasting to the system means propagating a block to the network through its peers. Its peers also relay the block information to their peers, and eventually all nodes connected to the bitcoin network will receive the block.

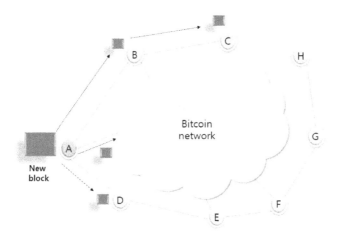

Figure 3-5 Broadcasting of a newly created block

Figure 3-5 shows the process where node A succeeded in creating a block and broadcasts new block to the entire bitcoin network. Each node that receives the created block validates that this block has been created by strictly following the specified rules. If the validation fails, the received block is immediately discarded. However, if the validation process is passed, then the block is to be accepted and thus to be added to the blockchain data stored in local computer of the user, thereby increasing the length of the entire blockchain data by one. At this point, all nodes admit their defeat for this specific round and discard what they were doing so far. Then they start new race for next competition round again to create next block.

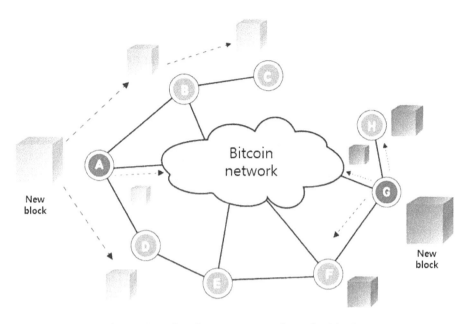

Figure 3-6 Simultaneous creation of a block

Sometimes, unexpected situations happen. Figure 3-6 shows the case where two different nodes succeed in block making almost at the same time. Nodes A and G each successfully created a block and then broadcasted their blocks to the system at approximately the same time. At this point node A and G have no way to know whether other nodes also created block or not. Due to the network latency, B, C, and D received only the blue block created by A, and H and F received only the red block sent by G. Furthermore in case of node E, it could get two different blocks at the same time! In this case, as long as the blocks created by A and G are valid, B, C, and D will add the blue block created by A to their blockchain data not knowing the existence of red block, H and F also will add the red block created by G to their blockchain data also not knowing the existence of blue block. Then they will start the next block making competition. In case of E, it is completely up to E's discretion which block to choose (and therefore discard the other) and thus to add to its local blockchain data as both blocks are valid.

At a particular moment, nodes may have different blockchain data.[10] However, over time, B, C, D, F, H and E will find that their blockchain data are not the same, and the de-centralized consensus is used to finally synchronize data following the heaviest blockchain data. In this race, we never know which node will make the heaviest chain at the end. We'll discuss how this eventual consensus actually proceed later at *3.5. Decentralized Consensus.*

3.2. Transaction

Context related to a bitcoin trade are described in a transaction. The interesting point here is that a transaction of bitcoin itself is a bitcoin. A bitcoin does not exist as a coin with a face value, but the remaining balance after the transaction becomes a bitcoin itself! In the end, a remaining transaction balance of the transaction itself become new bitcoin face value. So if you've ever imagined a bitcoin as something stored individually somewhere like a coin in blockchain data, then let's break it. All of the new issuance of a bitcoin in terms of block subsidy as described in Chapter 1 are also paid in transaction. Let's take a closer look at transactions.

A bitcoin transaction is similar to a balance sheet. Figure 3-7 is a conceptual diagram in which the balance sheet used in accounting is compared to a transaction of bitcoin. The basic concept of a balance sheet is the record of income and expenditure. It records all income items on the left and expenditure items on the right. If you look at Figure 3-7, you will find the page number ① that tells the current page you are on and you have the total income recorded at ②. Under income, which is denoted as 'input', reference pages are stated in parentheses. In the figure, there are 2 incomes, which are 120 and 300, their details are to be referred to pages 20 and 17, respectively. Also, the sum of those incomes is 420 and is shown at ③.

---

[10] Actually, it is more natural for nodes to have different blockchain data at a specific given moment due to network latency. All local blockchain data will eventually become identical as time goes by and may differ at all times at a specific given moment.

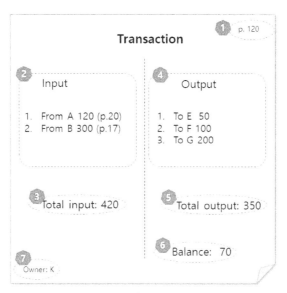

Figure 3-7 Conceptual comparison of bitcoin transaction with balance sheet

The right side of the sheet records expenditures, which is denoted as 'output', and if you look at ④, all the expenditures are recorded in detail. According to the figure, 3 expenditures of 350 in total were made. The sum of expenditure is recorded at ⑤, and the remaining balance of 70, which is the sum of income (420) – the sum of expenditure (350), is recorded at ⑥. ⑦ is the name of the owner of this page, K, who is the owner of the income from ②.

Now, let's turn a few more pages of the ledger and see how the transactions that were paid to E, F, and G are written on their respective pages.

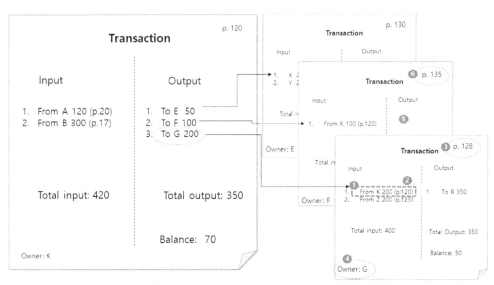

Figure 3-8 After turning a few more pages of the ledger

Figure 3-8 shows how the transactions are recorded on pages of E, F, and G. The first yellow page in front of you is the transaction page of G, let's take a closer look.

- You can see the income items of G at ①. The income item of 200 received from K earlier is listed at the top.
- There is a reference page that allows you to check the transaction in which G received 200 from K. It says 120 which is the page number owned by K from Figure 3-7. Therefore, if you go to page 120, you can find out the transaction which this 200 originates from.
- As shown in ③, G's transaction is recorded on a separate page, and the page number is 128. On this page, only the transactions of G are recorded, and the owner name is G in ④.

- ⑤ is part of F's ledger, but F hasn't spent any of the income received from K, so its expenditure area remains empty.

- As shown in ⑥, F's ledger is recorded separately on page 135, the page number is much later than 128, which is G's page number. From this, we know that the order of expenditure doesn't necessarily correspond to the order of record.

Let's look at another page.

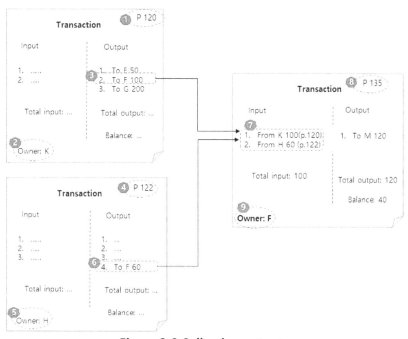

Figure 3-9 Collecting outputs

Figure 3-9 shows situation where F is collecting scattered output to accommodate his expenditure of 120. As combined sum 160(=100+60) is greater than F's due expenditure(=120), now F can successfully pay his or her amount.

Like this, someone's expenditure is someone else's income, and these records are scattered all over the ledger. Such items that are scattered over ledgers and haven't been spent yet are called Unspent Transaction Outputs or UTXO in short. We have seen a bitcoin wallet gathering all the inputs scattered over multiple blocks and display the sum in Figure 2-9, and that was the process of gathering

UTXO information. From previous explanations, we can assume that income and input mean the same thing, and expenditure and output mean the same thing. UTXO will be explained later at *3.2.3. UTXO: Unspent transaction output*

3.2.1. Coinbase Transaction and Normal Transaction

To put it differently, to transact bitcoin is basically equal to transfer the ownership of bitcoin from one person to another. This is technically the same concept as handing over paper money. Handing over paper money is, in other words, transferring the ownership of the paper money to another person. So far, it was repeatedly explained that someone's input is someone else's output, and all the inputs discussed earlier originated from outputs of previous transactions.

If you keep following along the continuous thread of inputs and outputs, you will be able to trace back to the very creation moment of the first bitcoin source of the thread. Some readers may have already guessed that, yes, it is when block reward is issued. It was said that if one makes a block then one gets a reward. The first transaction of every block is a transaction in which the maker is given due reward for mining the block. Since this transaction is about new issuance of the bitcoin, there are no previous inputs. The transaction which gives a block reward, and thus the first transaction of each block, is called a coinbase transaction. It literally means transaction which is the base of a coin. All transactions other than coinbase transactions are called normal transactions. Thus, all the transactions discussed up to this point were normal transactions.

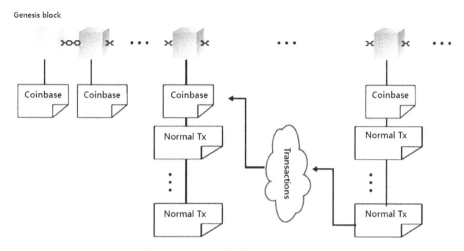

Figure 3-10 Coin-base Transaction

Figure 3-10 shows how one always ends up with a coinbase transaction if one traces back to a normal transaction's source of its inputs and outputs. Also, we can see that the first transaction of every block actually is a coinbase transaction. Every time a block is created, a coinbase transaction is also created, so the total number of coinbase transactions is the same as the number of blocks in the blockchain data.

One question arises here. Earlier, we witnessed a situation where two nodes created a block at almost the same time in Figure 3-6. In this situation, each node that received a different block added the received block to its blockchain data without knowing what happened. In this case, who gets the reward? A coinbase transaction is created always when a block is created. Thus, A and G both get the reward. However, ultimately, according to decentralized consensus, only one block survives and the other will be discarded. Then, all the transactions in the discarded block will also become invalid, so the coinbase transaction in that block will disappear naturally.

When multiple blocks are created at the same time and some blocks are discarded by decentralized consensus later, all the transactions recorded in the discarded blocks go back to the transaction waiting room. In this case, if a person spends the bitcoin given by the coinbase transaction before the block gets discarded, there could be a lot of confusion. In other words, it is possible that block reward that is supposed to be discarded could be used and get scattered over a number of blocks, and then all of a sudden, all the transactions that involve this reward could be canceled at once. This is never a simple confusion and could potentially threaten the stability and reliability of transactions. Therefore, in order to prevent such a problem from occurring, bitcoin system forbids a reward to be used until 99 more blocks are created after it is added to blockchain data (in other words, 100 confirmations). Theoretically, as 144 blocks are created per day, it can be easily thought that a newly created bitcoin by a coinbase transaction has to wait for almost a day until it can be spent. One thing that shouldn't be misunderstood here is that even if a block gets discarded and its coinbase transaction is canceled, its normal transactions that were included in the block don't get canceled or discarded. Normal transactions simply move back to the waiting room and wait until they get reprocessed. As long as a transaction itself is valid, it will get processed eventually and never get discarded.

3.2.2. Submission of Transaction

Previously, I explained that a transaction in bitcoin system is not a direct communication between two parties but is broadcasting to all nodes. Now, let's find out what really happens when a transaction is submitted to the system.

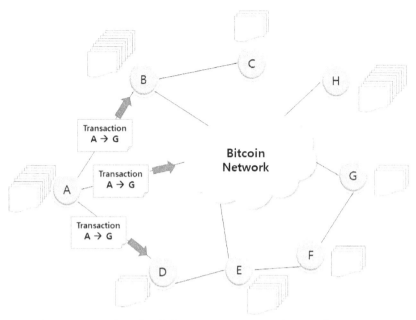

Figure 3-11 A is submitting a new transaction to the system

In Figure 3-11, A is broadcasting a transaction in which A pays G a certain bitcoin. As it was explained earlier, the submitted transaction will continue spreading throughout the system, and ultimately every node will receive the transaction and store it in the waiting room.

If you take a closer look at figure, you can see that A has a bigger number of waiting transactions than node C does. Once a transaction is submitted to the system, it will certainly reach every node in the system, but you never know in what order or how fast your transaction will be broadcasted. This is because every node has a different network speed and different software/hardware specifications. Now, the nodes will compete against each other to create a block before anyone else and record the transaction. And transactions in the waiting room are waiting for some node to make a block so that they could exit the waiting room.

If you are not lucky, your transaction might have to wait for a long time if the nodes your transaction are waiting keep failing to make a block. However, basically every transaction gets delivered to all the nodes in the system and at least one node will definitely succeed in making a block, so your transaction might take long to be recorded but it will be recorded for sure. After a transaction is successfully recorded on a block and added to blockchain data, it is finally considered to be valid (of course if there is a conflict between blockchain data and the block has to be discarded according to decentralized consensus, your transaction may have to go back to the waiting room).

After time, the output transaction in which A pays G is stored in every node's blockchain data. Thus, every node can open and see this transaction.[11] However, the right to use this output is strictly limited to G. Then, how can you ensure that only G can use this output and no one else is allowed to use it? Some readers who remember about the hint from earlier might have guessed that it could be related to bitcoin address. To put it easily, all transaction in fact have locking mechanism, and only those with keys are allowed to open transactions. In the case of the figure, only G has the key to unlock this locking mechanism. In order to understand how one can unlock these locking devices, you must know about encryption. So, we will stop here shortly and come back after learning about *4.2. Cryptography.*

3.2.3. UTXO – Unspent Transaction Output

Previously, we learned that records scattered over blocks that have not yet been used by owners are called UTXO or unspent transaction outputs. These unspent transaction outputs are locked so that only their owners are allowed to use them. Assume that A has submitted a transaction to the system where A pays B, C, and D 0.1 BTC each, and this transaction has become an UTXO and been scattered and recorded on blockchain data. Let's look at the following figure.

---

[11] We will discuss on privacy issue separately at *5.2. Personal information protection* Personal information protection

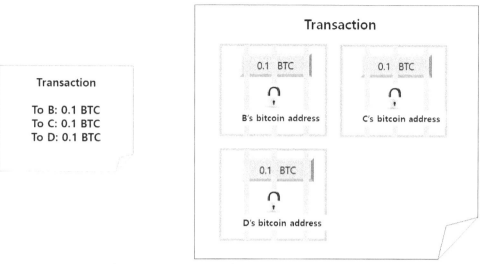

Figure 3-12 UTXO and its conceptual diagram

Figure 3-12 shows UTXO and a conceptual diagram about locking mechanism. Each output is confined and locked in a box. If you look closely into this locking device, you will learn that it is actually locked using bitcoin address information of whom directly involved in each transaction. So, we can guess that there really is something about bitcoin address indeed. The locking mechanism is mainly formed with the bitcoin address of the recipient. Try to recall that a bitcoin address has information about the bitcoin recipient's public key.

When filling out a transaction, a locking device is activated so that it can only be unlocked by its owner using the owner's key. Although every node has this transaction saved in its blockchain data, there is no way to unlock the locking device without the key. **Appendix 5 –Transaction Script** has detailed information about locking device, key, and secret behind bitcoin address.

3.2.2.1. UTXO Tracking

Previously, we compared transaction details to a balance sheet. Back then, the description in the figure wasn't perfectly accurate and that was just for the convenience of explanation. Surprisingly, actual transactions of bitcoin don't have total amount information in the income category.[12] The income category actually doesn't even have individual amount information at all and only have reference pages. This is why bitcoin blockchain is called blind blockchain as it does not keep track of any global status information at all. We have to construct current global status again by looking up previous blocks every time we need information.

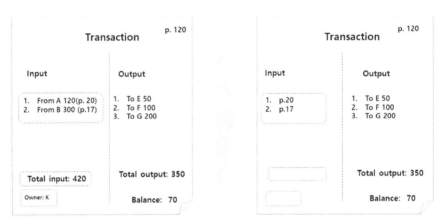

Figure 3-13 More realistic version of Figure 3-7

Figure 3-13 is a conceptual diagram that represents the content of Figure 3-7 more realistically. Do you see the differences between the new figure(=right side) and the original figure(=left side)? Red dotted areas are the changed parts. Take a closer look at the income category. In the original figure, it showed income amounts and total sum. However, on the right, the income amounts have disappeared let alone total amount and only reference pages are present. Even, there is no information about senders! Also, the name of the page's owner at the bottom is also gone.

---

[12] Do you remember the explanation of 'blind' blockchain at memo box of ***2.3.1.3. Management of bitcoin balance*** ?

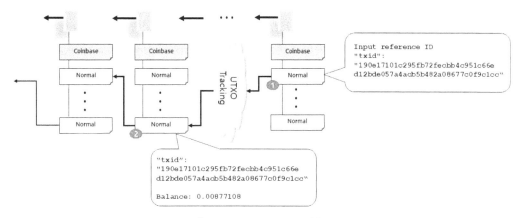

Figure 3-14 UTXO tracking

In Figure 3-14, information about balance is acquired by tracking the input reference number at transaction ①. txid is a transaction identifier and plays the same role as a page number of a ledger. In order to fully apprehend the transaction at ①, it is necessary to directly follow the input transaction reference number. In the figure, the corresponding balance is revealed to be 0.00877108 after tracing back several blocks. Of course, this strenuous task is done by bitcoin wallet, so the users don't have to worry about this inconvenience.

Actually, UTXO tracking has more to do with protection of personal information than with inconvenience. Fundamentally, bitcoin protects users' personal information by using only bitcoin addresses and not using any other personal information including real names while processing transactions. Nevertheless, it is still possible to trace back a certain output through its transactions and look up the contents of it. In other words, anyone can apprehend the transaction type of a certain 'bitcoin address' at a single glance. Also, as previously mentioned, everyone is allowed to examine all the transactions of the past 8 years since the creation of genesis block. We will discuss more about this in *5. Security and privacy*

The number of transactions began to increase significantly since 2015. Early blocks have only around 100 transactions. However, starting from

2015, there were around 1,500 transactions per block. Recently over 2,000 transactions in a block is very common. The total number of transactions stored in all the blocks from genesis block(Jan 3rd, 2009) up to # 500,000 block(December 18th, 2017) is around 290 million.

3.2.4. Transaction Fee

Every transaction has to pay a fee. This fee is given to the maker of a block in the form of reward. In early bitcoin system, feeless transactions were possible. Before, there existed ways to do transactions without paying any fees. 50KB of free space was reserved in every block, then transactions that declared not to pay transaction fees were processed using this reserved space chronologically from oldest to the most recent. 50KB of space is capable of containing around 300 transactions, which is not a small amount considering current transaction capacity. Thus, if the process was not so urgent, there was a way to trade without paying any fees although it took some time.

However, there are no more reserved space of 50KB since Feb 23rd, 2016, and all transactions must pay appropriate fees for process. It was then when concept of minimum fee came about, and the current minimum fee is 1,000 sat. However, it will take a very long time for processing a transaction if one pays only the minimum fee (to be explained again in *8.1.2. The fee strikes* back, it could take up to more than a month). Transactions that are pending at each node are supposed to be processed in the order of arrival if it has same fee rate, but transaction with higher fee rate is always preferred in processing priority of course. The miner of a block determines which transactions to be processed first. In this case, transactions with lower fees are only processed when there are no more transactions with higher fees or the waiting room has enough space to store all the waiting transactions in the block. Miners who make blocks usually prioritize the process order by fee rate which is the ratio between the size of a transaction and its fee. Fee rate is calculated by dividing transaction fee by transaction size(byte), so it is basically fee per unit byte size. It means that the profit maximizes as the fee rate of a transaction gets higher, so the order of priority is determined by fee rate. Recent bitcoin wallets automatically calculates system fee rates dynamically and give recommendations for you. If a user chooses this recommended fee, then he can expect an average processing time, but if he insists on the lowest fee, he cannot know how long it will take.

Bitcoin transaction fees are calculated by transaction size per byte rather than the amount. Your transaction fee would be minimal if you have only one output even if you are paying big amount, let's say 100,000 BTC, but if you have many outputs, then your fee would be very big even if the payment is very small like 0.0001 BTC. This is because the number of bytes increases proportionally to the number of outputs. Transaction fees being proportional to byte size instead of payment amount looks reasonable in the eyes of computer, but it's quite odd from commercial point of view. It is usually considered more natural for fees to be proportional to be the amount of trade. Bitcoin is practically incapable of micro payment because the transaction fee would be much more than the payment itself. Currently, transactions of less than 30 USD are practically meaningless since the transaction fee would gobble up the transaction. Satoshi Nakamoto used to argue that banks' high transaction fees hinder micro payments, but it seems quite self-contradicting that bitcoin created by him annihilating micro payments. Also, because transaction fees are designed to be proportional to size, a block's total fee cannot surpass 5 BTC as of now due to 1M block size limitation. Design philosophy of bitcoin seems to be more focused on the stability of the system rather than its function as a currency. This point is ultimately related to future stability of bitcoin. Let's discuss more about this in *8.1.2. The fee strikes back.*

In general, a block can store about 2,000 to 3,000 transactions. If we assume that 2,500 transactions are to charge only minimum fees, then it's only 0.025 BTC per block (= 2,500 x 1000sat). Then, what about things in real life? In practice, there are almost no transactions that pay only the minimum fee. I randomly sampled 30 blocks from those created in December, 2017 and analyzed. A block stores an average of 2,206 transactions, and the average transaction fee per block is 3.3232 BTC. That is 0.0015(= 3.3232 / 2206) BTC per transaction. It is 150 times the minimum fee of 1000sat! According to the current market price, it is about 30 USD per transaction. This point will be very important later when we discuss the future of bitcoin in Part 2, so make sure to remember it. Bitcoin wallet automatically calculates transaction fees and estimates processing times based on the average transaction handling time. Table 3-2 is estimated processing times per recommended transaction fees automatically calculated by bitcoin wallet as of December, 2017.

Estimated processing time	Recommended transaction fee (per KB)	Converted to USD (1BTC = 20,000 USD)
20 min (2 blocks)	0.00556052	111.2104
60 min (10 blocks)	0.00477993	95.5986
24 hrs (144 blocks)	0.0016287	32.574

Table 3-2 Estimated processing time per recommended transaction fee

As shown in Table 3-2, bitcoin transaction fee is never cheap and ever increasing. It is estimated that a transaction of 1 KB in size would take 24 hours to be processed after paying 32.574 USD. In short, it will take 24 hours to transfer money, and about 30 USD will be thrown away for the sake of fee. This is a critical flaw of bitcoin which makes it difficult to function as a currency. Problems of transaction fee will be investigated further in *8.1.2. The fee strikes back*

i   Currently, the only way to get bitcoin is to buy from someone who already has it because it is practically impossible for individuals to mine new bitcoin now. At this, so called bitcoin exchange connects buyers with sellers for trade. Though it is called bitcoin exchange, it never operates like stock exchange which coordinates all orders together and process with unified price for a certain property, but only acts as a broker matching buy-sell requests. Therefore, market prices vary by countries and even vary by brokers within the same country. In case of bitcoin, its price is 20% to 30%

more expensive in South Korea than USA. Brokers charge 0.1% to 0.2% of the total transaction amounts from both buyers and sellers as commission. For convenience, we will assume broker fees as 0.1% in all calculations in the book. 0.1% is 10 times the online HTS fee of stock firms. When transaction happens, 0.1% of the transaction amount is taken from the buyer as commission with legal tender, and the rest is given to the seller. Also, 0.1% of the cryptocurrency is taken from seller as commission, thus buyer only gets 99.9% of what he or she actually ordered. As a result, the broker takes 0.1% of the legal tender and 0.1% of the cryptocurrency being traded for commission at the same time. We will discuss more about brokers in Chapter 5 and Part 2 of this book.

3.3. Trust vs. Proof

The core of decentralized financial transactions is to eliminate the need for a trusted third party. The role of a trusted institution in financial transactions is to guarantee accuracy and reliability. You can use credit cards at stores because store owners trust the credit card transaction system not because they trust you. Also, bank transfers are possible even though only digitized numbers are come and go instead of actual money because the numbers' accuracy as well as people's belief that they can convert their digitized numbers into money at any time. In this point of view, transactions through financial institutions are transactions based on trust. There is only single truth on transaction history stored in central server of a financial institution. Regardless of question on whether we really can trust bank or not, anyway there is only one unique truth as everything was processed by the centralized server only. Thus, as long as the financial institution is trusted, then transaction history is always reliable as truth.

On the other hand, bitcoin system is based on proof instead of trust. Each one participating in the system could record transaction history. There is no one to be trusted because participants don't know each other. However, even in these cases, if there is a way to determine whether a given transaction history is correct, then the truth can be maintained.

Let's look at the following figure.

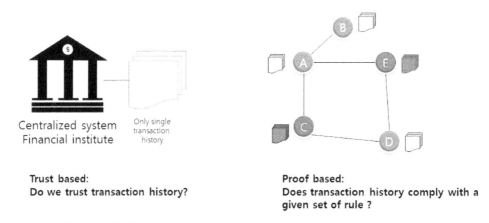

Trust based:
Do we trust transaction history?

Proof based:
Does transaction history comply with a given set of rule ?

Figure 3-15 Trust-based transaction and Proof-based transaction

Figure 3-15 compares trust based transaction with a proof based transaction. The left side of the figure is the trust-based transaction that uses a financial institution as a trusted writer. Everyone does a transaction through the centralized server, there is always only one version of transaction history. Therefore, if you can trust this financial institution, its transaction history can be considered true. Meanwhile, the right side of the figure shows the proof-based transaction. In the figure, A, B, and D have always followed the rule, but C and E broke the rule and recorded fake transaction histories. These fake transactions are colored in red. However, the problem for C and E is that they don't really have a good way of hiding the fact that they recorded fake transactions. Blockchain has solved this problem by being able to immediately detect fake transactions, not by forbidding fake transactions to be recorded. In this case, C and E's fake transactions get discarded from the system right away. In principle, there is no way of recording fake transactions. Even if everyone else but me records a fake transaction, it won't be a problem as long as I can tell the right transaction because all the fake transactions will be discarded by my software.

For fabrication, one would have to follow the rule otherwise it would be detected right away. There exists 2 common ways to cheat the system while not breaking the rule. One is to double spend and the other is to maliciously expel existing blocks from blockchain, which will be explained in detail in the next section. Nevertheless, this kind of manipulation is also practically impossible because it requires a prohibitively expensive cost to fabricate an already written record. How it's done will be explained in detail in the next section.

i In order for a manipulation to be prohibitively expensive, one basic assumption must be satisfied. The sum of computing powers of honest nodes must be greater than that of malicious nodes. The secret for this assumption to be valid in bitcoin system is that the system is actually designed in a way that acting honestly regardless of the actual intention is always much more economically profitable than cheating the system. Thus bitcoin system works not because there are always more good people than bad people but because acting honestly is much more profitable in bitcoin system. Since participants will pursue a behavior that is more economically beneficial to them regardless of their intentions, this assumption can be deemed valid. However, this also can be basic flaw of blockchain and implies how important it is to have an appropriate design on the contrary. For this assumption to be valid, a perfect design that include things like reward system must strongly back it and thus so called 'incentive engineering' is quite crucial. If not, the basic assumption will be broken, and manipulation would be out of hand. In that case, decentralized consensus would be void as well. We will investigate this matter again in Part 2 of this book.

3.4. Double spending and Authentication

3.4.1. Double spending

In Figure 2-6, we briefly examined how Alex attempted double spending. Double spending refers to a malicious attempt to use the same bitcoin multiple times. Previously, Alex broadcasted two different (conflicting) transactions to the system at the same time to use a single bitcoin twice. It was explained that the result is either having both transactions discarded or passing only one of the two transactions as valid and discarding the other.

However, what bitcoin blockchain solved the double spending problem is not quite useful for commercial point of view. Although it is true that bitcoin system has blocked any possibility of double spending bitcoin, but it cannot prevent malicious abuse. In Figure 2-6, if a transaction that pays to Alex himself gets recorded first or both transactions get discarded, Diana would be rooked. As a result, the so called trading justice implemented by bitcoin blockchain only means the state of no contradiction or disagreement. It doesn't take into account basic rule of faithfulness in commercial activity.

Then, isn't there a way to get bitcoin safely? Well, there is. Problems will be solved if you wait long enough. What are the criteria for "long enough"? It was said that a block takes an average of 10 minutes to be made. Thus, the minimum time it takes for a transaction to be recorded on a block after bitcoin has been paid is at least 10 minutes, and it could be longer depending on the transaction fee and network status. As discussed earlier, you cannot rest easy even after your transaction is recorded on the block and added to blockchain data because it can still be discarded if things go wrong. However, as the number of block confirmations increase, blocks become exponentially stable.

Number of confirmations	Status	Minimum waiting time
0	Safe only when the other party is completely trustworthy	immediately
1	Trustworthy to some degree	10 min
3	Trustworthy	30 min
6	In case of an expensive transaction	60 min

Table 3-3 number of recommended confirmations

Table 3-3 lists the numbers of confirmations recommended by bitcon.org per type of transaction. As shown in the table, it is wise to wait a long time if big amount is at stake for a transaction. If you were at a coffee shop whose owner is very distrustful, you might be seized for at least 30 minutes to an hour after you pay for your coffee with bitcoin. The owner who suspects double spending could hold you for 3 to 6 confirmations before you can leave the shop. This is very critical defect of bitcoin when it comes to ordinary everyday micro payment. It will be discussed further in Part 2.

i Blockchain only solved the double spending problem in terms of algorithm, not in terms of commercial activity. For the present, in order to eliminate double spending that also doesn't contradict the principle of faithfulness, the only way is to wait longer than recommended time in table 3-3. This completely violates the immediacy of exchange which a currency should have. In many aspects, contrary to Satoshi Nakamoto's claim, bitcoin is improper for everyday life usage, which requires a lot of micro payment.

3.4.2. Authentication

Another problem to be solved regarding digital transaction is verifying the owner of the cryptocurrency being used. In other words, there has to be a way of knowing if the person that submitted a transaction to spend bitcoin is actually the owner of the bitcoin. In fact, this is a very fundamental function for both a centralized and decentralized system in digital transactions. Even if there is a centralized control system, it is still necessary to verify the node attempting a transaction is the actual owner of the account. The same principle applies to a decentralized system. Fortunately, a solution to this problem has been around for a long time. The solution is called asymmetric encryption technique or commonly known as electronic signature by most people. Asymmetric encryption technique allows specifying owners of digital currency. This will be more explained in

4.2.1. Asymmetric cryptography. Like this, verifying an owner of a property is called Authentication.

3.5. Decentralized Consensus

Previously in Figure 3-6, node A and node G created blocks almost at the same time. Then, the peer nodes received two different kinds of blocks. Node B, C, and D received A's block, and nodes H and F received G's block. As a result, the two groups believed the blocks they received were valid respectively, added them to their blockchain data, and started a whole new round of competition again. When something like this happens, there exist two different blockchain data in the system temporarily.

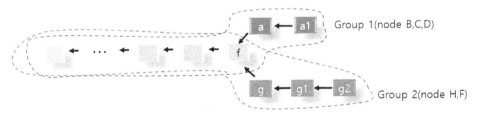

Figure 3-16 Conflict of two different blockchain data

Figure 3-16 shows a conflict between two different blockchain data within a system. The nodes in Group 1 surrounded by the blue dotted line believed a blockchain data starting with a and ending with a1 to be valid and saved that, while the nodes in Group 2 believed blocks g, g1, and g2 to be valid and added them to their blockchain data. Thus, even though the two groups' data agree with each other from genesis block up until f where they split up into a and g, but then they don't match each other.

Bitcoin system must choose only one data when it detects a difference among blockchain data during its nodes exchange data with each other. Then, rules need to exist for the selection. When the blockchain data held by the nodes in the system is not consistent, a set of rules that allows bitcoin system to identify the identical blockchain data so that all the nodes in the system can have a consistent status is called decentralized consensus. Decentralized consensus doesn't only mean expelling a block that has broken the rule. It also refers to all the rules which set criteria so that all nodes in the system to choose identical single blockchain data. In this process even a blockchain data which perfectly comply with given set of rule also could be discarded due to rule. Decentralized consensus mechanism of bitcoin is surprisingly simple. When two nodes conflict with different blockchain data, they firstly check if each other's blockchain data followed all the rules. Once they have checked that both blockchain data are normal and followed all the rules, then they compare to see whose blockchain data is heavier.

The losing node has to update its blockchain data until it synchronize all blocks with the winning node's data. In Figure 3-16's case, if both sides have the same difficulty, Group 2's blockchain data becomes heavier as block g2 is created, so the outcome of the game is decided, and all the nodes in Group 1 now has to discard blocks 'a' and 'a1' and should add 'g', 'g1', and 'g2' instead. Blockchain data of the two groups is finally consistent as a result. Blocks 'a' and 'a1' that were initially added to blockchain data as normal but got discarded later are called orphan blocks.

Decentralized consensus is enforced upon every node, and by this rule, all nodes are able to eventually maintain a single blockchain data that is always identical for every node. When a violation of any rule by the opponent is detected, the comparison immediately ends, and the opponent's defeat is confirmed. In addition, if ever the weight of two blockchain data was the same, the comparison ends in a draw, and then a new competition for another new block starts in order to outrun their opponents. As this competition continues, the balance would be lost at some point. Once the competition ends, all the blocks created by the losing contestant during the competition would be discarded and become orphan blocks.

> *i* Decentralized consensus discussed in this section does not describe the general character of blockchain but only the method taken for bitcoin blockchain. Bitcoin chooses the heaviest chain through the method of PoW, but this can also be applied in many different ways while implementing blockchain. Also, it could be implemented in a different way from PoW. Therefore, decentralized consensus may be defined differently. We will learn more about this in the next section which describes poW and ***9.3.3. Decentralized Consensus Rule***.

3.6. Proof-of-Work – Finding Nonce

Proof-of-Work(PoW) is a concept suggested by Cynthia Dwork and Moni Naor in 1993, and it is a technique devised to prevent a service from being abused by various acts such as DOS (Denial-Of-Service) or spamming. It is important to require service users to carry out a certain task that is quite demanding but achievable. Here, task means work that requires computing resources of a computer. Though the concept was introduced in 1993, the term PoW first appeared in a paper by Markus Jakobsson and Ari Juels in 1999.[N]

The simplest and most common example of PoW is when you have to type in a string of hard-to-read letters or numbers as you sign up to a website in order to prevent automated subscriptions. Meanwhile, the type of PoW applied to bitcoin system is one of the most difficult and demanding on earth, and its difficulty is exponentially increasing in time that it looks like it will soon devour all the electricity in the world. One of the most important concepts when it comes to designing a PoW is asymmetry. That is, verifying PoW has to be as simple as possible while actually doing it should require a formidable amount of efforts and resources. PoW of bitcoin system requires a huge amount of resources but its verification can be done in an instant.

PoW of bitcoin as part of the rules which must be obeyed when creating a block is finding a nonce that is an answer to a hash puzzle. A nonce is usually a very big integer. Let's see how big nonce values are by sampling some blocks that were recently created. # 400,000, # 450,000, and # 500,000 blocks were randomly selected for investigation.

Block number	Nonce	Block creation time
400,000	657,220,870	2016-02-25
450,000	2,972,550,269	2017-01-25
500,000	1,560,058,197	2017-12-18

Table 3-4 Comparison of 3 nonce of randomly selected blocks

Table 3-4 compares the nonce values of 3 different blocks. Nonce of # 400,000 block is about 650 million, while that of # 450,000 block is over 2.9 billion. Earlier, it was said that a nonce is an answer to a hash puzzle. Usually, if a nonce is big, then it generally means that the hash puzzle was difficult to solve.

Previously, asymmetry property of PoW has been explained. Verifying PoW should be as simple as possible while doing PoW itself should require lots of effort. In order to do PoW of bitcoin system, you have to repeat your calculation process over billions of times to find a nonce as seen earlier. However, checking if this calculation satisfies the given conditions only takes an instant. In other words, bitcoin system fulfils asymmetry property perfectly. After all, creating a block can be summarized as finding a nonce and calculating your block hash value, and it takes an average of billions of times of repeated calculating process. The hash value of the previous block is used in the process of calculating a block hash as mentioned in *3.1.1. Structure of Block*. In other words, it is necessary to know the hash value of previous block to calculate the hash value of current block.

If you use the hash value of the previous block to calculate the hash value of current block, the property shown in the following figure builds.

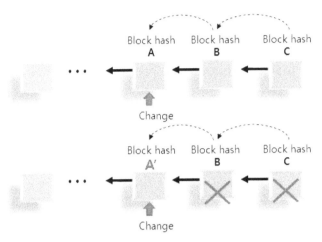

Figure 3-17 Change of block hash and chain reaction caused by it

The top of Figure 3-17 conceptually describes how each block hash is calculated by using the predecessor block hash value with dotted lines. Block B at the top of the figure used the hash value of A, which is predecessor of B, to compute its own block hash and block C used B's hash value likewise. Let's assume that part of A has been changed and its hash value was affected by this change as a result. The bottom of the figure illustrates the situation in which hash value of block A has been changed to A'. When hash value A changes to A', all the blocks that follow it are sequentially affected because B originally used A, not A' to compute its hash value. For the same reason, hash value of C will change, and all the other blocks will see the same effect. When a block changes, bitcoin blockchain is designed to require all the blocks after the changed block to do their PoW over again. This practically makes modifying blockchain data almost impossible. Not only PoW is difficult, but also you have to make the heaviest chain to pass decentralized consensus. Therefore, even if you did a PoW after manipulating blockchain data again, all your efforts will be wasted if you can't make the heaviest chain. Changing blockchain data is so difficult that nobody would ever even think of attempting it, thus blockchain data becomes prohibitively irreversible and thus practically immutable.

The underlying reason that ecosystem of bitcoin blockchain can sustain itself is not because each node is honest but because it was designed in such a way that putting resources into good work is more profitable than attacking the system at all times. Nevertheless, we will discuss whether or not it was actually designed in that way in Part 2.

A more detailed explanation of hash puzzle can be found in *Appendix 2 – Concepts of hash puzzle concept*, and its details are found in *4.1.5. Nonce and block hash puzzle*

> The heuristics behind PoW is to make malicious act costly. The counter effect though is that it is also very costly to virtuous activity. From the nature of decentralized ledger, blockchain cannot outperform centralized system at all in terms of processing speed due to synchronization overhead. So if someone is seeking for faster performance with blockchain, he is completely in wrong page. Blockchain is more for safer distribution of record in immutable way, which possibly could remove the necessity of intermediary. This is where you need to look for its value.

3.6.1 Proof-of-Stake

Previously, it was explained that decentralized consensus of bitcoin system always chooses the heaviest chain. This method was chosen by bitcoin blockchain, so it doesn't mean that all blockchain have to use this method. Rule of bitcoin blockchain to choose the heaviest chain is based upon PoW method. A selection method based on PoW fundamentally looks for who spent most energy, so it can be quite inefficient at times. Recently, a lot of research is being done to achieve irreversible immutability without using PoW. One of the ideas is Proof-of-Stake(PoS). To put it simply, in PoW, the most powerful one always wins, while in PoS, anyone who has the most accumulated contribution or stakes always wins. Like decisions of corporation are always made by the ones that have the most share, when there exist different views, PoS seeks to solve the problem by following the decision of someone whose accumulated contribution or share is the most. This follows the basic assumption that the more accumulated contribution you have, the more you have contributed to the development of a system. One idea along the line of PoS is to let whoever has more bitcoin win when a conflict between two blockchain data happens. However, this can easily cause a monopoly over the system by those who have more bitcoin than others. Therefore, if it were implemented without an appropriate countermeasure against monopoly over system, then PoS would cause even bigger problems than PoW. Alternatives of PoW are mostly at the idea stage. Though it was announced that ethereum would launch a new type of blockchain which has adopted a PoS method called Casper, the development of it should be watched yet.

One thing that is clear is that PoW implemented by bitcoin needs to be improved in many aspects. Difficulty control, decentralized consensus, and PoW heavily depends on deterministic methods only. Since there is almost no randomness in winning PoW, so whoever spends more energy than the others will win the game. Also, winner always takes all. It is all or nothing game. If your opponent puts in more energy, then you must put in even more energy accordingly to win the game. There is no 99%. It is game of either 0 or 1. There is no strategic dominance[13] in this game. This is a chicken game in which you must not lose, so the only strategy is to be interlocked with your opponent's strategy and control your energy input. At last, it rushes into a chicken game where spending more means winning, then reaches Nash equilibrium on its own at which you and your opponent spends most of the available energy and a balance of competition is achieved, and then it becomes the worst possible waste of energy. During the time, difficulty control system of bitcoin increases the difficulty exponentially in order to react with the shortened block creation time due to massive and competitive influx of energy, and more energy would be required, so a totally vicious cycle forms eventually. This level of difficulty won't be achievable by nobody but large-scale miners. A complete polarization of mining has been fixed.

---

[13] Strategic dominance is a term from game theory. It refers to a situation where one specific strategy is always advantageous regardless of opponent's reaction.

Nash equilibrium refers to a situation where each contestant has reached the best strategy so no one changes their strategy any more and a kind of equilibrium forms. It is a balance theory suggested by a genius mathematician, John Nash. A film "A beautiful mind" starred by Russell Crowe, directed by Ron Howard' is a story about John Nash. John Nash is regarded as genius who changed the paradigm of game theory fundamentally.

The PoW method implemented in bitcoin blockchain induces an unnecessary waste of energy and polarize mining power. This is critical defect of bitcoin blockchain which eventually could kill the entire bitcoin ecosystem.

Many discussions are on-going around PoW of bitcoin blockchain. Some even claim that the PoS or other consensus mechanism is the only answer to cure the defect of bitcoin. These alternative mechanisms may possibly improve defects of bitcoin indeed. However it should also be clearly noted that most of the PoS or Delegated PoS(DPos) algorithms which are in heavy discussion today are actually not a cure of bitcoin system but rather a solution to a different problem domain. For example, PoS or DPos would not work in absolute anonymous environment just as PoW of bitcoin and on top of that PoS and DPoS are not a theoretically proven algorithms in terms of stability and security. PoS and DPos also put lots of different conditions and assumptions which are in some respect far from decentralized system. So it is also arguable that those algorithm may not be referred to as decentralized consensus algorithm but may be as a 'centralized decentralized algorithm'.

There are many improvement points for bitcoin PoW. If some randomness mechanism is combined with bitcoin PoW, then the polarization problem will be much more smoothened and alternative hash algorithm could be tried also. With these improvement, PoW still could have a chance to do much better job than PoS.

For further knowledge on additional decentralized consensus, please search for document on RAFT and Paxos.

3.6.2. 51% Attack

Bitcoin system is dominated by those who have the computing power to find a nonce of a block before anyone else. This computing power is called hash power in general, and it means a power to solve a hash puzzle. Assume that a certain group has gathered all their hardware together, and as a result, achieved the absolute hash power to win in the block making competition at all times. In this case, every block in bitcoin system will be dominated by this group, and this group will generate all the blocks. A situation like this is figuratively called 51% attack. In other words, it symbolically refers to a situation in which a group has dominated majority of the system hash power.

If a certain group dominates hash power and takes over the production power of blocks, the weight of blockchain data produced by this group will always surpass that of anyone else. Even this group would be capable of catching up last 5 to 6 blocks of other blockchain data with no problem, so the latest 5~6 blocks of previous heaviest blockchain data might be discarded. In this case, the rewards that were given to those discarded blocks will be thrown away, and those who have caught up blockchain data will take away those rewards. Also, they could be able to selectively process only transaction that are in favor of themselves since transaction processing is entirely up to the miners' discretion.

Although 51% attack is possible, it is not an efficient way of attack, actually. The biggest reason is that 51% attack requires a huge amount of resources such as hardware and electricity, but the benefits achieved after attacking the system are not very big. Earlier, I explained that with dominating hash power it is possible to catch up 5 to 6 blocks to plunder others' block rewards. However even with this dominating hash power, catching up more than 6 blocks is theoretically impossible, so there is a limit in plunder. Also, in *3.5. Decentralized Consensus*, I explained that the first thing that each nodes check when they validate blockchain data with each other is whether or not every block in the blockchain data has been built by complying with the given rules. Therefore, even if some group dominated the production of blocks, it still has to stick to the rules! If not, its blocks will be discarded by decentralized consensus algorithm through validation process. Thus, one has to find a way to do bad things while keeping all the rules. So, taking others' bitcoin is impossible from the beginning. Some of the bad things one could do while keeping the rules would be double spending or catching up 5 to 6 blocks and stealing the reward. Of these, double spending would be always effective if one could completely control the production of blocks. Because dominating the production of blocks means to have the right to choose which transactions to be processed. Nevertheless, double spending itself is basically using one's own bitcoin twice, not taking someone else's bitcoin. Also, double spending is destined to fail if the recipient waits long enough. As a result, you can never put your hands on others' bitcoin even if you have control over the production of blocks.

However, if this group begins to abuse its power to take control over the rule of the system, then the problem gets serious. A decentralized program is obviously different from a centralized program in system maintenance method. Every software must be updated by each node voluntarily, so maintenance can't be done in systematic nor in scheduled manner. Meanwhile when some group has dominating hash power then they can abuse its power through soft fork which will be explained in the next section. Even though there is an obvious limitation which one can do with soft fork but still soft fork can change rule itself through dominating hash power. We'll discuss on this further at next section.

Meanwhile regardless of profit, once some group has dominating hash power there are numerous way to crash the bitcoin system. For example, miner could refuse to process transaction. In this case all transaction cannot be processed. Then this miner can request tremendously high transaction fee for processing. However again, this profit may not be that much compared to the investment required to dominate a hash power. Actually a bitcoin system is already taken by few miners. In fact, they are ready to execute 51% attack anytime. But they won't just because of cost efficiency.

By the way, these node with dominant hash power would become clear target of hackers. As explained earlier blockchain is the safest from hacking due to its decentralized property. However as some nodes dominate hash power, the system become more like centralized system and thus now there are obvious targets for hackers to attack. Current bitcoin system is not a decentralized system but a centralized system taken by few miners with dominating hash power.

 It is a still long far future story but once quantum computing become real, the system controlled by hash mechanism would fail to conduct its role. For example, the PoW of bitcoin implemented with SHA-256 would be void in front of quantum computing.

3.7. Hard fork and Soft fork

Bitcoin coin system is still in beta version and nobody guarantee its integrity. For last 8 years lots of security bleaches and bugs were found and fixed, still many improvement points are reported constantly. When comparing a centralized system with a decentralized system, the biggest weakness and dilemma of decentralized program is the maintenance of the system. In case of a centralized system, changes to the system will be reflected in perfect order once a certain server is upgraded at a certain scheduled time. Modification of software, upgrade, etc. can be executed according to a pre-established schedule plan. But in a blockchain ecosystem where thousands or tens of thousands of users gathered voluntarily, it is impossible for everyone to update their software to the latest version all at once. It is also impossible to execute such a plan according to a predetermined schedule. Thus, modification and update in decentralized software goes through totally different methods and procedures.

As having all the nodes upgrade at the same time is practically impossible, nodes that have upgraded themselves and nodes that haven't will inevitably coexist for some time. Then, there may be a collision between the new rules and the old rules. There are two types of rule changes that cause this collision.

- Validating a rule that used to be invalid
- Invalidating a rule that used to be valid

For convenience, let's adopt some notations. Firstly, capital letters A and B mean certain group of nodes. In other words, they are sets of nodes. Small letters α and β refer to blocks built by group A and B respectively. α refers to a block built by group A, and β is a block built by group B. We can break notation of block further down into α/α' and β/β'. Blocks without ' mark are recognized as valid by all of groups, while blocks with ' mark are only recognized as valid by respective groups. In other words, block α' is perfectly valid for group A but is an invalid block for B, whereas β' is perfectly valid for group B but is invalid for group A. Lastly, group A is a set of nodes which did not yet upgrade their software, so they follow the old rules, and group B is a set of nodes which did upgrade to the latest version of the software and thus follow the new rules.

Now, let's look at the following figure and table.

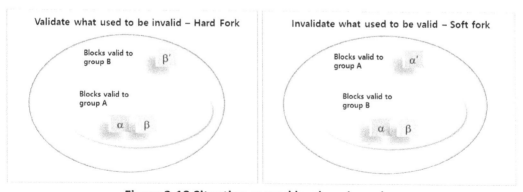

Figure 3-18 Situation caused by changing rules

Block	Block creator	Valid for
α	A (no upgrade, following old rules)	A and B both
α'		Only A
β	B (upgrade, following new rules)	A and B both
β'		Only B

Table 3-5 Table of blocks categorized by creator

Figure 3-18 and Table 3-5 summarizes the notations explained so far. If you look at Figure 3-18, you can see that the range of blocks each group accepts varies depending how the rules are changed. The left side of the figure shows validating rules that used to be invalid. In this case, the group that follows new rules can build much more various blocks because it can now produce blocks that used to be invalid in the past also. The right side of the figure, on the other hand, is invalidating rules that used to be valid before. In this case, the group that obeys old rules has a greater range of blocks. The group with the latest version of the software can't produce now invalid blocks, while the A group that uses a previous version of the software will continue to produce blocks without knowing that the rule has been invalidated. Now, let's closely examine what could happen in each situation.

3.7.1. Validating rules that used to be invalid – Hard Fork

As rules that used to be invalid in the past became valid, now group B is able to generate much more types of blocks than group A. As a result, some of the blocks produced by group B would not be accepted but be discarded as invalid by group A. Those unaccepted blocks are β'. On the other hand, all the blocks produced by group A are to be accepted by group B, so they all become α and there cannot be any α'.

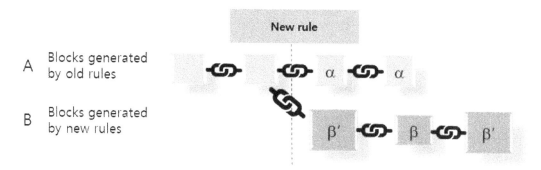

Figure 3-19 Hard Fork

Therefore, at some point of type there could be a conflict of two different blockchain data in the system. Blockchain data generated by group A according to their own rules and blockchain data generated by group B will grow separately from each other in the system.

These two different blockchain data cannot be combined into one. In group A's point of view, B's blockchain data, which includes β', has violated the rule, so it doesn't even need to be compared during decentralized consensus. Thus group A simply ignores blockchain data which contains β' and discard as invalid regardless of the weight of opponent blockchain data. Then A will simply choose heaviest blockchain data only from within group A. Meanwhile if ever group B was successful in creating a heavier blockchain data than group A, then group B will follow their own chain as their chain is heavier than group A's blockchain data. Eventually, these two groups' blockchain data will never be unified until every node in the system updates its software and thus will stay separated in the system forever. Of course, this problem will be solved if everyone in group A finally upgrade their software. However, this is very unlikely to happen. Realistically speaking, it is quite unreasonable to expect that every node in group A to update its software.

As soon as group A adopts new rules, all the blocks previously generated by group A between rule change time and upgrade time may be discarded, and A has to accept blocks of B instead. Then, all the rewards that were given to A will disappear. Unless there is an enough compensation for giving up their old rewards, group A won't give up their blocks. Thus, two totally different blockchain data will grow separately in the system, and such a situation is called a hard fork. Hard fork refers to a situation where there is a change that validates rules that used to be invalid and the only way to unify blockchain data is to have every node migrate to the new system.

> *i* The term fork originates from the shape of a fork and is widely used in computer science. When a process is ramified into another parallel process, it is also called fork. Also, a software project that copies an entire software and build a new one upon it is called a fork software. In blockchain data, the term fork was used to describe a situation where multiple blockchain data are divided into separate branches.

A typical case in which hard fork is necessary is to change the capacity of a block, that is currently limited at 1 MB. Current blocks can only process about 3,000 transactions at most, but transaction demands are constantly increasing. Thus, there is a constant debate on increasing the capacity of a block. If a rule is changed suddenly on some day, and the capacity of a block is increased to 2MB, nodes that have reflected this change would produce blocks of 2 MB in capacity and add them to their blockchain data, but the other nodes that follow the old rule won't accept blocks with 2 MB of capacity as valid and then discard them. As a result, there will be two versions of blockchain data in coexistence: one with only blocks of less than 1 MB capacity and the other that has accepted blocks of 2 MB capacity as well.

3.7.2. Invalidating rules that used to be valid – Soft Fork

This is an opposite case to hard fork. It invalidates rules that used to be valid. For example, if some rule is found to have a serious security breach, then that should be invalidated. This case, as shown on the right side is opposite case to hard fork. Group A can produce more blocks than B, so α' becomes invalidated by B because the block violates the new rule. Meanwhile, blocks produced by group B are all valid to group A, so there is no β'.

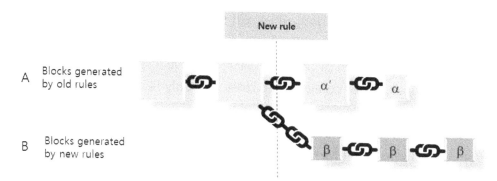

Figure 3-20 Soft fork

Figure 3-20 illustrates soft fork. As in hard fork, there could be a conflict of two different blockchain data, however the situation is quite different. Unlike hard fork where every single node has to upgrade in order to have one unified blockchain data, in soft fork if ever blockchain data produced by group B becomes heavier than group A, blockchain data will immediately be unified according to the decentralized consensus rule regardless of the software upgrade. This is because all the blocks generated by group B are valid to group A.

When there is a change that invalidates a rule that used to be valid, and everyone begins to follow the new rule as the nodes which follow the new rule become the majority, it is called soft fork.

As discussed earlier, soft fork is only successful when nodes with new rule dominates hash power. If group B cannot dominate, then the new rule can't settle. At this point, there are two types of full nodes which can reflect the new rule: full nodes which also do mining and full of nodes which don't do mining. Even though full nodes which don't do mining cannot generate blocks but they still can participate in validation of blocks and transactions. Thus, they can have an influence on the validation of blockchain data. The method of launching soft fork without considering mining power is called User Activated Soft Fork(UASF).

Meanwhile, the method of proceeding with soft fork by relying on the opinion of miners who have an enough hash power is called Miners Activated Soft Fork(MASF). Usually, soft fork proceeded by MASF has a low probability of failure and is capable of a quick reflection, while soft fork proceeded by UASF could fail depending on cooperation of the miners and can't reflect the change as quickly as MASF. However, if abused by miners, MASF can have a serious adverse effect on the system because they could spread rules that only favor miners, exploiting the logic of power.

So far, bitcoin core used soft fork 3 times but never allowed (official) hard fork to happen.[B] Though there are still many opinions and arguments about the necessity of hard fork, bitcoin community does not allow hard fork. On the other hand, a lot of alt cryptocurrencies have already used hard fork, and each has a unique characteristics. The problem related to hard fork is very serious and closely related to the stability of bitcoin system. We will discuss this in Chapter 5.

> The funny thing is that although bitcoin community never let hard fork happen, there actually happened many hard forks. One of them happened on August 1st, 2017 when 'bitcoin cash' branched off from bitcoin through hard fork, and the block size was increased up to 8 MB starting from #478,559 block. Also, in October, 2017, 'bitcoin gold' which has a new type of hash puzzle called equi-hash instead of the conventional SHA-256 in its PoW method, was created through hard fork starting from the #491,407 block. These two hard fork incidents may not be official but they are still hard forks. There is no way to prevent a hard fork if a group of users, that is big enough, begins to use a core software with their own rules. They are just not official hard forks. Because of this, it is often called as User Activated Hard Fork(UAHF).

3.7.3. Segwit and Segwit 2x

Earlier, I mentioned the limitation of block size as an example of situation where hard fork is necessary. Since changing block size which is not allowed before is to validate what used to be invalid, this requires hard fork. However, an idea that can have the same effect as increasing the capacity of blocks without doing a hard fork was introduced. In other words, a soft fork that can effectively increase the capacity of blocks virtually was introduced, and it is called Segwit. Segwit is an abbreviation for Segregated Witness. A witness is related to the unlock script that unlocks locking mechanism in transaction script which will be explained in **Appendix 5 – Transaction Script**. Since nothing about transaction script has been explained, readers only need to understand it as a readjustment of a transaction components without violating the existing rules. This can be thought of removing duplication to accommodate more room.

0100000001829725198 5
9d27dba0bd0f9161ccba
06d91657a50462a7c596
9613814cd15a6e010000
008a4730440220710606
5addb9389617baa15d6f
be0fc0e9f8e97d36a969
7f1b832e718666b56402
20776a864e92427871fd
9c6399bf7a2536c526b0
e3d5bca86e9c24d022eb
2832ef014104f191bd8a
1e966cfb402b65ae9305
42e37b38a710fcfe1fb2
4a05af7769d93b0f5fbb
b2b1ad589214d30dddfe
f1f2253529fbb8290a2c
738d80fb7b413a7b49b9
ffffffff0280841e0000
0000001976a914296a1c
3939c5250271f0db2a70
1ce62ae7aeac0488ac00
3e490000000001976a9
14d2349b0232f9ce2c60
5b97695973103326e2f5
1c88ac00000000

Input

Output

Figure 3-21 Source data of a transaction and a part highlighted by JSON Format

Figure 3-21 shows part of actual transaction data. Details of transaction data will be explained in Appendix, so it is perfectly ok even you don't know about it at all. Nevertheless, let's focus on the dotted red box on the right of the figure. This specifically lengthy looking part is about the ownership of UTXO. Segwit is a claim that argues for modifying this part. In other words, the structure of the configuration script data of the transaction is changed slightly, but it is readjusted to be a valid transaction even to the existing rule. Through this sort of readjustment, a block's availability can be virtually increased up to 1.8 MB. That is, it will virtually accommodates transactions as if it is 1.8M bytes in size even though physically it is still remained to be 1MB. Segwit was launched through soft fork technique.

On the contrary to this, a claim that the capacity of a block should be increased immediately using hard fork is called Segwit2x. Although, there has been a long debate on applying a hard fork from November 16th, 2017, it failed to reach a consensus, so Segwit2X actually didn't happen and looks like it won't even in the future.

Summary

- A block can be compared to a page of a ledger, and blockchain data to an entire ledger book.
- Block header is a place where all information in the block are summarized and stored, and its size is fixed at 80 bytes.
- A transaction can be compared to a balance sheet, and it consists of incomes and expenditures.
- UTXO or Unspent transaction output is an output that is unspent and scattered over blockchain data.
- The first transaction of every block is a reward transaction for block miner. This transaction is called coinbase transaction, and all other transactions are normal transactions.
- A transaction is not direct activity between stakeholders but is broadcasted to every nodes. Transaction become valid only when some node makes a new block and records it.
- A transaction requires a fee, and the minimum fee is 1000 sat. However, most fees cost 0.0015 BTC on average which is 150 times the minimum fee.
- Bitcoin system has eliminated the necessity of a trusted third party. It suggested a method that replaces trust with proof.

- Authentication is process of verifying the ownership of bitcoin to be spent, and it can be solved by asymmetric encryption.
- Decentralized consensus is a rule that chooses an identical blockchain data when there are multiple versions of blockchain data conflicting with one another. The heaviest (= most resources and efforts were put in) blockchain data gets selected.
- PoW should be designed in a way that proving should require lots of resources and efforts but verifying it should take an instant. This is called asymmetry.
- PoW of bitcoin system is to find an answer to the hash puzzle of a block. This answer is called a nonce and is a huge integer.
- When a rule that used to be invalid becomes valid, a hard fork occurs, and multiple different blockchain data could grow separately. These chains are unified only when every node updates its software.
- When a rule that used to be valid becomes invalid, a soft fork occurs, and multiple versions of blockchain data could appear as a result. These blockchain data get unified when the number of nodes using the new software become majority and thus exceed in weight.

4. Details of bitcoin system working principle

So far we covered all basic fundamentals and necessary concepts for bitcoin system and blockchain. This chapter will further detail on some specific parts where a detailed explanation is required.

Beginning of chapter 4 covers 2 core technologies of blockchain and bitcoin system, which is a secure hash and cryptography respectively. Later we'll discuss how these 2 techniques are implemented and utilized in block and transaction.

This chapter is mainly devoted to technical part of blockchain and could be quite difficult to some readers. As I mentioned several times, it should be perfectly ok for you to skip this entire chapter if you feel difficult. You may immediately skip to chapter 5 and return to this chapter again on demand. Anyway, most part is accompanied with precise diagram and concise comments for easy understanding.

Chapter 4 covers following topics.
- Hash function
    - Hash collision
    - Checksum
    - Byzantine general problem
    - SHA-256
    - Nonce and block hash problem
- Cryptography
    - Asymmetric cryptography
- Transaction
    - Merkle tree
    - Submission of Transaction

4.1. Hash function

Hash function is one of the most 2 important fundamental technologies of blockchain. Here we will shortly discuss what hash function is and how it is utilized in bitcoin system.

Hash function is a function which maps arbitrary size of input to a fixed length output. Hash function could be used in many purposes and sometime it also is used for efficient data search. However the biggest purpose of hash function in blockchain is not for efficient search but for easy detection of document modification.

Firstly let's look at the following figure

1	2	3	4	5	6	7	8	9	10	11	12	13	14	15	16	17	18	19	20	21	22
A	B	C	D	E	F	G	H	I	J	K	L	M	N	O	P	Q	R	S	T	U	V
23	24	25	26	27	28	29	30	31	32	33	34	35	36	37	38	39	40	41	42	43	44
W	X	Y	Z	a	b	c	d	e	f	g	h	i	j	k	l	m	n	o	p	q	r
45	46	47	48	49	50	51	52	53	55	56	57	58	59	60	61	62	63	64	65	66	67
s	t	u	v	w	x	y	z	0	1	2	3	4	5	6	7	8	9		,	.	!

Bitcoin = B(2) + i(35) + t(46) + c(29) + o(41) + i(35) + n(40) = **228**

input   output

Figure 4-1 Simple hash function

In Figure 4-1, we developed one of the simplest hash function that one can think of. The hash function rule is a quite straightforward. Each alphabet, numbers and some of most frequently used special characters are mapped to its matching unique numeric number. Then we sums all corresponding numbers to get a single integer. If we apply this hash function to word 'Bitcoin' we can get the result 228 as shown in the figure. However, this simple hash function has several significant defects and one of the most severe drawback is that the length of integer is not fixed and is a direct violation of basic property of hash function which should guarantee a fixed length regardless of input size. The size of current hash output could be shorter for the short word whereas it could be quite a longer for a long sentence. For example, the hash value for "Hi" is just "H(9)+i(35) = 44" and thus is only 2 digits, which directly violates the assumption of 'fixed length'.

Now let's fix this simple rule to comply with the fixed length principle and add up a little bit complex rules to make our hash function more reliable one.

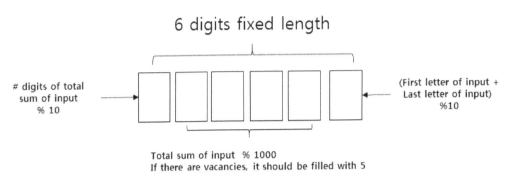

Figure 4-2 New hash function with augmented rules

Figure 4-2 shows new hash function with enhanced rules. Now it seems a bit complex. Firstly the length become fixed with six digits and complies with basic rules. Secondly we added some more rules to escalate complexity of a function. % symbol is modular operation which calculates a remainder of a division operation. For example 12 % 3 means a remainder of 12 divided by 3. If we divide 12 by 3, the quotient is 4 and remainder is 0 and thus the value of 12 % 3 is 0. Similarly 13% 3 = 1 (quotient is 4 and remainder is 1) and 22 % 5 = 2. If we look at the overall rules again, the first step is to calculate the first slot, which takes a remainder of division of overall sum by 10. Second step is to calculate the 4 yellow slots in the middle, which is to calculate a reminder of division of overall sum by 10,000. If the result of a second operation got less than 4 digits then all vacancies should be filled with digit 5. The last step is to calculate final slot, which is to calculate remainder of sum of first and last letter of input divided by 10.

Our new hash function sounds a bit complex but actually it is quite simple. Now let's apply new hash function to word "Bitcoin" again.

1	2	3	4	5	6	7	8	9	10	11	12	13	14	15	16	17	18	19	20	21	22
A	B	C	D	E	F	G	H	I	J	K	L	M	N	O	P	Q	R	S	T	U	V
23	24	25	26	27	28	29	30	31	32	33	34	35	36	37	38	39	40	41	42	43	44
W	X	Y	Z	a	b	c	d	e	f	g	h	i	j	k	l	m	n	o	p	q	r
45	46	47	48	49	50	51	52	53	55	56	57	58	59	60	61	62	63	64	65	66	67
s	t	u	v	w	x	y	z	0	1	2	3	4	5	6	7	8	9		,	.	!

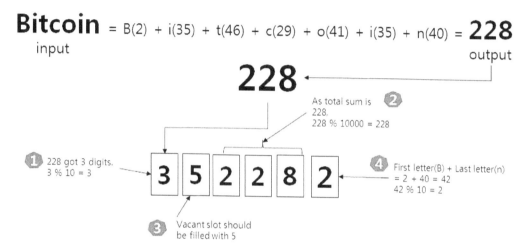

Bitcoin = B(2) + i(35) + t(46) + c(29) + o(41) + i(35) + n(40) = **228**

Figure 4-3 Hash value of "Bitcoin" with new hash function

Figure 4-3 shows how to calculate hash value of "Bitcoin" with new hash function. Above all, we need to identify all corresponding digits for every letters in "Bitcoin" from mapping table and then sum them to get 228. When we apply rule ①, as 228 is 3 digits, the first bin becomes 3 because 3 % 10 = 3. At ②, 228 % 10,000 becomes 228 itself and therefore there left 1 vacant slot and this vacant slot should be filled with 5 according to rule number ③. The last bin is calculated by applying rule ④, which adds the first and the last character of input then apply % operand. 42 % 10 = 2. Finally we get the result, which is 352282

Input	Output Hash value
Hash	351142
Bitcoin	352282
Blockchain	353752

The purpose of this hash function is to easily explain what hash is	428495

Table 4-1 Hash function applied to various inputs

Table 4-1 shows the hash values of several different inputs. Looking at table, despite its crudeness, our hash function behaves quite well. Firstly it perfectly converts every input into 6 digits fixed length output. The simple word like "Hash" and a bit long sentence like in the last row, both are mapped to 6 digits hash value. On top of that, the resulting 6 digits don't have any obvious clue on what might have been the input.

4.1.1. Hash collision

One noticeable point from Table 4-1 is that that final hash value of short word looks a bit similar and naturally raises one question. Is it possible that two different inputs could have an identical hash value result? To make a long story short, yes it could have. Our coarse hash function could have many cases where the output is the same from different inputs. When the hash result is the same despite the different inputs, it is called a 'hash collision'. The probability of hash collision would reduce inversely proportional to its output length and properness of a formula. For an important usage, hash function should absolutely be free from hash conflict.

4.1.2 Checksum

At this point, some curious reader might wonder whether the output of the lengthy input sentence of the last row of Table 4-1 is really 42849 or not. Some may have a non-productive doubt on the truth of that number thinking that I might have filled some arbitrary numbers in the row as it is not easy to check. Please don't try to calculate yourself for the long number. It would take long as well as quite a waste of a time. I did it with program so no need to worry about me. Then, as it is quite a work to check the truth of a number, is there any way to do simple sanity check? Let's take a look at Figure 4-3 again. All rules seem to require calculation of entire numbers of input but actually there is one exception. The rule number ④ doesn't need entire input.

Rule ④ simply requires the first and the last character of an input then find a remainder after division by 10. It means that we don't need to calculate full summation of entire input to get the hash number of 6th bin, which is calculated by rule ④.

1	2	3	4	5	6	7	8	9	10	11	12	13	14	15	16	17	18	19	20	21	22
A	B	C	D	E	F	G	H	I	J	K	L	M	N	O	P	Q	R	S	T	U	V
23	24	25	26	27	28	29	30	31	32	33	34	35	36	37	38	39	40	41	42	43	44
W	X	Y	Z	a	b	c	d	e	f	g	h	i	j	k	l	m	n	o	p	q	r
45	46	47	48	49	50	51	52	53	55	56	57	58	59	60	61	62	63	64	65	66	67
s	t	u	v	w	x	y	z	0	1	2	3	4	5	6	7	8	9		,	.	!

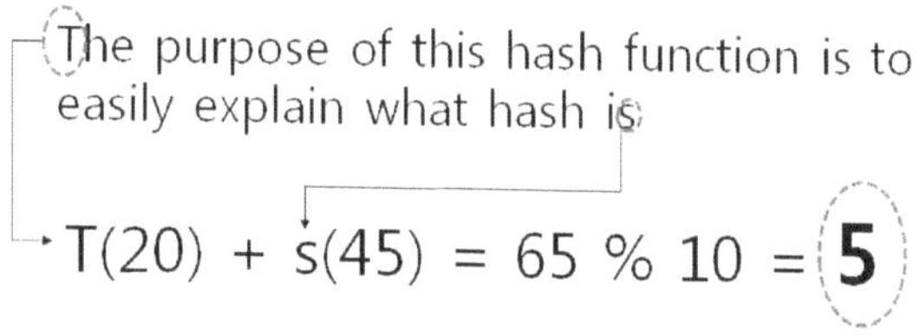

The purpose of this hash function is to easily explain what hash is.

$$T(20) + s(45) = 65 \ \% \ 10 = 5$$

Figure 4-4 Rule using only the first and the last character

Let's take a look at Figure 4-4. Even though calculating entire hash value is a bit complex, to find the last digit of a hash value is simple. Let's apply the rule ④. The first character T(=20) and the last one which is s(=45) sums to 65. As 65 % 10 = 5. The last digit should be 5. Now look at the Table 4-1. The last digit is 5 indeed. With this method we cannot tell whether 428495 itself is correct one at least we can tell it could the correct one. If the last digit were something between 0 ~ 4 or 6 ~9 we could have easily identified that it is fake. As such the simple method to check the sanity of a rule is called checksum. Please remember the checksum as it will be used at bitcoin address calculation at appendix.[14]

---

[14] Actually in most of the cases, checksum involves entire input. The checksum formula here is just for convenience of explanation.

4.1.3. Byzantine general

Imagine a situation where our forces confront enemy. During a battle, our forces are split into separate areas and enemy set up a stronghold in between. Individual battle with enemy will result in defeat whereas united attacks at the same time will obviously win the battle or may retreat at the same time to some place to gather together to fight back in the future. What is important here is that forces should act the same way at the same time whether to attack or to retreat.

The problem is that there is no reliable communication tool. The only way to communicate is to use raven. However raven should fly over the enemy and possibility of getting caught to reveal our strategy and also enemy may make fake message to deceive our forces. In this case how the general of each troops could identify that the message is not forged and thus behave the same way?

Our forces   Enemy   Our forces

Figure 4-5 Situation where enemy forged message

Figure 4-5 shows situation where enemy forged message and changed attack signal to retreat signal then forwarded the message to our forces. However if we take a closer look at the message we could identify six digits at the bottom. Yes, the hash value was included at the message and the enemy was not aware of the meaning of the digits and just forwarded as it is.

Figure 4-6 Mismatch of hash values

Figure 4-6 shows a situation where our forces compare hash value written in the message and a hash value newly calculated over the sentence using hash rule. Our forces detected that the newly calculated number 357600 is different from hash number 417955 written in the message and thus could conclude that the message has been forged.

This example briefly describes what Leslie Lamport and his colleagues presented to ACM programming language in 1982.[i] Isolated spread byzantine generals has to have an identical opinion either attack or retreat. There is no reliable communication media for several reasons and what is worse is that there even could possibly be betrayers among generals. The problem is to find a solution to have an identical consensus among all generals. This is an easy analogical mapping of a common problem on distributed network of how to find the truth of a signal received by other nodes in an extremely unknown environment. What differentiates byzantine general formulation from former distributed consensus works is that in byzantine general problem, nodes are supposed to be arbitrary, which means that nodes could not only crash but also could behave maliciously at its own will. This is much more complicated formula than previous crash-stop model where each node could only either crash(and stop operating) or behave correctly. Nodes are not supposed to be maliciously behaving in crash-stop model.

Decentralized consensus in bitcoin system is one possible solution for byzantine general problem. Each nodes are byzantine generals themselves. Each node keeps its own copy of blockchain data. There is a need for checking whether a given data is a truth or lie. Blockchain itself is basically one of proposed solution to byzantine general problem. Bitcoin blockchain used 'decentralized consensus through proof-of-work' to find a truth against false information.

4.1.4. SHA-256

As every readers may already realize that the hash function used in bitcoin cannot be that simple as we developed just before. Let's point out just 2 biggest problems in our hash function.

- Hash collision potential – Big risk of two different inputs to be hashed to the same hash value
- Prediction of hash rule – Rule is so simple that with several trial and error, hash rule itself could be revealed.

Once hash rule is revealed, the document protection capability become void.
The hash that strongly comply with the second rule is called secure hash. As it is impossible to reverse engineer the hash rule, it perfectly protects original document. In this respect, our hash function is far from secure hash because it is too simple to not to be disclosed its underlying rule.

SHA is an acronym of Secure Hash Algorithm and is developed by NSA. The first hash algorithm was SHA-0 developed in 1993 but was abandoned due to reported hash collision. Afterwards it was enhanced as SHA-1 and SHA-2 family. SHA-0 and SHA-1 are designed to produce 160 bits hash value but with advent of SHA-2, it become various versions like 224,256,384 and 512 bits. SHA-256 as its name suggests generates 256 bits hash value. Unlike SHA-0 there has never been an actual collision in case of SHA-1 but is proved to have a possibility of collision. Now only SHA-2 family is being used for secure hash. SHA-2 is a secure hash function which is believed to be perfectly free from above 2 problems.

Although SHA-256 looks very complicated, the basic concept is more or less the same as our coarse hash function. It is just an extension in terms of hash calculation operation with more complicated rules.

0xb4056df6691f8dc72e56302ddad345d 65fead3ead9299609a826e2344eb63aa4

Figure 4-7 SHA-256 of "Bitcoin"

Figure 4-7 shows a result of SHA-256 hash applied to "Bitcoin". The resulting number looks a bit familiar? Yes, this is exactly the same 32 bytes pattern of block hash value we saw before. What we mentioned as a hash function just before actually was a SHA-256. It generates 32 bytes a fixed length output regardless of input length. Whether the input is just 1 character short or composed of million characters long, the output length always remains the same, a 32 bytes. Let's remember this property.

Now, let's apply SHA-256 to the inputs in Table 4-1 and compare the result with our simple hash result.

Input	Hash output
Hash	351142
	0xa91069147f9bd9245cdacaef8ead4c3578ed 44f179d7eb6bd4690e62ba4658f2
Bitcoin	352282

	0xb4056df6691f8dc72e56302ddad345d65fea d3ead9299609a826e2344eb63aa4
Blockchain	353752
	0x8a347e1afd785d0c88500c16fbaa234029bd 41d9af5ee2c7da6cf98c5b8af3e7
The purpose of this hash function is to easily explain what hash is	428495
	0x5d666552fba37e81793806700340405f3cbc 400888a230099189588ed319590b

Table 4.2 Comparison of our hash function and SHA-256

Table 4.2. compares our hash function with SHA-256 result. The upper 6 digits of the right side of a table per each input is our hash value whereas the lower 256 bits(32 bytes) is a result from SHA-256 function. Even a short glance could tell that new hash value does really look strong enough to be free from hash collision or any prediction of a rule. Especially, the hash values of "Hash" and "Bitcoin" never look similar this time, which were quite similar in case of our old hash function. Also there is no clue at all regarding whether the input is short word or long sentence, etc.

Figure 4-8 Even a tiny difference cause a big difference

It is definitely obvious that SHA-256 is not predictable if we look at Figure 4-8. Figure 4-8 compares a hash value between "Bitcoin" and "Bitcoin." Two input has only dot(.) difference at the end but resulting hash values are completely different from one another. SHA-256 can be regarded as the most advanced secure hash that is free from hash collision and predictableness.

Another interesting feature of SHA-256 we already discussed is that its output length is the fixed size regardless of input. From this characteristics, multiple application of hash function always generates completely different but the same length output.

Figure 4-9 Double hash

Figure 4-9 shows situation where hash is applied twice directly in a row. As such, to enhance security, sometimes hash function is applied multiple times.

4.1.5. Nonce and block hash puzzle

Previously it is explained that the answer to hash puzzle (which is required to make a new block) is called 'Nonce'. Here let's investigate about that hash puzzle more in detail.

```
Bitcoin0    : c118cf0671c5ddc5706967a3eb7c5a55685a113a8bf4667f5daa128f3174fcf3
Bitcoin1    : f1a4bf6b4b78ce172c51c778a144ace04c3b4fb9dfdc05a242434b18efd42690
Bitcoin2    : e6cc5201223f94c6a57541c065e7ba9aa05922c34f35a5f7abb8ca32654bbb5c
Bitcoin3    : e67520be2df787378f6ba454fca8daa469edbbe71febd266f7247a5d5a001737
Bitcoin4    : 4194d1f4259f651ec23173660cf8c3fbaa3dcab216a07635063b634338c5d589
Bitcoin5    : 6015369392f19b4c29b520d9dbfc2fd1b543dd0d19f5c80ff2218e4d1323a268
Bitcoin6    : fcd6dbfcbe63b111b1c8e099db4d960a55749862708eb7f5d656df5b757f73f4
Bitcoin7    : 27cf89eab4ad49f56e8a90846e1fb1dc88b1884bb7b7bf78c9e9857a182d5095
Bitcoin8    : b2fa975eabd52aeae55dc9299c924f9ab89649cdead2a16aa988a7ddd7d65416
Bitcoin9    : 17d1cd8974c4034422802891a614ecf5ed48822d02d13c7a629f85428ff3789b7
Bitcoin10   : 2a605c43fc09cd5ddb43f68db40554afa2f4219899c533d5c7e255cfc3e9ed09
Bitcoin11   : 1a2f13efdaf9eb0e001f8c2f3874d286504ff7d499faf9bc0295d07db7e946e8
Bitcoin12   : b34b60c26b7c0b707a5ae4563e3fb5f323cef6cb4ec41575c41c48f9b3dcba9a
Bitcoin13   : dddd8d46caf8fa6539ff7d87039be3964146c43ffc78aa59853ccc26a3421b32
Bitcoin14   : 043d5eed99bc5c4f022509096f808c63ae2f56aa65fcba781b1bf83f259aa4b5
Bitcoin15   : 7bce098148d1b5f59ae22ae6f8573944a20a0fd77b6ff616824247272716a6c6
                                  . .
Bitcoin73   : 63a8a1063b67281f1e42fdcb50fe3f40864adfac26b7e2b192f0d3c7b6c019cb
Bitcoin74   : c5094c692868698883b392dd38e648ac9c1d02d1a85ae8ff8bb1b726ec4499e5
Bitcoin75   : c7c24c4c4872d855bd4632a2808bfe67879c9441ec337eda1940aac926f847f9
Bitcoin76   : 00e499e27d0e0a2edd4ecd5e089bcd97647d7b1aa678e03812e569dc9f3c6229
Bitcoin77   : a1758cd05e73e40069a8488e5b0b9286a4c988bf13c1ffeca4548a2072d5b223
Bitcoin78   : fa0e684f5fbbde4f5d3e3b8cc8053b4840b98b14a33e10971917cd7a6f5d8bc5
Bitcoin79   : 6baec470abec203bd1e81d0d2a07b1878ac2f455b5ec1555b9bbd93ccfa65853
                                  . .
Bitcoin96   : 479902adca33327dffcabcc25d25bfd57f66e05a3b4a9e7ac43638aec89b52c2
Bitcoin97   : e476a35704a06be232817dc562b51a383d6b466515829e13be568471d5b391c8
Bitcoin98   : 744fa2e8ce627d228e06efc94fae63b4c8e08f6b4becd14c061800aea93bd8f9
Bitcoin99   : c28b5df37fade968fc0d3157fc7ebfe0d3eb8fb33087f06dafdce823af9b5d84
Bitcoin100  : 7ac5356e484f67ef54ec0cf5b4ad16feafe0b2827c735a25303523609a18993e
```

Figure 4-10 Hash value calculated by changing number from 0 to 100 at the end

Figure 4-10 show what happens to the SHA-256 hash value result when we change a number at the end of a word "Bitcoin" from 0 to 100. Closer look at Figure 4-10 shows that there occasionally happen to be cases where the hash value starts with 0 and sometimes with several leading zeros. For example if we add 14 to 'Bitcoin', the resulting hash value happened to starts with 1 leading zero and similarly when we add 76 to 'Bitcoin', it generated 2 consecutive leading zeros at the beginning of a hash value.[15]

In the same fashion if we increase the numbers in experiment, there are cases where more consecutive leading zeros happen. Table 4-2 shows the results of an experiment where we increase number 1 by 1 up to 100,000,000. When number

---

[15] As this is hexadecimal notation, two leading zeros in hexadecimal is 8(=2x4) leading zero bits.

reaches 4,457, we got 3 consecutive zeros and got 4 and 5 leading zeros when the number increased to 13,562 and 26,949 respectively. The number looks still manageable. However the number which was required to get 6 consecutive zeros was 10,920,353! A huge increase from previous one. As you have seen before, this pattern is completely unpredictable and we have no idea when we can get how many consecutive leading zeros.

# leading zeros	numbers	Hash Value
1	14	0x043d5eed99bc5c4f022509096f808c63ae2f56aa65fcba78 1b1bf83f259aa4b5
2	58	0x006ac0f2f56172bdb073a3433852d61cb6bd51388325c1ff 275a8462e14d1e69
3	4457	0x0001ce656b8bff026345ee54f0a1c0bbacba5d0f1d721a76 f92dcbadc40689c8
4	13,562	0x00009b90178d06701ce50fd1a59a2f958cf229a0eca9e2ca f5e45717cedd23a0
5	26,949	0x00000892155c74f7e5b9babc9c260c01f22f14f7e622f645 0df295d3b82d9e37
6	10,920,353	0x000000f4e09bf1d08fa1f4f6011e9a19d2268346f14d2ef1 dd797840ca29848a

Table 4-2 Leading zeros in hash value as we increase numbers

It has low chance of having a leading zeros in hash value and the probability is exponentially decreasing proportional to the number of leading zeros.[16] Hash puzzle is to find an integer which makes resulting hash value to be less than a given target value and we call this integer a Nonce. Let's look into actual target value of a block # 500,000. The target value of # 500,000 block is as follows.

3608622922776648000000000000000000000000000000000000000000.

---

[16] Roughly saying, when we need k bits of leading zeros, the probability of one specific SHA256 result to have k bits of leading zeros is 2^{-k} and it requires around 2^k trials to get the answer. Numbers in Table 4-2 is in hexadecimal notation and thus 6 leading zeros in bottom row is actually 6x4 = 24 leading bits in binary representation.

Please don't be overwhelmed by this huge number as this is actually quite a small number compared to other target numbers. This number is denoted in decimal and let's convert that into 32 bytes hexadecimal notation.

0x0000000000000000000025ad0000000002e63d3207a18525192c5ca80000000000

Ah ha, the hash puzzle is simply more or less just to repeat trying and checking whether some integer happens to result in specified number of leading zeros and consequently become less than the given target value. The integer which happens to make a hash value less than this target is a called Nonce! The according hash value will become a unique number of that specific block and is called 'block hash value'. The only way to find a nonce is a trial-and-error. With SHA-256, there is no other way around as we never can predict a pattern of a hash value.

Previously it is explained that block is being generated every 10 minutes in average. That's because it takes around 10 minutes to find a nonce which is a mandatory prerequisite job to make a block. There is a possibility of reduction in solving time of hash puzzle as degree of integration of semiconductor will double every 18 months according to Moore's law. Bitcoin is self-adjusting target value to come up with the development of hardware. It adjusts difficulty in every 2,016 blocks. Theoretically, as 144 blocks is to be produced a day, the time to produce 2,016 blocks should be 1,209,600 seconds(or 14 days, that is 2 weeks). If 2,016 blocks were produced in shorter than 2 weeks then system will increase difficulty to make a producing time longer but if 2,016 blocks were produced in longer than 2 weeks, the system will decrease difficulty to make a producing time shorter on the contrary. The maximum increase of difficulty in one adjustment is up to 300% of previous one depending on shortened time and the maximum decrease of difficulty is up to 75% of a previous level depending on exceeded time.

> Due to a system bug, an actual adjustment of difficulty is not per 2,016 blocks but per every 2,015 blocks. This could produce 0.05%(=1/2016) error from original theoretical adjustment.

4.1.6. Parallel block hash calculation

Obviously there is no alternative mathematical formula or method to solve a hash puzzle other than trial and error. However there are several tricks to solve a hash puzzle much quicker. As we discussed shortly before, every step of hash calcualtion is independent of each other and has absolutely no relation at all between each steps, which was the main reason that the only way to solve a hash puzzel is just a trial-and-error. From this very charatersitics, the hash puzzle can perfectly fit for parallel processing as each calculation is perfectly independent of each other.

Consider the case where we try to find 6 consecutive zeros in Table 4-2. Previously, we used only 1 computer and calculated 10,920,354(as we started from 0) times to find 6 consecutive zeros. What if we have 10 computers available? Can we divide this job 10 pieces and do a parallel computing? As each sector is completely independent, we can divide sectors and allocate the calculations to each of 10 computers. If we divide 100,000,000 into 10 equal pieces then it will become ten 10,000,000 pieces. Let's allocate a sector from 0 to 9,999,999 to computer 1, 10,000,000 to 19,999,999 to computer 2, as such 10th computer will compute from 90,000,000 to 100,000,000. This would reduce an average calculation time by 1/10. Let's take a look at following figure.

Single vs. Parallel – 6 consecutive zeros

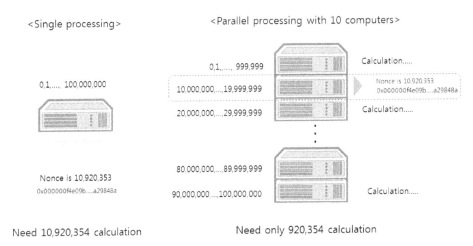

Figure 4-11 Nonce calculation with parallel processing

Figure 4-11 compares the performance between single processing and parallel processing to find a nonce for 6 consecutive zeros at Table 4-2. The left side of a figure shows a single computer computes 10,920,354 times to find a nonce whereas a right side of a figure shows 2nd computer finds a nonce only from 920,354 computations since it started from 10,000,000. It found a solution 11.9 times faster (of course with around 10 times more electricity consumption and 10 times bigger hardware investment) than single computer. The more the computer, the shorter the time to find a nonce. Parallel computing can be maximized with distributed networking. A pool could be formed to connect tens of thousands people together.

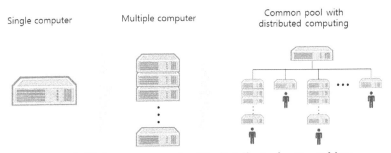

Figure 4-12 Common pool with distributed networking

Figure 4-12 shows a comparison between single computing and common pool computing. The more the number of participants, the more computing power one could utilize. Currently almost all big miners form this kinds of pool to mine a block. Block reward is to be distributed per contribution factors. This pool could be a closed pool where only professional miners form a pool or an open pool where even a personal user could join as a member of a pool. A normal pool could be composed of around several hundreds to more than 100 thousands. Thus each individual could hardly win the battle against this kind of expert pools. Accordingly, most of the individual joins to open pool to get a dividend per contribution. If they could use ASIC machine when they join a pool then he or she could have a better chance to get a higher dividend. (with expense of further investment of course)

 Parallel processing does not necessarily require a multiple computers. A single computer with multiple cores could do a limited parallel processing and can enjoy full parallel processing with GPU. Thus single computer also could do a parallel processing. Of course a networking of this kinds of parallel computing capacity computers would be better. As explained previously, mining bitcoin with CPU is impossible as of now.[17]

4.2. Cryptography

Up to now we have been discussed on secure hash function where it was impossible to guess input from its output. On the other hand, the cryptography which encrypts sentence then decrypts to recover to its original form is way different from secure hash function. Hash can easily detect the change of an original context but cannot recover input from output in any cases.

Cryptography comes from a Greek word 'Kryptos' which means 'secret'. This commonly refers to a method which camouflages original context by using scientific principles including mathematics. Ancient cryptography was usually a

---

[17] *Refer to 2.3.3 Mining – making block*

steganography where the method of disguise is a physical one. Wring a sentence with lemon juice which can only be seen with candle light or sealing an envelope with wax seal to protect to be unopen are typical steganography with physical method.

A transpose encryption used by a Caesar is one of the most well-known encryption method which uses letter position shift. Caesar is said to have used 3 position shifted character method when he deliver a secret message. That is, A is shifted to D which is 3 characters away in alphabetical order, B is to E and in this manner Z is mapped to C. When they decrypted the message, they shifted a sentences backwards 3 positions.[o]

Recent cryptography is mostly developed by mathematics, especially that of 'number theory'. In the movie 'Imitation Game' a Benedict Cumberbatch starred an Alan Turing who was a genius mathematician tried to decrypt Germany cryptography system called 'Enigma' during a second world war.

Cryptography method means any method which hides a meaning of an original context then decrypts to recover its original context on demand. In this section we will discuss another key technology component of a blockchain called an 'asymmetric cryptography'.

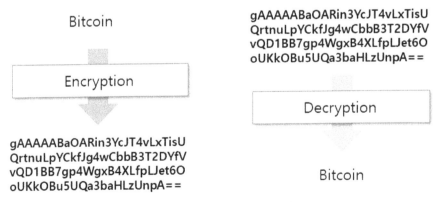

Figure 4-13 Encryption and Decryption process

Figure 4-13 shows the process of encrypting "Bitcoin" and then decrypting it back to get original text "Bitcoin". As previously mentioned, in case of secure hash, there is no way to recover original text but in cryptography, it is about protecting document by encryption and then recovering original document through decryption. In broad sense, there are 2 different cryptography techniques. The first one is a symmetric cryptography and the other one is an asymmetric cryptography.

Figure 4-14 compares symmetric cryptography with asymmetric cryptography. Cryptographic key is a data used for encryption and decryption. If the same key is used for encryption and decryption then it is called a symmetric whereas it is called asymmetric if keys used for encryption and decryption are different. In case of asymmetric cryptography, there always is a pair of keys. One of this pair is called a public key whereas the other pair is called a private key(also known as a secret key). A document encrypted with one of these key can only be decrypted with the other key of the pair.

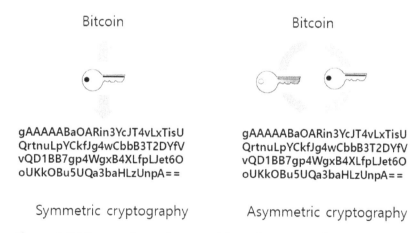

Figure 4-14 Comparison of symmetric and asymmetric cryptography

As it is shown in the left side of Figure 4-14 a single key is used for both encryption and decryption in case of symmetric whereas one key is used for encryption and the other key is used for decryption in case of asymmetric as right side of a figure. Modern digitized finance almost always use asymmetric one and bitcoin system also uses asymmetric cryptography. We will discuss asymmetric cryptography in detail from next section.

4.2.1. Asymmetric cryptography

In asymmetric cryptography, a pair of keys is used for encryption and decryption. Encryption is possible with both keys, however when document is encrypted with one of the key pair then it is only to be decrypted with its pair and cannot be decrypted with any other key including a key used for encryption. For example, if a document is encrypted with private key then it is to be decrypted with its public key only and if a document is encrypted with public key then it is only decrypted with its private key pair.

Generally, a private key is generated first and then according public key is derived from the private key. Thus person with a private key can be regarded as a person with both keys as public key could be derived from private key. However public key will never can derive a private key nor could give any clue on what the private key might be.

There could be 2 different usage of asymmetric cryptography depending on which key is used for encryption. For the convenience of explanation, we will draw private key as yellow and public key as white. Encryption will be depicted with green arrow while decryption will be depicted with yellow arrow.

4.2.1.1. Encryption with private key – Electronic signature

Encryption with private key is generally related to electronic signature. That is, a message maker can prove that the specific message is actually created by himself or herself through electronic signature. Let's take a look at following figure.

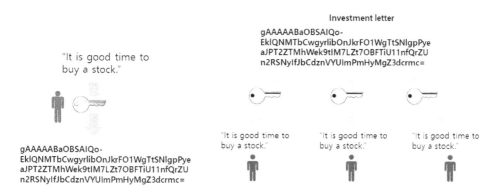

Figure 4-15 Encryption with private key

Figure 4-15 shows a situation where an analyst sends investment letter to subscribers. At figure, analyst, with his private key, encrypted message which tells that 'this is a proper time to buy a stock' then sent a message through email. A recipient of this email could decrypt this message with given public key of an analyst. If this message is successfully decrypted with analyst's public key then it means that this message has been truly encrypted by analyst's private key and thus automatically prove its authenticity. Normally as public key is accessible for many persons, this way of encryption is more for proof of authentication rather than protection of a contents. Thus the main purpose of this type of encryption is to sign on content.

4.2.1.2. Encryption with public key – Contents protection and Authentication

Encryption with public key then decryption with private key is a typical way of protecting secrecy. As this message can only be decrypted with according private key, it could perfectly protect document

Figure 4-16 Encryption with public key then decryption with private key

Figure 4-16 shows the situation where a document is encrypted with public key and then is decrypted with its according private key. As encrypted document could only be decrypted with a private key pair, it perfectly protects document and the fact that it is decrypted with private key proves itself that key owner is legitimate person to access document. Please recall that from **3.2.3. UTXO – Unspent Transaction Output** that UTXO is locked with some mechanism and could be unlocked only by a legitimate owner. The way UTXO is locked has to do with asymmetric cryptography.

With asymmetric cryptography, bitcoin system puts a lock using public key of owner of UTXO so that it would only be unlocked by according private key! We will discuss in detail at next section.

Table 4-3 summarizes what we have discussed so far regarding symmetric and asymmetric cryptography.

	Symmetric	Asymmetric
Key used	Single	A pair (Public and Private)
Key(s) used for encryption & decryption	Same	One for encryption , the other one for decryption

Table 4-3 Symmetric vs. Asymmetric cryptography

4.3. Transaction

As we have covered two fundamental technical building blocks of bitcoin system, this is proper time to discuss how it is applied to bitcoin blockchain. It has been explained earlier that a single block can store around 2,000 ~ 3,000 transactions. Also please recall that block header has a 32 bytes field called merkle tree root. At that moment, I explained that merkle tree is way of magically condensing all transactions information into just 32 bytes. Actually the root of this merkle tree is a hash information of all transactions such that any tiny modification of transactions is to be detected quickly. Now let's first take a little bit closer look at merkle tree then discuss on transaction which is a core part of blockchain.

4.3.1. Merkle Tree

There are diverse different logical way of storing data in computer. The logical structure which we store a data is called data structure and each data structure has its own advantages and disadvantages.

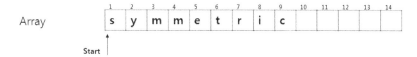

Figure 4-17 Data structure - Array

Figure 4-17 shows one of the simplest and basic data structure called array. Each data has the same physical order as logical order. The biggest advantage of this method is that once you know the starting point of data, all the rest of the data could be easily accessed as a relative position from the starting point. However the biggest drawback of this method is that when you insert new character in the middle, it costs a lot of efforts.

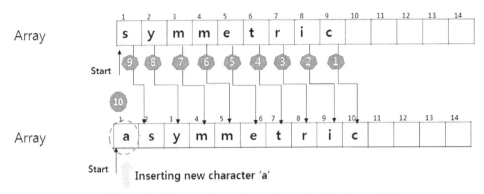

Figure 4-18 New character is inserted in the middle.

Figure 4-18 shows what happens if new character is inserted in the middle of array. To prepare a space for new character 'a', entire 9 characters have to be shifted by 1 position rightwards then finally 'a' is to be inserted into newly prepared vacancy.

Another common way of storing data is a linked list.

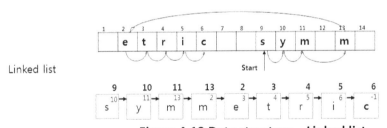

Figure 4-19 Data structure – Linked list

As seen in Figure 4-19 a physical order of linked list is different from its logical order. To keep logical order, every element needs to keep a position of its successor element. The very first data 's' has to remember the position of its successor which is 10 and 'y' has to remember 11 and so forth. As such, linked list has an inconvenience of having to remember the position of its successor but it is quite convenient when it comes to inserting new character compared to array.

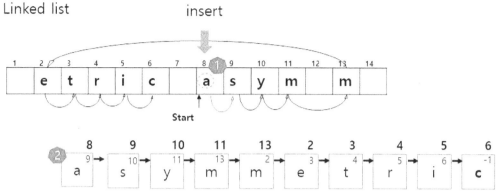

Linked list   insert

Start

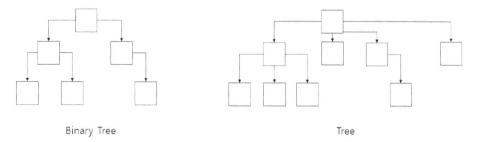

Figure 4-20 Inserting new character at linked list

Figure 4-20 show how to insert 'a' into existing linked list. Unlike array, the physical inserting position of new data is not important in linked list and thus no need to shift data to make a vacancy. All we have to do is to update a few links for newly inserted character as shown figure. In ② of a figure, we can see that 'a' is pointing its next data 's'. As such, a convenience of inserting new data is one of the biggest advantage of linked list. By the way, do you remember that in block header, there was a field which stores 32 bytes value of 'previous block hash'? The previous block hash value could be thought of as an address or a position of previous data. Yes, blockchain data itself is a linked list like Figure 4-19 chained together one by one!

Basically a combination of array and liked list can create lots of different variation of data structure. A tree is a bit complicated version of linked list.

Binary Tree   Tree

Figure 4-21 Binary Tree and general tree

Figure 4-21 shows a tree structure, which is a variation of linked list to accommodate multi dimension. Linked list has only 1 successor to form a long straight line whereas a tree can have an arbitrary number of successors. The top most node of a tree is called root. A directly connected nodes just a level below are called children nodes whereas a directly connected nodes just a level above are called parent nodes. The shape of tree structure resembles a tree upside down and the top level looks like a root of a tree. Thus it is called a root node.

A particular case of a tree where only 2 children nodes are allowed in maximum is called a binary tree. Tree at the left side of Figure 4-21 is a binary tree and as shown in figure it has only maximum 2 nodes as its children(left child and right child respectively). Merkle tree was developed by Ralph Merkle in 1979. It has binary tree structure.[M] Bitcoin uses merkle tree to store an aggregated single hash value of all transactions in a block. Following figure describes how merkle tree extracts a single 256bits(32 bytes) hash value out of all transactions.

Hash(x) = SHA256(SHA256(x))

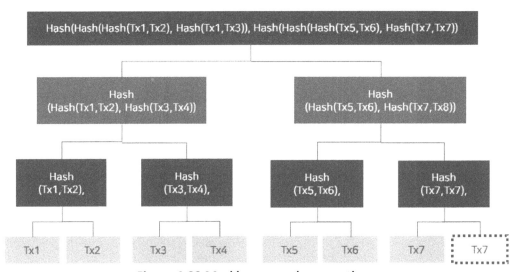

Figure 4-22 Merkle tree and transactions

Figure 4-22 shows a process of condensing information from 7 transactions into a single hash value. Even though it looks quite complicated, actually it is nothing more than a repetition of concatenating values of 2 children nodes and then apply double SHA-256 hash on them. Meanwhile we can notice that a leaf node Tx7 is duplicated, which is denoted as a blue dotted box at the right bottommost position. This is because merkle tree always requires even number of nodes due to its binary property. If there are odd number of nodes then we simply duplicate one at the end just like the one shown in above for Tx7.

As described at the top of the figure the hash function to be applied at each node is Hash(x) = SHA256(SHA256(x)). This means that we have to apply 2 consecutive SHA-256 in a row. Thus despite its complicated look, every node will have exactly 32 bytes value. In this way. around 2,000 ~ 3,000 transactions in a block is summarized into 32 bytes hash value as a merkle root and is stored at block header.

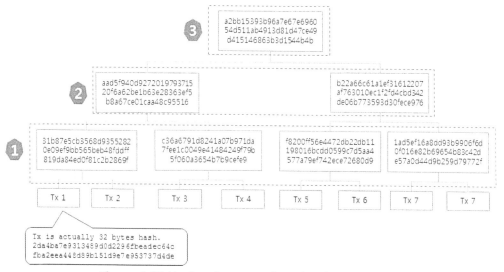

Figure 4-23 Hash value at each node of a merkle tree

Figure 4-23 shows actual 32 bytes hash value calculated from transactions. What is denoted Tx is transaction id(TxID). Transaction ID is a unique transaction number and it also is a 32 bytes SHA-256 hash value itself. It is a double hashed result value from serialized bits of entire transaction data. That is to make Tx1, firstly, serialize(=make every bits of transaction a long sequence of serial line) all bits of transaction and then apply SHA-256 twice in a row resulting in 32 bytes hash value. Step ① of Figure 4-23 is to pair each leaf nodes and apply SHA-256 twice. Step ② is a repetition of the same process with their children nodes. These repetitions continue until the process ends at root node as shown in ③. The final hash value at root is an aggregation of all transactions from leaf nodes and thus even a slightest change in 2,000 ~ 3,000 transactions will be easily detected at merkle tree root, 32 bytes final hash value. This is really a wonderful magic what mathematics can offer. Ralph merkle got his patent over this idea at 1979.

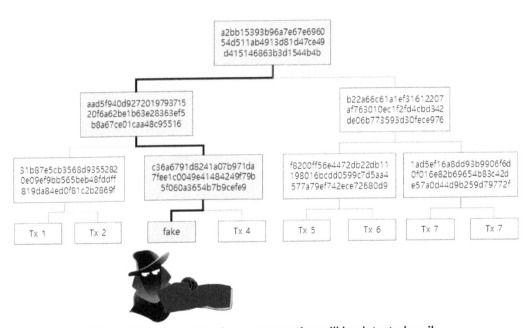

Figure 4-24 Attempt to change transaction will be detected easily

Figure 4-24 show the situation where a malicious individual tries to forge transaction. As soon as he change a bit of third transaction(Tx3) it will be immediately detected at merkle root as shown in cascaded yellow trail from leaf to root path.

4.3.2. Submission of transaction

Bitcoin transaction uses bitcoin address of a recipient. Previously it has been explained that bitcoin transaction does not mean direct exchange between stake holders but it is simply to broadcast transaction into bitcoin system for all participants with transaction locked by recipient's bitcoin address information. That's how only the recipient can unlock this submitted transaction by using his or her key. Here we discuss how bitcoin address is used in locking and unlocking of a transaction. It is good to know that all explanations in this section are related to asymmetric cryptography that has been discussed shortly before.

4.3.2.1. PTPKH

PTPHK is an acronym for **P**ay-**T**o-**P**ublic-**K**ey-**H**ash which means 'paying to someone who has according public key hash'. Literally, system allows someone who has public key hash to unlock transaction and this is basic approach how bitcoin handles transaction. As we discussed about bitcoin address and public key hash, let's redraw UTXO a little bit closer to its reality.

Figure 4-25 Lock mechanism using B's bitcoin address

UTXO in Figure 4-25 shows lock mechanism indeed contained in bitcoin address related information. As locking mechanism was installed with public key information, an according private key should be provided to unlock this(Actually it requires private and public key at the same time). Thus only B can unlock this lock mechanism. We will look more detail in coming section on how lock and unlock mechanism was described in bitcoin script notation.

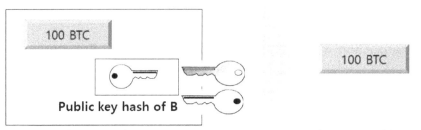

Figure 4-26 B is converting output to input using private key and public key

In Figure 4-26, B is unlocking UTXO using his or her keys. As this lock was installed using B's public key information, only B who got its private key could remove the lock. The more detailed explanation can be found at ***Appendix 5.***

 In 2012 bitcoin system added additional transaction method called P2SH[Pay to script hash] using soft fork. When transaction is using P2SH it uses bitcoin address which start with 3 not with 1. This book does not explain about details of P2SH. You can find more information on P2SH at bitcoin.org.

4.3.2.2. Smart Contract

Smart Contract was first conceptualized by Nick Szabo and was published through paper in 1996. Important contracts normally involve a third party lawyers in proving and executing. A contract implemented in this way is prohibitively impossible to breach in terms of executing and record. Here, 'prohibitively impossible' means that it may be possible but in a prohibitively expensive way requiring enormous cost. Traditional offline contract with third party described just before could also be breached by buying off lawyer and forging a document and thus not impossible but requires lots of efforts and cost.

The basic concept of smart contract is to seek a digital method which removes necessity of third party involvement in executing a promised contract yet preserves every core properties of offline contract with third party in conducting contract. It resembles a basic concept of blockchain. Its property of executing contract without an involvement of third party and irreversible from its characteristics of requiring extensive time and cost reminds us of PoW concept.

The simplest example of smart contract is coffee vending machine. Coffee vending machine is implemented not by software but by hardwired mechanism and thus functionality is fixed, but yet to provide digitized mechanism to fulfill promise of giving a cup of coffee by taking due coins. To execute this contract we don't need third party. Customer can get his or her coffee simply by putting coins to coin slot. Theoretically customer can break this contract by destroying vending machine and taking his money back. However, that sheer behavior will cost a customer money and efforts including possible criminal punishment.

> *i* The core of smart contract lie in its property of 'executing' and different from simple recording. A digital way of recording contracting called 'Ricardian Contract' is to provide efficient way of recording a contract and different from smart contract which is focused on executing a contract.

Bitcoin transaction is a sort of smart contract. It describes the way to find proper owner of a UTXO. By executing transaction script (without third party), we can check the exact ownership by observing if the script execution results in TRUE or FALSE.

Sometimes, UTXO could even be locked using by multiple keys from several persons. In this case UTXO is spendable only when n out of m persons(m > n) all agree to sign.

Bitcoin also could be time-locked when it is submitted to system. It is to be unlocked only when the contract is proven to be correct within a predetermined period of time. This could be used as a mechanism to protect a person from stealing a bitcoin without conducting his or her duty(Actually this mechanism of bitcoin has never been used and will be discussed in appendix).

One point to note is that bitcoin is not equipped with a true smart contract. What bitcoin use as a transaction script is a stack based Forth language. This language is simple and attractive but has clear limitation in expression. There are lots of different computer languages with different scope of expression. To categorize this scope, it used to be compared with turing machine.

To understand the definition of turing machine, it requires another knowledge and thus it's just ok to regard turing machine simply as a black box which is able to perform some task. Language is said to be 'turing complete' if and only if it can describe all the functionalities of turing machine whereas it is 'turing-incomplete' if it describes only subset of turing machine functionalities. Script language being used in bitcoin is turing-incomplete and got lots of limitations. You can just imagine a vocabularies of a baby whose sentences with the limited words cannot fully express many things happening in real life. Many developers are enthusiastic at advent of Ethereum. Ethereum is designed to support full smart contract from the beginning by adopting turing-complete script language. Its development environment platform including virtual machine is by far superior to bitcoin. Ethereum is said to be the first smart contract blockchain in the world and could be regarded an important evolution from bitcoin blockchain. Solidity is a turing-complete language adopted at Ethereum and it could accommodate every application which is to be expressed in contract. In fact it is hard to regard bitcoin system as a smart contract if we focus only on script language of a transaction. In this context, bitcoin is mostly for just simple recording whereas Ethereum is for execution and thus is the first general purpose blockchain.

i Ethereum has a concept of account which is different from bitcoin. There are two types of account in ethereum, the External Owned Account(EOA) is quite similar to bitcoin address, controlled by a private key, and its main purpose is just to transfer ownership of a coin. Another type of account called contract account is where actual smart contract script reside. EOA can call contract account and contract account can call another contract account just like function call. User can pass parameter when they call contract account.

There are five different script languages are available for ethereum development. Solidity, Serpent, LLC, Viper, Mutan. As of today Mutan is not used at all and most developers use Solidity.

4.3.2.3. Bitcoin transaction script

This section deals with technical details. Any readers who find difficulty in reading this section are ok to skip entire section as this section has no deep relation with a core context flow of a book.

Transaction in bitcoin system uses script. Originally it supported only PTPKH method and from 2012 it added P2SH method through soft fork and thus now there are 2 different ways to describe bitcoin transaction. One clear and obvious advantage of using script for transaction rather than hard-wired way is that it can easily accommodate a change of rules or an addition of new rules. It doesn't require source code modification but simply accept new rules as long as new rules comply with script grammar perfectly. This flexibility is inherited from the script language adopted in the system. As mentioned earlier, stack based Forth language adopted in bitcoin system bears lots of problems whereas solidity adopted for ethereum is flexible and accommodate turing-complete functionality.

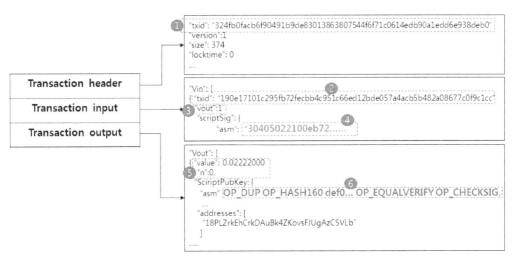

Figure 4-27 Transaction script

Figure 4-27 shows typical composition of bitcoin script. Topmost box shows header information that contains transaction id(txid), version, size and locktime. ① shown in the topmost box is a unique transaction id which is a 32 byte hash value[18].

Version tells which transaction rule should be applied to validate this transaction. As transaction rule itself could change as system upgrades, this number can be regarded as a rule number to apply. Size field tells total size in bytes of a transaction and in this case it is 374 bytes long. Locktime field is a timer introduced shortly in previous section. Transaction is to be hold without being processed until a timer expired specified in this field.

Transaction id specified at ② in input is a transaction where to search back to get the according UTXO as explained at

3.2.2.1. UTXO Tracking. If we trace back a transaction starting with 190e..., we could find that the actual amount of input was 0.01683108 BTC.[19] vout:1 specified at ③ tells that traced transaction is a second item, as index starts from 0 and thus vout:1 should be a second output of a traced transaction. Meanwhile, long blue font number at ④ is the place where electronic signature information

---

[18] Generation of transaction id was explained in ***4.3.1. Merkle Tree***.

[19] ***Appendix 5*** shows actual process of tracing.

resides and thus a place where to unlock UTXO lock mechanism. In this sense, this part is called an 'unlock script'.

In output part there is a spent amount as shown in ⑤. As this is n:0 we can guess that this would be the first output as index of output also starts with 0. ⑥ is the UTXO lock mechanism described previously and thus is called a 'lock script'. To remove a lock, unlock scrip specified at ④ should be applied to lock script specified at ⑥. If the result of executing a script turns out to be TRUE then it successfully removes lock mechanism while it remained to be locked if the result is FALSE. You can immediately find full detail on transaction script at Appendix 5.

Summary

- Hash function is to generate fixed length output regardless of its input with functionality to easily detect changes in document.
- Hash puzzle in bitcoin is to find a nonce which makes a resulting SHA-256 hash value less than a system specified target value.
- The only way to find a nonce is a trial-and-error. However there is a trick to boost a process by using parallel processing.
- Cryptography refers to a method which hides original context through encryption and then decrypt to restore its original context on demand.
- Asymmetric cryptography uses a pair of keys. A private key is to be kept personally and secretly whereas a public key is to be shared to others.
- Encryption with public key in asymmetric cryptography is related to secret protection and authentication of identity. This is what is used for bitcoin UTXO lock mechanism in transaction.
- 32 bytes hash value stored at merkle tree root can detect any tiny changes of entire transaction within block.
- Bitcoin transaction is locked and is to be unlocked only when a script with according keys is evaluated to be TRUE.

5. Security and privacy

This chapter discuss on security of bitcoin and blockchain. Many people confuse with terms and concepts when they spoke of bitcoin security. Someone even confuse security of bitcoin system with broker site security, which has no relation at all. This chapter firstly clearly define boundaries between bitcoin system and its surrounding environment and then discuss issues of security and privacy for each areas separately.

5.1. Security and safety

Figure 5-1 shows blockchain and its surrounding components.

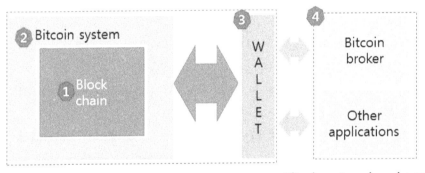

Figure 5-1 Blockchain and its surrounding environment

The very core area is depicted by ① and is a blockchain itself. Blockchain refers to suite of technologies comprising decentralized ledger and is not limited to a specific application. This area serves as a platform incorporating every concepts which includes decentralized consensus. ② is the area where blockchain is customized and applied to cryptocurrency called bitcoin. Bitcoin system refers to all application programs and its implementation methods applied to the world first blockchain based cryptocurrency. Thus this area incurs a brand new problems specific only to this application and is different from inherent problems from blockchain itself.

③ is bitcoin wallet. ③ is just an application software which is basically not related to blockchain nor cryptocurrency directly. Bitcoin wallet is just a convenience software serving for easy transaction of bitcoin. Thus wallet basically has all intrinsic problem what the general software can have such as defect of software itself as well as the carelessness of its users. This is why the area ③ has completely different security risk from ① and ②. However technically as users without wallet cannot transact bitcoin we can regard ①, ② and ③ as the minimum components to use bitcoin and let's call this area all in all as a bitcoin internal environment.

④ is outside environment. This has no relation to bitcoin nor blockchain at all. There is no restriction in using bitcoin at all even without ④. ④ exists mostly to enhance a convenience of people in trading bitcoin like broker site or other application programs. So security problem occurring in ④ is completely isolated from blockchain or bitcoin.

There is one ambiguous gray area in this distinction. Person who are trading bitcoin at broker site usually use broker provided wallets. In this case wallets have tight relationship with ④ and sometimes is the same. Here we leave a detailed discussion at this point up to coming chapter and just assume that every components are clearly separated as depicted in Figure 5-1.

Table 5-1 summarizes what have been explained just before.

Area	Description	Example	Remarks
Blockchain inherent security	Security of decentralized concept itself (Inherent security)	Blockchain	
Bitcoin system security as an application	Security as an application of a crypto currency using blockchain (Application security)	Bitcoin system	Bitcoin internal
Wallet to use	User environment program	Wallet	

bitcoin	security and user's carelessness. This layer is irrelevant to underlying technology (Individual security)		
Convenience programs outside bitcoin system	Separate services or other applications for convenience of use but no relation to internal bitcoin system at all (external security)	Broker	Bitcoin external

Table 5-1 Bitcoin, blockchain and their surroundings.

Figure 5-2 is a concept diagram which shows all areas discussed so far. The reason for repeated visualization of each sector is to help reader clearly differentiate each area, otherwise clear understanding of security problem is impossible. Now as we clearly defined each areas and discussed concept let's take a look at each sector individually.

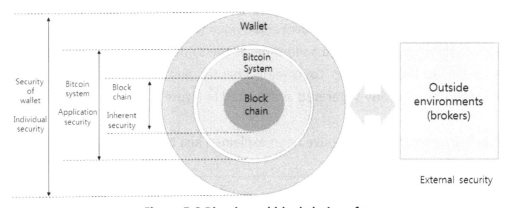

Figure 5-2 Bitcoin and blockchain safety

5.1.1. Blockchain – Inherent security

Security of blockchain means security of a concept itself and thus every application that use blockchain will be inherited this intrinsic security property. Blockchain can be regarded immune to hacker's attack. This is inherited from basic property of being decentralized and the absence of centralized control

168

system. The best policy that hackers can take is to attack the server which has the most of the control power with the most of the data available. In blockchain which has decentralized nature in principle has no clear target to attack. Only individual node could be a target but to get a control of an individual target never gives a hacker any goods. It has almost no effect to network by having some nodes conquered by hacker. Actually hacker doesn't even need to hack any individual node because he can get the same amount of information easily by just participating as a node! Unless hacker occupies a certain amount of hash power in the system, it cannot really affect system due to integrity by decentralized consensus mechanism.

However, blockchain is always vulnerable to 51% attack due to its decentralized consensus mechanism. When 51% attack really happens, it can seriously damage entire network. 51% attack could become real when malicious forces get together to attack system. 51% attack directly violates basic assumption of blockchain which states that "In system, collection of all virtuous computing powers always exceed that of malicious one." Once there comes a force that rules the system, it become no longer decentralized one but become a centralized one.

Blockchain is invincible to any threat except 51% attack. 51% could be always a big threat to blockchain system. To protect blockchain from 51% attack, it needs to be delicately designed and implemented. We will discuss again on this matter at *9.3. Implementing a blockchain: Composing new ecosystem*

5.1.2. Bitcoin system – Application security

5.1.2.1. Security of a core software system

Bitcoin system is the first application which uses blockchain in cryptocurrency area. Application implies that it redefines basic concept of blockchain so as to tailor it to some specific purpose. Thus on one hand blockchain based application will have intrinsic blockchain internal security inherited from basic blockchain concept and also on the other hand it will have an additional security concerns depending on its own definition irrelevant to blockchain fundamentals. However, this additional security concerns has no relation to blockchain itself but only specific and limited to that application. Therefore this security area is called application security.

Bitcoin system is being maintained by voluntary nonprofit organization. To the surprise, bitcoin core which is a sort of operating system of bitcoin system is still an experimental software. Apart from conceptual integrity, integrity in respect to real implementation is a different story. Bitcoin system maintained by nonprofit voluntary organization probably could secure maximum transparency. However security in policy making is another story. Different side of maximum transparency of is an absence of decision control tower. There is no clear mechanism to solve an opinion conflicts when it happens. Failure of Segwit 2X discussion in 2017 clearly have shown this kind of weakness. Opinions are being exchanged with no active nor aggressive mediation. Bitcoin definitely needs system upgrade which absolutely includes hard fork to remove reported problems and secure stability but still no clear progress is made regarding hard fork and others.

5.1.2.2. Security of application design

Bitcoin is the world first instantiation of blockchain and also a blockchain based cryptocurrency. So despite a great effort towards perfect integrity, it happens to have an unpredicted problems as no software can be perfect. Bitcoin blockchain is different from general blockchain and is only specifically tailored to bitcoin cryptocurrency application. All components of a bitcoin ecosystem such as decentralized consensus algorithm, transaction handling, controlling difficulty of block making, hash puzzle and transaction puzzle are all specific only to bitcoin. Other 1,400 cryptocurrencies all inherit blockchain fundamental concept but with different algorithm by redefining on their own way. Especially, other cryptocurrencies improved many reported problems in bitcoin and thus evolved in many ways to be a better coin than bitcoin.

Basically as bitcoin inherited blockchain fundamental concept, it is clearly safe from hacking threat but many application problems specific to bitcoin are reported. Here we discuss 2 of most important aspects among them.

- 51% Attack
- Hard fork and others

5.1.2.2.1. 51% Attack in bitcoin system

PoW and difficulty control system adopted in bitcoin system needs a lot of improvement. Current bitcoin PoW and difficulty system is an extremely deterministic. Deterministic means no involvement of randomness in decision process. The opposite concept is called non deterministic structure where there is a random elements involved in the decision process. In current bitcoin system the success rate of mining is directly proportional to invested energy. So mining can never be a progressive investment based on rational assumption but needs to be ruthless investment enough to crush opponent. As defeat means total loss, only chicken game rules the bitcoin world. The stepwise deterministic success probability which is directly proportional to invested energy drives participants not to hesitate in putting every resources available to crush opponent by grouping themselves for common enemy. So under bitcoin design of PoW, the strategy to reach Nash equilibrium is to do chicken game through endless investment in energy resources as explained previously.[20]

---

[20] You may refer to *3.6.1 Proof-of-Stake*

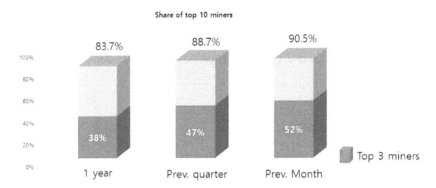

Figure 5-3 Share of top 10 miners (source: each miner's homepage)

Figure 5-3 shows activity of top 10 miners. During last year, the proportion of blocks produced by top 10 miners was 83.7% and now become 90.5% for the last one month. The bitcoin reward that top 10 miners got over the last 1 year is 83.7% of a total block which amounts to 676,874 BTC from 46,933 blocks. 676,874 BTC amounts to 13.5 billion USD. Meanwhile, what is depicted with red bar represents shares from top 3. The proportion of top3 used to be around 38% but now is over 52% exceeding half of entire system hash rates! Thus mining in bitcoin is now completely occupied by only top 3 mining nodes out of around 15 ~ 20million nodes.

Top 3 miners are all Chinese and top 10 miners are either Chinese or Chinese-invested companies. In fact, all bitcoin mining is literally taken by Chinese and it is never an exaggeration to say bitcoin is a centralized system run by China and not a decentralized system. It is estimated that over 20 million people installed bitcoin wallet. However 20million wallet users rely on transaction processing only to top 10 miners. Bitcoin miners perfectly copied the role of fee-based traditional banks where 99.99995% of users just rely on 0.00005% miners for transaction processing to be on time. As the mining difficulty now become 1.9 trillion times of a genesis block, only these top class miners with giant monster machine and outrageous energy can do the job. This is a perfect and permanent polarization in mining power! Also as shortly explained in *5.1.2.2.2. Hard fork and others,* if this mining forces try to abuse their power in soft fork or hard fork to control a rule system in bitcoin, that's it. No one can stop them. They surely can abuse their power towards higher fee rate and so on.

Actually these forces already have enough power to succeed in 51% attack. But simply there is no specific reason to do 51% attack at this moment because mining is much more profitable than 51% attack. [21] However further decrease in subsidy will bring tremendous change in profitability of mining and thus eventually cause big threat to the system. In extreme case, miners can stop mining and abandon bitcoin system or move to another cryptocurrencies. Once they leave, system will completely stop because no miners except them can handle current difficulty any more. By the way, please don't even dream of starting mining again expecting system difficulty to be lowered down after big miners are gone. Theoretically even though the system lowers down the difficulty to its maximum, it would take 1,371 days for current difficulty to be lowered down back to 1. [22] At some extreme scenario, the difficulty will never be decreased. To decrease difficulty level, some nodes have to make at least 2016 blocks but this may not even be possible! It will be like all banks in the world stop operation.

> *i* Another threat of dominant mining force is that now hacker can have a clear target to attack. This is almost the same risk of centralized system. Now hacker can effectively affect entire system by just attacking a couple of nodes.

Some of new cryptocurrencies targeting to overcome this dominancy is Z-Cash or Bitcoin Gold. What they did were to change hash function from SHA-256 to Equi-Hash. The result of this change in hash puzzle is to prevent miners to use massive ASIC machine in mining. Equi-Hash function has memory-hard characteristic meaning that it requires tremendous memory to implement in ASIC thus cannot

---

[21] Refer to **3.6.2. 51% Attack**
[22] It is explained *in* **4.1.5. Nonce and block hash puzzle** that maximum decrease of difficulty in one round(=2016 blocks) is 75% of previous one.

be cost-effective. This is a good example of preventing dominancy of a system and many others started to follow the case.

5.1.2.2.2. Hard fork and others

Officially bitcoin community never allowed hard fork yet. It tried to solve problems only with soft fork and never broke this principle.[23] However soft fork alone cannot resolve all the problems. Most of other cryptocurrencies already launched couple of hard forks. This is quite natural because no one can be perfect in designing and implementation of software from the beginning and once for all. The problem is that it is never straightforward to launch a hard fork (and even a soft fork) for bitcoin as of today. This is mainly due to conflict of interest from the change of a system rule. Every hard fork and soft fork could affect some parties in a beneficial way while the other in an unpleasant way. The person who would be affected a bit in a harmful way will never accept hard fork because the money involved might become astronomical nowadays.

However problems would never be fully fixed with just soft fork alone and it definitely needs to be accompanied by hard fork also. Many other cryptocurrencies including ethereum already launched a few hard forks. The most urgent requirement for bitcoin hard fork is to enlarge its block capacity. There has long been a discussion on doubling the capacity of a block size, which is called Segwit 2X, but eventually ended up as a failure due to disagreement among diverse stake holders.

Another aspect to be considered for bitcoin is its characteristics as a commercial purpose. As shortly mentioned before, when I explained double spending problem, many features of bitcoin is designed only in technical point of view. Even though bitcoin system is perfect in blocking bitcoin from being spent twice but it cannot effectively block double spending cheating in commerce activity. It has no functionality to discriminate a proper transaction nor to process the prior

---

[23] Actually there had been UAHF twice. Please refer to *3.7.2. Invalidating rules that used to be valid – Soft Fork*

one in a timestamp. There is not even a timestamp for transactions issued and is never guaranteed to be processed in the submitted order! The first one which is recorded in block depending on network traffic would be regarded as the winner, regardless of its actual time order.

i The transaction order in blockchain is not in the order of submission but is the order of its being processed. Transaction with higher fee will be processed prior to transaction with lower fee and thus has a little relation to its submission time. This is intrinsic limitation of decentralized network and cannot overcome due to network latency and conditions.

Current bitcoin maintenance community is composed of so called voluntary people and thus no clear motivation in proactively making new features or add much of commercial functionalities. On top of that there is no leading group or person to redesign a functionality. Bitcoin has never deeply been designed for commercial purpose. This is quite different from many brand new commercial purpose cryptocurrencies which seek to provide functionalities of user black list management , fast transaction handling, connection to commercial bank.

In commerce point of view, bitcoin is nothing more than just an inconvenient digital toy of little use. Then why people buy this useless thing with so much money? We'll examine that in Part 2 more closely.

5.1.3. Bitcoin wallet – Individual security

Bitcoin wallet is a software program which enables people to interact with bitcoin system to transfer bitcoin actually. This software have no direct relation to bitcoin community and are being provided by various (sometimes safety is unknown) vendors. This raises 2 types of new threats to security and safety.

5.1.3.1. Problem of Wallet software itself

First problem is a wallet software itself. In the market, there are numerous number of wallets published by many vendors of which security level are mostly unknown. Some of the application may have top-edge security capabilities but some of them could even be a disguised booby-trap of hackers. In this way users are exposed to these kinds of risk irrelevant to blockchain itself. Hackers usually are targeting wallets because attacking this wallet has relevantly many profit than others and also quite easy to attack. Resistance to hacking is dependent on wallet design and as these wallet software are freely distributed, when actual hacking happens no effective way to recover the loss. When wallet is hacked, everything in the wallet become hacker's!

5.1.3.2. Problems of users of wallet

Another security issue regarding wallet is user's carelessness. Wallet generates private key and public key for users and this is managed by password set by users themselves. However if users ever forget their password it cause irrecoverable damage to users. As bitcoin system is P2P network with anonymous participants there is no way to recover the damage. This instigate criminals to abuse recipient with many attacks such as voice phishing and other scams to steal private keys.

Equally dangerous as key stealing is key loss. When user forgot his or password or lost keys through broken device then there is no way to recover. In centralized system like bank has contact center to assist this kind of situation, but in decentralized system there is no place nor method to assist this kind of disaster. Thus it's solely each person's responsibility to backup and not to be stolen keys. From the beginning, this type of transaction system is never easy nor comfortable to ordinary people. Many readers already will question themselves that why we need this kind of uncomfortable and unfriendly currency system and yes, in most of the aspects you are right. Bitcoin is not suitable in many aspects for new currency system. We'll see more on this at Part 2 of this book.

What I explained so far about security of bitcoin wallet is all individual and thus when security is broken, the damage belongs to some individual. It does not affect others and this is why this danger is classified as an individual danger.

There are many variations in bitcoin wallets. It could be a wallet provided by bitcoin core itself or it also could be a wallet provided by bitcoin brokers. What has been explained in the book is individual wallet software not embedded in any other applications.

5.1.4. External environments, brokers and others – External security area

Bitcoin broker is there to accommodate trading convenience between sellers and buyers. This broker is never a necessary element in bitcoin system and just provides a little convenience. This kind of environment is completely separable from bitcoin and even without them, using a bitcoin is perfectly OK. Each of these brokers has its own level of security mechanism and the security level varies greatly from one broker to another. Most of people uses (sometimes fake) wallet provided by brokers and in this case user's asset is completely in hands of security level of brokers irrelevant to blockchain. Unlike the other components explained so far which causes individual damage, breach to broker site is not an individual damage but a group damage.

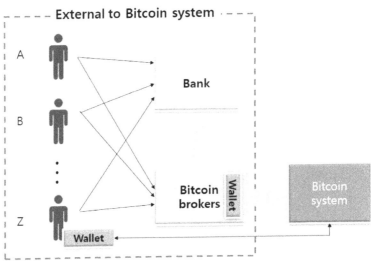

Figure 5-4 Bitcoin trade through broker site

Figure 5-4 shows typical cryptocurrency trade between users. A, B and Z depicted in figures are doing bitcoin trading for gain. Thus they all have illusion that they are using bitcoin themselves. In fact they are not. Actually they have never been used bitcoin at all! All they did were to wire transfer their legal tenders to broker sites and rely on them to purchase due amount of bitcoin from someone. In this process, no actual activity of using or even a mere contacting to bitcoin system happens from user's point of view. Thus even they are heavily trading bitcoins, they have no direct access to bitcoin at all. All their coin is stored somewhere on broker site.

In fact, many brokers don't even conduct trade between sellers and buyers at all. What they actually do is to pretend trading and simply to change numbers in virtual user account in their site. In this case, actual transaction has never happened but broker site fakes trade as if real deal were happened. When customer asks for cryptocurrency, brokers simply send cryptocurrency they themselves have.[24]

---

[24] Brokers typically charge 0.1% of commission for trading. Thus what they get from seller is 0.1% of a cryptocurrency. Thus 50% of broker income is legal tender from buyer and 50% of income is cryptocurrency from seller.

Let's look at the Figure 5-4 again. In case of person A and B, their wallets are stored at broker site and they don't have their own. When A purchases bitcoin, A believes that broker will buy due amount of bitcoin from someone else for him and that's why he pays commission of 0.1%. However what many brokers actually do is simply to change A's virtual bitcoin account figure and never conduct actual purchase. In this way, brokers can save transaction fee and can encourage A to trade quickly again for brokers to exploit further commission. Broker site consistently incites customers to heavily trade to get a maximum commission out of it. If you are curious about whether your broker site also does this cheat or not, there is handy way to check. Simply make an order for bitcoin, then check the time for actual purchase and then try to sell it back again. If this is less than 20 minutes then it is 100% fake. As you learned from previous chapter, making a block takes at least 10 minutes. This means that the fastest time for your order transaction to be processed is at least 10 minutes, and depending on transaction fee sometimes it could be days and even weeks (as you'll see in coming chapters). Thus real time trading of bitcoin can never be possible but magically, with high probability you'll be able to trade bitcoin repeatedly buy and sell in real time in your broker site!

Meanwhile Z in Figure 5-4 is a bit different. Z himself installed a separate wallet of his own and thus he is able to store his bitcoin outside of broker site. However to transfer his cryptocurrency from broker site to Z's own wallet, he needs to pay extra commission to broker which normally amounts to around 0.003 BTC! [25] All in all, very ironically most of the users of broker site have never been used bitcoin system at all.

The broker site has no relation to blockchain technology at all and their system is fully centralized trading system mimicking stock home trading system. However

---

[25] To withdraw your coin from broker site to your own wallet, you have to pay around 0.002 ~ 0.003 BTC, which amounts to 40 ~ 60 USD. We'll discuss this later at *8.1.2.2. Brokers*

they are dominating opinions of cryptocurrency world by fully utilizing huge money got from broker fee.

Meanwhile, this outside environment always is a wonderful target for hackers as these broker site is a centralized system with abundant information of users and cryptocurrency. When successful, hackers can extort astronomical amount of money, which actually happened several times which includes Mt. Gox. This kind of hacking will continuously happen all over the world because the security level of broker site overwhelmingly varies from one to another.

5.2. Personal information protection

Earlier, we learned that transaction in bitcoin is broadcasted to all nodes and thus every nodes can see the content of the transaction. On top of that, without looking at previous transaction output, which is UTXO, further transaction is not possible. So basically everybody can see which bitcoin address spent what amount to whom fairly conveniently. Then what about privacy?

Simply saying, there is no mechanism of protecting information in bitcoin. In principle every information is to be shared and to be read with no limitation. However even though there is no protection for information, there is no breach of private information neither. This means that as bitcoin system does not use private information such as name, there is no way to identity the owner of a given information. If we can't match information with its owner then it is simply information and not a personal information. Bitcoin uses bitcoin address when it does transaction and bitcoin address no information related to particular person's identity. However, this private information issue itself is a kind of built-in problem of blockchain from its properties and thus application which involves personal information is normally not suitable for blockchain.

Even in bitcoin system where no personal information exist, user needs to take care not to reveal any hint on any information. Consistently changing bitcoin addresses is a good start to make trace complicated. It is explained that bitcoin address is produced from public key. Therefore when initiating a new transaction, it is advised to generate new public key and consequently change bitcoin address. In this case, bitcoin address is used just twice. Once for receiving address, and once for unlocking UTXO lock script. CoinJoin is another functionality of bitcoin system which can be utilized to weaken traceability. Multiple person put transactions together then spend in mixed combination output. In this way, now each output is not necessarily comes from identical source and thus make trace complicated. However all these efforts just make trace complicated but not don't mean that it can completely block traceability.

As a summary, there is wide open information but no personal information in bitcoin system. On the contrary, this is can be another perks of blockchain system, which allows everybody to access big data information (not personal information). Now this big data no longer belongs to only to specific financial institutes anymore.

Summary

- Security areas surrounding bitcoin system can be classified as following 4 different types.

    1) Blockchain – Intrinsic security: Security of blockchain concept itself. Resistant to most of attacks including hacking, but vulnerable to 51% attack by nature.

    2) Bitcoin system – Application security: There could be a bug or defect in application design regardless of blockchain concept.

    3) Bitcoin wallet – Individual security: Wallet bears problem of application software and carelessness of users.

    4) Brokers and other external environment: External service for convenience. These services are exposed to hacker's attack and have a various level of security issue depending on service provider.

- In bitcoin system, information is open to everyone but it is not a personal information because identifying owner of a given information is not possible.

Part 2 *Cryptocurrency and economy and the future of blockchain*

So far, we have discussed concept of blockchain and basic operational principles of bitcoin as well as its technical details. 5 chapters in Part 1 were devoted to technical aspects of blockchain and bitcoin in order to explain the difference between general blockchain and the particular blockchain implemented by bitcoin as clearly as possible.

Part 2 will explain bitcoin and blockchain in financial point of view.

Chapter 6 investigates bitcoin as a currency from the definition of currency. Also, by discussing the difference between speculation and investment, it will be explained why bitcoin speculation can't be an investment. Chapter 7 will illustrate who maximize profits through cryptocurrency and discuss two different types of commercial cryptocurrency: commercial cryptocurrency led by tech companies to create functional intrinsic value and speculative commercial cryptocurrency that only pursues speculative value.

Chapter 8 will discuss the necessity of system maintenance, conspiracy surrounding cryptocurrency, and the future of cryptocurrency including bitcoin. Lastly, Chapter 9 will discuss technological innovation that will be brought by blockchain and explain precautions on implementation of blockchain in detail. Finally, a complete definition of blockchain will be explained

6. Currency and Bitcoin

Cryptocurrency was already conceptualized in the name of e-cash by an American cryptologist, David Chaum 35 years ago in 1983 and was even implemented in the name of DigiCash in 1995. Bitcoin itself was just another epigone of cryptocurrency in the context of cypherpunk spirit as explained earlier. The world was surprised by bitcoin only because it used blockchain technology not because of the appearance of cryptocurrency. If you take away blockchain from bitcoin, it is just a combination of existing technologies that are not new at all. Therefore, confusing between cryptocurrency technology and blockchain technology is the same as confusing between asymmetric encryption and decentralized consensus.

i   In fact, most of the technical components were already implemented far before bitcoin. Cryptocurrency were firstly implemented by David Chaum in 1983, hash puzzle was introduced (conceptually) by Wei Dai in 1998, PoW was introduced by Adam Back in 2002. What distinguishes bitcoin from previous works is that bitcoin actually and physically implemented concept to reality. Bitcoin is succession of cypherpunk spirit.

Bitcoin is barely used as a currency despite its name 'currency'. The total number of daily transactions involving bitcoin amounts to almost 300,000 and daily exchange volume is well over 13 billion USD which is about 5% of the overall asset. However, all these transactions are trading bitcoin using legal tenders, and there is practically no commercial transaction activities. Then, is bitcoin really a currency? Can it be a currency in the future?

In this chapter, we will analyze bitcoin in terms of currency. To do so, we need to look for the history and the definition of money. Afterwards we will discuss speculation and investment. Chapter 6 covers following topics.

- Gold and Dollar
- Definition of currency
- Speculation and Investment

6.1. Gold and Dollar

6.1.1. Gold

One cannot tell the history of money without discussing the story of gold. Gold has a very long history as a money that it even appears in the Genesis of the Old Testament. Gold of which atomic number is 79 is a yellowish shining metal and doesn't get corroded by water.

Figure 6-1. Gold

Professor Andrea Sella of chemistry department of London University claimed in an interview with BBC in 2013 that gold is the most ideal material of all atomic structures known on earth to be a currency and explained as follows. First, we exclude anything from the periodic table that is liquid or gas at room temperature. Then, from the metals, we exclude anything that either dissolves or explodes when met with water. Also, don't forget to exclude radioactive substances such as Uranium, Plutonium, and Thorium. Metals like iron, copper, and lead should be excluded as well because they rust. Aluminum is too weak to be a coin, and titanium is too solid to be smelted in the ancient times. Finally, we are left with 8 final metals, which are iridium, osmium, ruthenium, platinum, palladium, rhodium, silver, and gold. Except for gold and silver, these metals are extremely rare and thus barely meet the demand. Also, their boiling points are very high, so extraction is very difficult. At last, silver and gold remain. Gold and silver do qualify for currency in most aspects, but silver has a relative weakness in that it easily discolors when met with even a tiny amount of sulfur in the air. Therefore, there is no other material on earth that is more appropriate for currency than gold.[V]

> *i* Of course, the reserves and outputs are more important than their atomic features. But the analysis that gold is most suitable for currency due to its atomic characteristics is very interesting. As of 2013, the gold supply around the world is 163,000 tons including the reserves, and the gold held by central banks, national treasuries, and the IMF stands at 31,868.8 tons, which is worth 1.7 trillion USD assuming that 1 ounce of gold is worth 1,500 USD.[U]

The first paper money of the world was said to have been issued by Banque Generale which was founded by John Law in 1716.[26] John issued bank notes as a certificate for the silver that people deposited in the bank. It was like a silver receipt certificate or silver standard note. John realized that people wouldn't withdraw all of the silver at once and thus issued bank notes more than actual silver deposit. Later, he began colonization business and founded a corporation named West India Company. During the same time, John became the French government treasurer, merged his bank and West India Company, and had his bank manage the national debt. As a result, he was able to decorate his bank notes as a legal tender. People were eager to buy West India Company stocks, and the stock price skyrocketed. Meanwhile, his colonization business was facing serial failures, and John, not being able to pay the promised dividends, hid that failure and issued even more bank notes to pay dividends. People got even more excited when they were paid promised dividends, and the stock price increased. The funny thing here was that these people were buying john's stocks with loans

---

[26] Actually, the first paper money was used in China far before than John Law.

from John's bank, which was a paper money by John! The bubble didn't last long. With a deathly annual inflation of 26%, the bank notes became completely worthless and became just a paper literally in October, 1720.[W]

John's method of issuing more bank notes than actual silver reserve still forms the backbone of financial system. It is now legalized under the name of reserve requirement ratio or just reserve ratio. Banks around the world are generally allowed to lend 10 times the money deposited by their clients as long as they hold about 10% of reserve according to laws. The financial world has glamorized this act by calling it credit creation.

> Actually bank also uses capital adequacy ratio. This is a ratio of a bank's capital to its risk. The threshold number is set by banking regulator and varies from one country to another but normally it is also around 10%. Bank for International Settlement(BIS) usually set recommendation threshold for the world.

John's silver deposit certificate has become the model of gold standard in most countries starting with England by the 19th century. The gold standard is a system which compels to match a certain amount of gold with the unit of currency. Therefore, in order for a country to issue a currency, it had to have the proportional amount of gold in deposit, and currency was always guaranteed of exchange with gold. After the First World War, more and more people began to store actual gold instead of unstable currency and prefer gold to currency. As a result, procuring gold became very difficult, and the gold standard faced a crisis. However, as the United States began to gain supremacy over the world after the Second World War, gold began to stand out once again. At this time, gold was pretty much the single united currency of the world. Though it was through US dollar, gold was the single currency of the world if you look at the root.

The United States engaged in the Second World War due to Pearl Harbor attack by Japan on December 7th, 1941. Then it completely changed the course of the war. The United States, which mainly performed the role of a huge logistic base supporting the allied forces, was able to make an excess profit after the war when 44 countries around the world gathered in Bretton Woods, New Hampshire in 1944 and concluded Bretton Woods System.

Figure 6-2 Pearl harbor attack on December 7th, 1941(source: Wikimedia)

The main content of Bretton Woods System was that US dollar become key currency and other countries fix their currency exchange rate to US dollar. Each country can have 1% range of discretion from fixed rate. At the same time, 35 USD is fixed to 1 ounce of gold and is guaranteed to be exchanged with gold at any time on demand. Also, in order to support this system, IMF and IBRD were founded to take charge of liquidity provision of US dollar in international transaction and international monetary system.[2] IBRD has changed its name to World Bank later. Through this agreement, US dollar, which was the world key currency, has become the gold certificate receipt for which 1 ounce of gold is 35 US dollars, and the world has been eager to collect dollars ever since because collecting dollars was almost the same as collecting gold. This monetary system is called gold standard monetary system.

It may have seemed like US dollar was coming to the front, but it was actually gold that became the single currency of the world. However, issuing currency and thus to match gold reserves was not quite easy to handle, and the price of gold skyrocketed as everyone began to collect actual gold instead of US dollar since the situation of the world became increasingly unstable. Not one person in the world would sell his gold for 35 dollars per ounce, and the US government was faced with a tremendous crowd asking to exchange their dollars with gold. Hence, President Nixon abrogated Bretton Woods Agreement in 1971 and got rid of the gold standard, so US dollar was freed from the bondage of gold. At least up to 1971, collecting dollars was basically collecting gold, and therefore US dollar was able to perform the role of key currency well. Of course, there has been a continuing series of efforts to maintain US dollar as the key currency such as limiting payment of oil purchase only to US dollar[27], but the power of US dollar is not as good as it used to be.

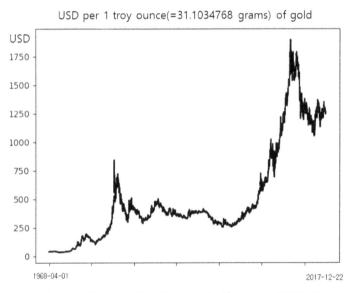

Figure 6-3 Changes in the London gold trading market(source: FRED, Economic Reserve)

Figure 6-3 is a graph made from data downloaded from FRED[28] which shows the US dollar price of gold per ounce in the London Gold Trading Market. The price of gold stayed at 38 dollars until 1971, then began to increase drastically and reached its peak of 1896 dollars. After that, the price kept falling until it began to

[27] This is said to be thanks to Kissinger, a Secretary of State, under Carter administration, who successfully persuaded Saudi Arabia.
[28] FRED, Federal Reserve Bank of St. Louis: https://fred.stlouised.org/

suddenly rise again to 1281 dollars as of November 30th, 2017. This is a 29.8-fold increase from 43 dollars in 1972, and it is equivalent to the annual complex interest rate of 7.83%.

> The ounce used in gold transactions is troy ounce(31.1034678g), which different from the traditional ounce(28.349523g). Troy ounce is about 10% heavier than the traditional ounce. It is not clear who began to use this unit and when it began to be used. The term is known originate from Troyes, which is a French trade market.

James Rickards, who has been active as a monetary system analyst and crisis manager, evaluates gold as the best insurance and claims as follows.

"Attraction of gold is in that it preserves wealth in both states of the world. In inflation, the gold price just goes up as we saw in the 1970s. In deflation, the gold price also goes up, not by itself, but by government dictate as we saw in the 1930s. Gold has a place in every investor's portfolio because it is one of the few asset classes that perform well in both inflation and deflation. That is the best kind of insurance. "[v]

6.1.2. Dollar

US dollar, which was liberated from the bondage of gold in 1971, finally stripped itself off the shackles of gold reserves which had been the biggest obstacle to the issuing dollar bill. Since then for about 50 years, we are living in debt based monetary system instead of gold standard. Debt incurred by printing new paper money is basically backed by taxes from people's labor force.

In United States, authority to print new dollar bill is held by the Federal Reserve Bank. The Federal Reserve Bank is surprisingly a civilian bank, not a government institution. Funnily enough, the US government, whose dollar is performing the key currency of the world, doesn't have the authority to issue paper dollar. When the government is in need of money, it issues government bond. In other words, the government incurs new debt. Issued national bonds are mostly purchased by the Federal Reserve Bank, though some of them are sold to the public. The Federal Reserve Bank purchases these national bonds with newly printed US dollars. The Federal Reserve Bank, which is a civilian bank, prints as many US dollars as needed and buys US national bonds with the printed dollars. All it did was basically printing dollar on demand and using that to buy the national bonds, which is like making something out of nothing.[Y] As a result, the national debt will increase, and stock holders of the Federal Reserve Bank are paid their interests. The more dollars issued by the Federal Reserve Bank, the more interest earnings the Federal Reserve Bank makes. Such profits made by the Federal Reserve Bank are returned to its share holders in the form of dividends of 6% every year[F]. It must be very difficult to believe that a government is paying an interest to issue a currency instead of issuing it on its own. It is a very unique way of issuing currency adopted in United States.

> "All U.S. dollar bills have 'Federal Reserve Note' engraved at the top. There are $1.3 trillion worth of these Federal Reserve Notes in circulation according to the current Federal Reserve Balance sheet. Federal Reserve notes are listed under the liabilities section of the central bank's balance sheet because U.S. dollar bill is essentially unsecured debt issued by the Federal Reserve that has no maturity and pays no interest."[U]

6.2. Definition of Currency

So far, we have discussed the history of currency. For a very long time, the human has been used gold, which has its own intrinsic value, as a currency. However, since 1971 in which the gold standard was discarded, the world greeted the age of fiat money.

Nominal money refers to a currency that is used according to the displayed amount regardless of its actual worth. When nominal money becomes a legal tender and assigned certain worth by the law, then it is called fiat money. The word 'fiat' means order or command. A king's order is often called a royal fiat

Fiat money doesn't have a value in itself because it is just a piece of paper. However, it is assigned an intrinsic value enforced by law. As long as the law is in effect and the attached value is stable, intrinsic value of fiat money is respected. Though fiat money is a method of legal tender used around the world, there is still a big debate on its stability as well as its future. Some argue that bitcoin doesn't have an intrinsic value, but our own fiat money doesn't have an intrinsic value either because it is just a piece of paper. There may be a law-enforced value in it, but if hyper-inflation occurs, then fiat money could become completely worthless anytime. Therefore, when analyzing value of bitcoin as a currency, the analysis may not be complete if we use only conventional definition of currency. Thus, we will examine properties of bitcoin as a currency not by traditional definition only but by comprehensive functional characteristics of a currency.

The most generic and universal definition of currency is that it is a medium of financial exchange and storage of purchasing value. When people actually spend money, people are usually thinking of exchange in mind. Here, a means of exchange should be universal rather than selective. Legal tender is forced in its circulation. Not accepting euro in a US store is a selective behavior, but USD must be accepted. Therefore, when discussing currency as a medium of financial exchange, it must be supported by universality as significant as forcibleness. A currency that is limited and circulated selectively is considered incompetent as a currency. Meanwhile, as a means of storing purchasing value, currency is all about how much of purchasing power it can store. This is related to the matter of stability as well.

Now, let's think about whether or not the definition of currency can be complete with just the aspects of medium of financial exchange and storage of purchasing power.

William Henry Furness, an American anthropologist, has an interesting perspective in his book, The Island of Stone Money, published in 1910. Aboriginal peoples of Yap of Federated States of Micronesia, Northeast of Australia, put a hole in the middle of a stone and use it as a currency. The size of a stone varies from 30cm to 3.6m, and each stone has a hole in the center so that it can be carried around easily. These stones are all acquired by sailing all the way to Palau with raft. Palau is over 500 km away from Yap. Though value of stone is usually proportional to the size, it is sometimes appreciated of its additional value if the limestone is whiter or has finer grain. If a stone is too big, people would stay in Palau for years to rub and shave until it is small enough to be transported back to Yap. Not only the fact that stones are being used as a currency, but the way of exchanging these stones is even more interesting. In the case of a small stone, it is physically moved to new owner's place, but in the case of a huge stone, it couldn't be moved easily, so huge stones normally just stay where they were. Even when the ownership is moved, there aren't any special marks made on these stones. Yet, there hasn't been a single conflict over the ownership of these huge stones. Contracts were established orally, and these trust-based promises were strictly obeyed at all times.

Figure 6-4 Stone Money on Yap(source: Wikimedia)

There is an even more interesting story. A very huge stone owned by someone in the island has never been witnessed, but people have been using it for a long time with no problem. This stone is a legendary stone and was lost in the middle of the ocean long time ago as one of ancestor was transporting it from Palau to

Yap. Everyone that accompanied this ancestor testified for the man, and this legendary stone has been accepted and used well without causing any problem even though it is sitting at the bottom of the sea from the beginning.[G]

Stone money may be carrying out its role as a medium of financial exchange and storage of purchasing, but its usability is terrible unless absolute trust is backed. The people of Yap who are based on complete trust each other may find maximum mobility from the stone money, but it is obviously inappropriate to be used for other countries. Of course, convenience of use in currency cannot solely be an absolute requisite, but it is true that the development of currency has always been pursuing better convenience of use, and it shouldn't be ignored. Thus, a true currency must possess the property of convenience of use.

Zimbabwe is a country in Central South Africa, which achieved complete independence from the UK in 1980. In the early days of independence, Mr. Mugabe was the independence hero, and the country was relatively stable in terms of economy. However, with the prolonged dictatorship by Mugabe, economy of the country began to sink, prices skyrocketed, and the monetary value of Zimbabwe currency kept dropping due to an inflation. The inflation in 2008 was almost 231,000,000%, and the country even issued a 100 trillion-dollar bill at last which was unprecedentedly huge in the history of mankind. At that time, 100 trillion Zimbabwe dollars could only buy around 3 eggs, and a piece of paper was actually more valuable than a 100 trillion-dollar bill.

Figure 6-5 100 trillion Zimbabwe dollar bill(source: Wikimedia)

The biggest hyperinflation in the history was actually in Hungary at July, 1946, and it was 4x 10^{29}%. There are 29 0s that it is even hard to read the number. If you don't really get the seriousness of it because the number is too big, consider that prices doubled every 15 hours. There was basically an inflation of 207% a day. Compared to this, monthly inflation rate of 79.6 billion% in Nigeria doesn't seem so big.[W]

A currency should fundamentally be stable. US dollar has been able to maintain its status as the key currency for a long time because its value is stable. In the case of deathly inflation of Zimbabwe, a currency cannot function properly. Therefore, requirements of a currency must include the stability of value.

Another primary function of a currency is measure of value. It is one of key functions of currency explained by Marx in his book, 'Capital: Critique of political economy' and related to the intrinsic value of a currency. In other words, if a currency has a purchasing power in itself, then a monetary economy is possible where all goods can be expressed as certain amounts of the currency. For example, if gold were a currency, then the currency would have inherited gold's intrinsic value and be able to measure relative value of other object. If a gold coin could buy a cow, value of cow can be assessed from that gold coin.

After the gold standard was discarded and paper money became just piece of paper, some economists argue that function of a paper money as a measure of value ended, but it can still be seen that it has a value as a fiat currency. In this case, the corresponding intrinsic value of money is not formed naturally but enforced by law. In order for a fiat money to function as a measure of value, stabilization of price must be supported. If a cup of coffee that was 5 dollars in the morning suddenly costs 7 dollars in the evening, then the fiat money will lose its measure of value. A function of money as a measure of value is a very important issue when we discuss properties of cryptocurrency as a currency. We will examine more about this in *6.2.3. Stability of Value(measure of value, storage of value).*

Now, a requirements of money or functions can be summarized as follows.

- Medium of financial exchange

- Convenience of use
- Stability of value (measure of value, storage of value)

6.2.1. Medium of financial exchange

In order for bitcoin to work as a currency, it must possess the universality of exchange. In other words, bitcoin should be accepted in any stores in any countries. Currently no cryptocurrencies including bitcoin have this feature or even similar yet. The reasons would be the instability of its value, inconvenience of use, low level of recognition and inexistence of intrinsic value.

Pokémon cards, which are also just pieces of paper, are traded among kids at 1 USD. Someone might argue that its value is 1 USD, but you can't buy anything with a Pokémon card at a store. The store owner is not a kid, so he or she wouldn't value Pokémon cards at all. Therefore, Pokémon cards don't have the universality of exchange. Children would continue to exchange legal tenders of 1 USD to acquire Pokémon cards, but those transactions only happen between them. Likewise, transactions that involve cryptocurrency and use legal tenders may be happening a lot, but these transactions are only happening among themselves, in real-life actual cryptocurrency transaction is hard to be seen.

Meanwhile, if we limit our focus back to bitcoin, value as a medium of financial exchanges is hard to find. Especially, the claim that bitcoin doesn't require foreign exchange between currencies is simply a naïve misunderstanding. It is actually the opposite of it. If you try to buy something with bitcoin in a foreign country, the store will ask you to pay the price converted by the price of bitcoin linked with legal tender of the country. You would have to consider not only the market price of bitcoin but also the exchange rate of currency of that country because 1BTC has different purchasing power from one country to another. Besides, the instability of value caused by the difference in market price of bitcoin is in serious level. For example, market price of bitcoin in South Korea is 20 to 30 % higher than that of USA. Therefore, it means that a bitcoin purchased at 130 USD in South Korea only has 100 USD of worth in America. If you consider the transaction fee of 30 USD, then the actual value drops to 70 USD, which is only half of the original value. Thus, there is no merit in using cryptocurrency to do a transaction instead of digitized legal tender or credit card. As long as cryptocurrencies are traded by legal tenders and their prices are different by countries, cryptocurrency is unlikely to have value as a medium of exchange. In addition, it is certain that cryptocurrencies are going to be traded by legal tenders forever and the prices will be set differently from country to another, so bitcoin won't be able to have a universality in exchange now and in the future.

6.2.2. Convenience of Use

A bitcoin transaction is only valid when it is recorded on a block. As discuss in detail in *3.4. Double Spending*, it takes at least 10 minutes or even a couple of hours in some cases to feel safe about a transaction. If exchanging currencies always takes more than 10 minutes in real life, then normal commerce activity would not be possible. In case of small transactions, if people closes transactions immediately believing others, then there will be lots of people trying to abuse the double spending. As examined earlier, it is impossible to know if the normal transaction will be recorded first or the cheating transaction will be recorded first when double spending is attempted because that is entirely dependent on the network situation. Also, the average bitcoin transaction fee is over 30 USD and consistently increasing. After all, if you pay for your coffee with bitcoin, it would be like the price has increased by 30 USD. For example, you will be paying 33 USD to get a 3 dollar cup of coffee. Thus, small expenses are practically impossible because your bitcoin will be wasted more on fee. There is no reason to use bitcoin instead of stable legal tenders. You may attempt to pay a lesser fee than the average transaction fee, but in that case you can't be sure of when your transaction will be processed. In short, the current Bitcoin system is impossible to use as a currency in real life.

The way bitcoin blockchain process transactions based on PoW doesn't go along well with real life. This clearly shows that bitcoin was originally designed for the purpose of implementing the concept of blockchain rather than considering its function as a convenient tool of monetary exchange. Many cryptocurrencies after bitcoin have been improving this problem a lot. Nevertheless, these improvements only mean that cryptocurrency is becoming closer to digitalized legal tender and doesn't mean that it's easier to use than traditional legal tenders.

i Basically decentralized system cannot outperform centralized one due to network latency in distributed data synchronization. Thus from the beginning, blockchain is never meant for better performance. If someone claims that he developed blockchain system which outperforms centralized one then he is 100% scammer. He either lie on performance or disguise centralized system as decentralized system.

A 'transaction without intermediary' may sounds wonderful. However there are countless situations where we definitely need intermediary. Human is bound to error and to correct error, we need intermediary. Imagine the world where no error is allowed in all activities. Is this really a better place to live? The advantage of that horrible situation may be just a possible reduction of small fee.

6.2.3. Stability of Value (Measure of Value, Storage of value)

Bitcoin is too volatile to be a currency. Let's consider a situation where you buy a cup of coffee in the morning. Assume that a cup of coffee costs around 4 USD. The price of coffee is set at 4 USD whether you buy it in the morning or in the evening. This is why we can live a stable economic life. Earlier, it was explained that fiat money can carry out its role as a measure of value faithfully as long as the prices remain stable.

Now, take a look at the example of bitcoin. Let's assume that the price of a cup of coffee is set at 20,000 sat. Since 1 BTC was 20,000 USD, the coffee cost about 4 USD. Then, as you are about to pay for a cup of coffee, the price of bitcoin has sharply risen to 25,000 USD per bitcoin. A cup of coffee now costs about 5 USD. In a situation like this, no one would pay 20,000 sat because a cup of coffee costs less in USD than bitcoin. There is also the opposite situation. If the price of bitcoin suddenly dropped, then the store owner would refuse to take bitcoin as payment because selling his coffee in dollars is much more profitable.

As shown in the previous example, bitcoin cannot function as a measure of value because bitcoin doesn't have intrinsic value or legally enforced value like fiat money does. The only way to assess value of bitcoin is through market price tied to legal tender, which is of no use as a measure of value when price is in big fluctuation. If people stick to use only bitcoin under fierce volatility then it is equal to cause hyperinflation of tens of percent by oneself. This seriously violates the function of storage of value as a currency because the purchasing power of a currency changes rapidly by hour. Therefore, it can be said that bitcoin cannot function as a currency in the aspects of measuring value and storing value. The only way bitcoin can function as a measure of value is to enforce value of it by law. However, such a thing will never happen. The reason is quite simple. There is no need for that.

> *i* It is reported that total asset of bitcoin surpassed 320 billion USD, and for this reason, some people argue that bitcoin can store value. However, storage of value as a currency doesn't simply means storage but to mean storage of purchasing power which always exert a stable purchasing power. In other words, it should accompany a stable and equal purchasing power as well as storage. Therefore, volatility of bitcoin prevents it from being able to store persistent purchasing value. This is just like the case of Zimbabwe dollar where the Zimbabwe dollar was expelled for not being able to store consistent purchasing power. Then can bitcoin do role as a storage of an asset in long term which doesn't require immediate purchasing power? We will discuss this more in **8.1. Future of Bitcoin**.

6.2.4. Bitcoin as a currency

We have so far examined bitcoin by comparing it to the definition of currency. It was concluded that bitcoin, after being examined in three aspects, cannot function as a currency at all. Especially, bitcoin was found to be so inconvenient that it cannot be used as a currency. The biggest reason was that bitcoin was originally designed by technicians who simply wanted to remove intermediary and thus never been sophisticatedly designed for the purpose of real life currency.

As long as bitcoin is traded with legal tenders and its prices are different by countries, all the value of bitcoin is indirectly through legal tender. So bitcoin doesn't qualify for a currency which should function as a measure of value on its own. If a currency can't function as a measure of value, then an economic crisis like hyperinflation will be caused. After all, it is hopeless to wish that bitcoin will be used as a currency in the future.

i Then, can other cryptocurrencies function as a currency? There are many cryptocurrencies which improved weakness of bitcoin. The instantaneity of transaction has been greatly improved. However, none of these cryptocurrencies can function as a measure of value. Intrinsic value of money is formed from trust and never by technology. How a cryptocurrency can truly have intrinsic value will be explored in *7.3.1. Commercial Cryptocurrency with functional value*

In fact the biggest value for stable money should have is a 'Trust'. In fact, gold itself could be regarded that it has no intrinsic value at all. Gold is useless metal except ornamental purpose. It is too rare to be used as an industrial purpose. What people see value in gold is its proved 'trust' accumulated for thousands years as a valuables among human being. This explains why stone in Yap is a good currency for them but cannot be for ourselves. The answer is trust. Yap has accumulated trust on their stone, which we don't have at all. Well... trust in bitcoin? Let's find out more in coming chapters.

6.3. Speculation and Investment

It is difficult to distinguish between a speculation and an investment. The difficulty is because what makes difference is the attitude towards the object, not the object itself. In other words, some people may speculate on a stock, but others could be investing on the same stock. The same applies to the case of bitcoin. Most people may be speculating on bitcoin now, but there could someone who sincerely analyzing the market and making investments in bitcoin(Unfortunately I have never seen such a person).

Benjamin Graham, who is also famous for Warren Buffett's mentor, has given clear definition on speculation and investment in his book, "Security Analysis". It was in 1934 when Benjamin defined investment. Meanwhile, there have been many attempts to explain investment differently, this 80-year-old definition is still considered to give the clearest standard on investment.

"An investment operation is one which, upon thorough analysis, promises safety of principal and a satisfactory return. Operations not meeting these requirements are speculative."[5]

Now, let's analyze the financial insanity surrounding cryptocurrency according to Benjamin Graham's definition.

6.3.1. Thorough Analysis

A laptop with intel core 8th generation 15-8250U 1.6G, intel UHD 8G DDR4 RAM, 15 inch LED backlight Full HD 1920x1080 is being sold at 799.99 USD. Would you buy this laptop? Some readers might be able to grasp the appropriateness of the price, while others might find this whole thing puzzling. But, this is not a problem because you can simply find out about it after some googling on the internet for a few minutes. Then, if someone recommends you cryptocurrency called Mixin, by saying that it is only 2,000 USD per Xin would you buy this cryptocurrency? It will be extremely difficult to find information about this cryptocurrency. There may be lots of search results on a programming language with the same name, but nothing much about the cryptocurrency. There is no way to know if the price is appropriate because there is no information.

You need information to determine if a price in appropriate. Information helps analysis and evaluation of value. In general, to assess a stock value of a company we can check recent balance sheet, liquidating value, composition of share holders, market research and future value, etc. Also, a listed company has an obligation to disclose its financial situation including financial statements to the public. Thus, there exists a methodology and objective basis to determine the appropriateness of a stock value of a company apart from accuracy.

Bitcoin may also could be an objective of investment if its value could be evaluated through a modeling based on information. However, bitcoin cannot be an investment for following 3 reasons. The first reason is that value of bitcoin is not decided by market but is being controlled and manipulated by some forces. Thus mathematical formulation or analysis is impossible because market does not follow reasons but follow manipulation. Secondly, as bitcoin doesn't have an intrinsic value, in the worst case, its value is always 0. Therefore, there is no basis for evaluating its value because concepts like liquidating value don't exist for bitcoin. Last but none the least is there is so little information and no ground regulation therefore a sustainable and reasonable prediction is impossible. Its price varies greatly by over 8,000 brokers, and the differences are even greater by countries. Also, regulations on cryptocurrency are different by countries, so any assumptions you make about bitcoin will be overturned and the prices will shake when one government change some regulation. Stable prediction is never possible. All in all stable and long term investment is impossible from the beginning and only short term gambling or speculation is possible.

Technical reasons behind instability of cryptocurrencies are defect of blockchain design. There is no proven theory regarding sustainability of blockchain system. Blockchain basically relies on incentive engineering which should encourage people to invest resources for the operation of a blockchain system. Once the crazy bubble dies, all cryptocurrency would suddenly die because no one will invest resources in mining and others. There is yet not a single blockchain cryptocurrency which proved to be sustainable without crazy bubble in market price.

The current cryptocurrency speculative market looks really follow George Soros' theory of reflexivity. George Soros denies the concept of 'rational human'. In other words, he squarely denies a 'decision made based on a thorough understanding of assets' by Benjamin Graham. George Soros' so-called theory of reflexivity or theory of investment is based on mass psychology through the flock of sheep effect. For this, he would always mobilize instigation and fomentation to manipulate the market.[2]

Mixin, which was shortly mentioned earlier, is one of the 1,376 cryptocurrencies. If you visit its website, there is nothing but a picture icon. There is no information about who issued that or how much was issued. What is surprising is that the daily trading volume of this cryptocurrency is almost 2M USD. This is possible mostly because Mixin is listed on a broker website. It is impossible to know if those who bought Mixin actually visited its website. If you are trading cryptocurrencies, please ask yourself whether you have ever visited the website of the cryptocurrency for information. Also, please check if you ever be provided minimal information on cryptocurrencies from your broker. If you didn't get any information but a flash current price, you are actually gambling on the direction of the prices in a gambling house decorated as a broker. As the gambling continues, your money will slowly vaporize in the form of fee. We will get back to this point in *7.1. Cryptocurrency Broker.*

Meanwhile, there are people who try to predict price of bitcoin by using stock techniques. These people simply attempt to predict price with a graph of bitcoin price fluctuation and data on average trading volume. Even an analysts of a financial firm suggests an analysis opinion based on this kind of method. This is no different from trying to predict the artificiality of people and is definitely no better than gambling. If Mark Twain is here to see those who pretend prediction with only few statistics, he would have repeated his following saying again.

"There are three kinds of lies: lies, damned lies, and statistics."

6.3.2. Safety on principal

Although promising safety of principal is related to many things, it is especially in a close relationship with long-term investment. Let's compare equity investment to derivative investment. Generally while equity investment could be long-term investment, derivative investment cannot be a long term. This is because derivative investments have a maturity while equity investments don't. Derivative investments either become worthless or triggers a great loss when conditions aren't met at the time of maturity. On the contrary, equity investors have the choice of waiting until their principal is recovered by holding on to their stocks for longer when the desired prices aren't attained. Therefore, whether it can be invested in the long term or not is a very important element related to security of principal.

Also, if stocks were purchased through appropriate assessment based on the book value of company, the loss will be minimized even when the company goes bankrupt in worst case. There are actually stocks whose prices are even lower than their actual book values, and there are also stock items whose market price gaps against their book values aren't that big. Like this, investing based on assessment that can support the prices is the minimum device to guarantee the security of the principal, which is evaluating the intrinsic value. To check whether your financial activity is an investment or a speculation, you need to look for what mechanism you have which can guarantee your principal. If you are not sure what they are, then it is best not to do anything. Derivative products, which are the monsters of the financial world, is hard to be recognized as a vehicle for investment if we follow Benjamin Graham's criteria. In similar term, cryptocurrency doesn't have intrinsic value and thus there is no mechanism to safeguard minimum. On top of that, it is quite in doubt whether specific cryptocurrency will be still operating years later. It has risk of stop operation due to technical defects and also due to defect on incentive engineering. Thus basically there is no mechanism which can support safety of principal in case of cryptocurrency.

6.3.3. Satisfactory Return

The topic of satisfactory return is not only limited to bitcoin. This is something that should be considered as a principle for all investments and as a fundamental attitude. Because your investment on blue chip stocks can turn into a speculation any time depending on your attitude towards the profits. A satisfactory return is strictly subjective, and there is no such thing as an absolutely satisfactory return. Just like happiness is up to one's mind. The biggest reason for failing equity investments is that one can't be satisfied by return. This is because one wants bigger returns no matter how big current returns are just like one would wish to be much richer even if one is already rich. Thus, a satisfactory return means to set a certain target and then must be satisfied once the target is achieved. When you are able to act like you are satisfied even if you aren't really satisfied emotionally, then and only then it's considered an investment activity.

Isaac Newton, who is famous for his discovery of the law of gravity, had an extraordinary rate of return of 100% and made 7,000 pounds of profit in 1720 by investing in a company called South Sea which had the monopoly of trade in South America while colonization of Great Britain was at its peak. However, stock price of the company continued to grow after he sold all of his stocks, and he began to feel nervous watching his friend made even more profits from the company. Eventually, Newton decided to make an even bigger investment again and put most his wealth into South Sea stock again. But, the stock suddenly began to plummet, and Newton soon went bankrupt after losing all of his 20,000 pounds (about 3.7 million USD these days). After this incident, it became a taboo to talk about South Sea in front of Newton. There is a famous saying by him after this incident.

"I can calculate the motions of the heavenly bodies, but not the madness of the people."[D]

Even Isaac Newton, a genius scientist, couldn't handle his own greed. This anecdote illustrates how unlikely it is to have a satisfactory return. A lot of people fail in investment because they couldn't sell their stocks even though they invested in cheap price. They continue waiting for their stocks to go up a little higher or hold on to their stocks when the prices go down hoping for a rebound, and then some even lose all their investments in the worst case. Or, people also lose their investments by immediately reinvesting more in the same stock and incurring a greater loss after initially making a good profit in the short term, just like Newton did. After all, your investment turns into a speculation when you fail to be satisfied after achieving initially set return target rate.

6.3.4. Valuation Gain and Realized Gain

Total asset of bitcoin surpassed 320 billion USD. This is actually greater than the total asset of both Goldman Sachs and UBS combined. It is also greater than the total asset of Samsung Electronics.[29] Then, has bitcoin become something greater than prominent banks or Samsung? Let's think about valuation gain and loss and realized gain and loss for a while. Valuation gain and loss is an amount expected to be gained or lost after immediate total sales. In other words, it is the difference between the market price of an object and its purchase cost. For example, if you bought 1,000,000 shares of Apple for 170 USD each and the closing price went up as high as 190 USD, then you have made a valuation gain of 20 million USD because the profit per share is 20 USD. However, if the closing price of the

---

[29] It is around 304 Billion USD as of 28th, Dec, 2017.

following day was 150 USD, then you have the valuation loss of 20 million USD in total. You could even emotionally feel like you have lost 40 million USD because you could have sold the stock for 190 USD per share. Like this, a valuation gain and loss of stock is always virtual assumption until it is actually sold and thus it is called unrealized gain/loss

Meanwhile, when a stock is actually sold, the gain or loss after sale is fixed regardless of the stock price situation later, and this is called realized gain and loss. After all, valuation gain and loss is nothing but a virtual assumption of gain or loss unless it is liquidated and made a realized gain or loss. Here the problem is that normally one cannot sell all asset at once and therefore the selling price would varies significantly.

Matched sale is typical price manipulation scam. One person or a group pretends to be a multiple independent personals and then sell and back the stock each other. While doing this scam, they consistently raise stock price. Let's look at the following figure.

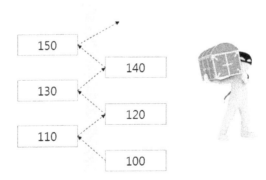

Figure 6-6 Price Manipulation through matched sale

In the figure, two persons are conducting a matched sales by selling and buying with predetermined plan repeatedly. While doing this they raise stock price from 100 to 150 quickly. Of course this kind of activity is not easy under current stock trading system as every transaction could be monitored and traced. However in bitcoin system where every transaction is anonymous, matched sales are just a piece of cake. If I were to pick two biggest reasons for current crazy bitcoin price, I would say scammers who manipulate prices and broker site which made that scam convenient. These two reasons has no relation at all with intrinsic value of bitcoin nor its future value. On the contrary people won't crazily trade bitcoin if it were to be a future currency, people buy and immediately sell it back because they also know about this scam. They just want exciting gain hoping to ride surf of this scam and not to be swept by the scam. However as far as I witnessed, somebody might stay a little bit longer surfing on this crazy wave, eventually they all fallen down and were swept away by the wave of scam.

> Cross trading is a legal act between stock firms and is distinguished from matched sale. Cross trading is reported to a stock exchange in advance, and two stock firms will legally trade stocks in quantity after having an agreement on price and volume. Since the price is fixed, it won't affect the market price in theory, but it actually causes an illusion from sharply increased trading volume and does affect price.

6.3.5. Daily Trading Volume to Total Assets

Despite the total asset of bitcoin which is around 320 billion USD, its liquidating value is 0. Thus current value is entirely an unrealized valuation (considering its brand value may, it not be 0). But, what would happen if all of the 16.7 million bitcoins were put out in the market at the same time to realize profits?

It was roughly 2016 when bitcoin began to draw attention of the public in earnest. Many indictors actually begin to sharply change around this time.

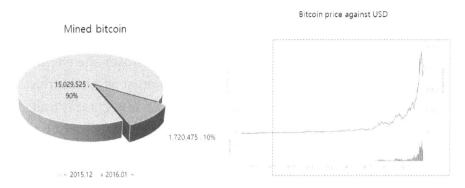

Figure 6-7 Bitcoin Production and Price to USD(source: CoinMarketCap)

Figure 6-7 shows the accumulated bitcoin minded and its price to USD. As shown in the red dotted box on the right side of the figure, price of bitcoin to USD began to slowly increase since 2016 and then skyrocketed starting from July, 2017. Let's compare bitcoin before and after 2016 in terms of several indicators for the sake of convenience. The last bitcoin of 2015 issued at 23:35:11 from the #391,181 block, which was created on Dec 31st, 2015. The total accumulated amount of bitcoin up to that point was 15,029,525 BTC. However, the number of newly issued bitcoin from Jan 1st, 2016 to the # 500,000 block was only 1,720,475 BTC. The amount of bitcoin issued since 2016 was only 10% of the total amount, but its price increase rate during the time was nearly 5,400%. This is after 90% of issued bitcoin has been taken beforehand. In other words, 90% of the total amount was already owned by someone before the price began to increase in earnest. Let's take a look at the following figure.

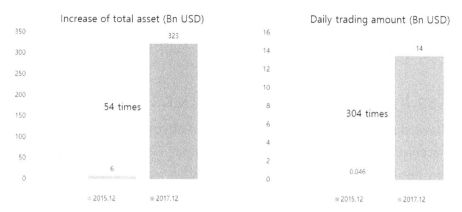

Figure 6-8 Changes of bitcoin asset and daily trade between 2015 and 2017

Figure 6-8 compares total asset of bitcoin and daily trading volume between the end of 2015 and the end of 2017. In two years, value of bitcoin to USD increased, and its total assets was multiplied 54 times, while its daily trading volume increased by nearly 304 times. This means that the daily trading volume was only 0.8% of the total assets until 2015, but now it is around 4% ~ 5% of the total assets, which is 5 times the previous percentage and is around 14 billion USD a day.

Korea is the most heated cryptocurrency market in the world. Around 5 ~ 6 billion USD is traded every day in Korea alone. Estimated daily trade to asset is almost 30%, which is around 6 times of US. How can we explain this? If you remember my argument on the formation of crazy bitcoin price in previous section, you will recall 2 factors that I picked as the most responsible for the crazy bubble, a broker site and forces who manipulate price. Thus the heat of cryptocurrency market is closely related to the convenience of these 2 factors, which exactly coincide with the situation in Korea. World most advanced mobile technology with no specific regulation in cryptocurrency market! This situation can explain the crazy market status of Korea with ease.

🔆 Usual daily trading amount of stock to total asset is around 0.5% ~ 1% around world. Thus daily cryptocurrency trading amount of 5% in worldwide and 30% in Korea can be regarded as way heated lunatic speculative situation.

6.3.6. Wise Investors and Unwise speculators

So far, we have discussed whether the mania for bitcoin is a speculation or investment according to the definition of Benjamin Graham. Much of the differentiation between speculation and investment is up to each individual's attitude. You may give an advice to someone who enjoys risks about joining the speculation but may not condemn the person morally. But, I only hope that my readers would understand that the word investment is no longer appropriate for cryptocurrency market. It is entirely up to each one's decision whether to seek for riskier profit or not as long as that is legal. However, I hope everyone would clearly establish standard for judging whether he or she is doing a speculation or investment.

Now in a slightly different perspective from previous aspect, I will introduce you three examples of an unwise speculation explained by Benjamin Graham

- Speculating while misunderstanding as an investing
- Speculating professionally without any appropriate knowledge or ability to analyze technically
- Putting too much money into a speculation

6.3.7. Temptation to invest in mining

There are many temptations that lure people into mining advertising huge profits. There are also lots of books being published whose authors claim to have made millions of dollars from investing in cryptocurrency mining. Since you get about 16 BTC in reward for creating a block, you can make around 320,000 USD according to the current price of bitcoin. That is almost 1.4 billion in a month. If you just look at the figures, you might confuse it for actual gold mining.

However, mining has already become the league of those who are heavily armed with professional hardware. It is impossible for an ordinary person to earn bitcoin through mining individually. Even those enterprise mining teams don't stand a chance of winning the competition against top mining companies. Mining is not about accumulating your efforts carefully and slowly.

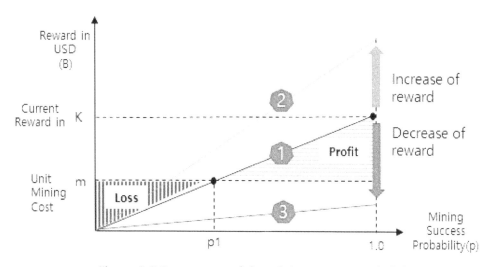

Figure 6-9 Revenue graph by mining success probability

Figure 6-9 shows the revenue graph when investing in bitcoin mining. p-axis refers to the probability of success in mining, and B-axis refers to the mining reward converted into USD. As of now, you can make around 16 BTC which consists of 12.5 BTC of direct mining subsidy and 3 ~ 4 BTC of transaction fee. Though the transaction fee slightly varies each time, let's assume it is fixed for convenience and the total reward is 16 BTC. According to the current price of bitcoin, 16 BTC is about 320,000 USD.

① is a break-even graph according to current block reward. This graph is dependent on mining probability and reward and forms a straight line with B = K x p. In other words, it is a straight line with a slope K along the p-axis. If mining reward K increases for some reason such as the dollar value of bitcoin changes or the block reward changes, the slope will increase, then the graph will become ②.

211

On the contrary, if the mining reward decreases and thus slope decreases, then the graph will become ③. m is the total unit cost required for one block generation cycle. Since the current block generation cycle is 10 minutes, you can calculate it by taking into account 10 minute worth of the depreciation cost, electricity bill, personnel expenses, rent, etc. The red shaded area in the graph is where you would suffer a loss with regard to the current reward K. In other words, it is where the mining probability is less than break-even probability, p1. The green shaded area is where you make a profit with regard to the current reward meaning that your mining probability is greater than the break-even probability, p1.

As you can find out from the figure, the profit and loss are dependent on three factors, which are mining success probability(p), unit mining cost(m), and mining reward in USD(K). Since the mining cost is in legal tender, the mining reward should be compared in USD also. Naturally, you can make more profits as the mining success probability increases or as the mining reward increases. Therefore, it is crucial that not only price of bitcoin to be kept reasonably high but also the mining success probability should be high enough. If we look at this in an opposite view, it means that if price of bitcoin is too low you cannot make a profit no matter high your success probability is. For example, you can't make any profit in any cases as long as your slope is ③. This is because you are destined to suffer a loss even if you can create a block for sure once the mining reward is less than the mining cost due to events such as bitcoin price collapse. We will discuss this again later in *8.1.1. Risks of suspension of mining*.

Currently, three major mining companies occupy more than half of the entire bitcoin hash power, and top ten companies occupy over 90%. So, it is extremely difficult for any of the remaining minor companies to win the competition and succeed in mining. Thousands of these minor miners barely have less than 1% of success rate. Simply saying, in order to make a profit after successfully mining with a probability of 1%, the reward needs to be over 100 times the cost. If the probability were 0.1%, the reward should be 1000 times, and 10000 times if it were 0.01% to pass the break-even point. In other words, in case of success probability of 0.1%, one block should generate more than entire week's expense, and in case of 0.01% success rate in order to make a break-even at least one block should generate 69 days' worth of expense.

At 6th, July, 2020, subsidy of bitcoin will further reduced to 6.12 BTC, which is exactly half of current subsidy. If this happens, the slope in fig 6.7 will decline towards ③ and it will affect mining profitability significantly. This is inevitable because it is hard-coded. We will revisit this in *8.1. Future of bitcoin.*

Summary

- Gold is one of few assets that can overcome both inflation and deflation.
- Gold standard of USA, which started at Bretton Woods Conference in 1944, was ended by Nixon in 1971, and dollar after the gold standard became the fiat money.
- For something to be a currency, universality of use is very critical as it should conduct a role of medium of financial exchange.
- Bitcoin is too much inconvenient to be used as a currency.
- Bitcoin is lacking function as a measure of value. Thus, it cannot function to store stable purchasing power, and ultimately damages the stability of value.
- Investment is making competent profits while securing the stability of the principal through a thorough analysis. Anything that doesn't satisfy this condition is considered as a speculative activity

7. Who makes money?

7.1. Cryptocurrency Broker

Just a few years ago, you would have to look for people who are willing to sell their bitcoin using chat programs such as IRC in order to buy bitcoin. If you found someone to sell bitcoin by luck, then you would have to negotiate with the person to decide the price and then trade in legal tender. This method is still being used when trading over-the-counter stocks. If there is no escrow service, then a trust issue may occur between you and the opponent. For example, it would be difficult to decide whether you will get the bitcoin first or the opponent will get the money first. In this sense, it is a very natural phenomenon that websites that directly connect buyers with sellers occur. Then, what is the matter?

Bitcoin, despite its name, is seldom used as a currency. Over 300,000 transactions that take place daily which amount to about 14billion USD are all just buy and sell bitcoin with legal tenders. No one really treats bitcoin as a currency. People rather treat it as stock item that is easy to buy and sell.

According to CoinMarketCap, as of the end of December, 2017, there are 7,717 registered cryptocurrency brokers around the world dealing over 30 billion USD a day. They typically charge around 0.1% of commission which is 10 times of online stock trading commission. Brokers charge 0.1% of commission to both seller and buyer. A broker would receive a legal tender from the buyer, deduct 0.1%, and give the rest to the seller. Meanwhile, the broker also deducts 0.1% of the cryptocurrency received from the seller and gives the rest to the buyer. In other words, the broker gets 0.1% of the trade cost in legal tender and 0.1% of the cryptocurrency being traded at the same time.

Traded volume is directly linked with broker's profit and therefore they provide every means possible to encourage people to more frequently sell and buy cryptocurrencies.

Stock turnover rate is the volume of transaction against balance. If a person who has 1,000 USD in his account buys 1,000 USD's worth of stocks and then sell 1,000 USD's worth of stocks, we say that the turnover rate is 100%. Sales personnel of security company used to get incentives proportional to the stock turnover rate. Therefore, in the past, it was often the case that customers were recommended to buy and sell unnecessary stocks, and there were many accounts that had 200 ~ 300% of stock turnover rate. According to a report by security company, customers who had over 300% of turnover rate actually had final earnings rates of -3% to -20%, and those with over 800% of annual turnover rate recorded -9 to -20% of earnings rates. In addition, it was analyzed that about 80% of the losses of those investors with high turnover rates were actually paid in transaction costs such as transaction fee. As a result, as the number of transactions increases, the profits decrease and the money will be wasted in transaction fee. Many security companies now excluded stock turnover rate from the sales incentive and try to warn their customers of the risks of high turnover rates.[a]

More often than not, it is misunderstood that brokers has tight relation to blockchain technology. As a matter of fact, brokers has no relation to blockchain technology at all. Rather brokers have tight relation to current bubble of cryptocurrencies. Brokers promote cryptocurrencies in various ways because trading volume has direct link with their commission. Cryptocurrency definitely has no value other than speculative tool or shelter for a black money.

Robert Shiller of Yale university and Joseph Stiglitz of MIT are both awarded Nobel economy prize. They both argued that the only role of cryptocurrency is a speculative tool or shelter of black money. However this kind of voice is not to be often heard in public. The public learn more of anthem for cryptocurrencies. That's because someone consistently spreads anthem by buying a media. That someone makes enormous fortune by convincing the public heavily trade cryptocurrencies. Currently we don't see any control over this potential fraudulent activities. Meanwhile in 'Global financial stability report October 2017' , IMF explained that China could well control financial risk against indiscriminate financial activities beyond regulation due to its enhanced financial regulation driven by Chinese government.[H]

7.1.1. The Power of Cryptocurrency Broker

The power of cryptocurrency broker in the cryptocurrency trading market is overwhelmingly tremendous. The life of cryptocurrency is directly linked to its exposure to public through broker. Then who on earth selects which one to be listed on broker site on what criteria? The answer is extremely simple. Brokers themselves select arbitrary cryptocurrencies on their will. Of course brokers themselves may have their own criteria but that criteria is not regulated nor reviewed by other authoritative institute.

Whether or not a cryptocurrency gets listed at a broker site is directly connected to the survival of it because ordinary people don't know how to trade cryptocurrencies other than through brokers. In some cases, when listed cryptocurrency is unlisted by broker someday then holders of the cryptocurrency has almost no way to sell it back. Thus the critical and immediate factor which significantly affects the market price of cryptocurrency is never its technical aspect but a how it is treated by brokers.

Imagine a situation where chairman of NYSE has omnipresent power to select which stocks to list and to make unlisted. He can make Apple unlisted today and also can list damnedest corporation tomorrow at his own discretion telling that "Trust me I have my own superb talent to identify a sound and excellent stock myself." The funny thing is that this crazy nonsense is actually a real situation in cryptocurrency market. All brokers select cryptocurrencies 100% on their own by saying the same argument of "Trust me I have ability to pick only the best one." However what they really select greatly vary from one broker to another. Except couple of very famous cryptocurrencies such as bitcoin and ethereum, rest of listed cryptocurrencies are almost completely different each other. It will never come as a surprise even if some coin developers bribe brokers for listing or brokers themselves develop certain mumbling bumbling coins and list those coins for maximum exploitation.

Therefore, the competition among cryptocurrencies to be listed on brokers is also very intense. Whether or not it is exposed to an environment where ordinary people can easily trade is a crucial factor in success or failure of the cryptocurrency. By the way, do you really want to put your money on this gamble?

7.1.2. ICO (Initial Coin Offering)

When a corporation goes public and collects external funds, it is called initial public offering or IPO in short. The company will explain the prospect of its business and issue new stocks. Investors will buy the stocks of an IPO company, and the investors can either make profits or suffer losses depending on performances of the company. IPO is a typical method of financing in a capital market which reasonably distributes risks and profits and efficiently collects investment funds for new businesses or projects.

ICO is an acronym for initial coin offering and an imitation of IPO to the cryptocurrency market. In general, ICO is a way of collecting funds by selling future cryptocurrency, which is planned and not in circulation yet, to public with other cryptocurrencies which are being actively traded in public. So, the investors will make profits when the price of newly given planned cryptocurrency is in circulation and forms an enough margin. Of course it could also be totally garbage with not a small probability.

In fact, ICO is not a well defined term or system but a newly made term in cryptocurrency market and broadly used to refer to a way to get fund in various ways which is related to cryptocurrency.

There are 2 major big differences between ICO and IPO. Firstly, IPO distributes stocks which can exert certain force over the company and by itself has a legal right on claim of information disclosure for transparency where as ICO distributes virtual coin which has no legal support. Amount of coin does not give an owner any legal right on monitoring and supervising the company.

Secondly, stock is sold in legal tenders while coin is sold with another cryptocurrencies. This create a big hole in that as all legal statements related to accounting and according compliance rule are based on legal tenders, there is no specific clauses at all regarding cryptocurrencies. Thus someone who took the cryptocurrencies instead of legal tender can be free from most of obligations and duties which applies only to legal tenders.

As a result, the problem of ICO is that it can easily be used in various crimes such as Ponzi scheme[30]. Because accounting standard for cryptocurrency is different from one country to another and most countries didn't even define the reality of cryptocurrency, ICO is easily abused as a tool to avoid obligations of supervision and monitoring from authorities and legal duties. So basically ICO investors are in a weak position in terms of investor protection as they cannot be systematically protected through well defined rule. It is known that (revealed) scams related only to ethereum ICO alone amounts to 10% of entire ICO.[L] It is said that 5.4 billion USD has been funded through ICO 2017.

Currently, many countries are preparing regulations for ICO, and South Korea and China have already banned or effectively blocked ICO since September, 2017.

---

[30] Ponzi scheme is a fraudulent investment where returns for existing investors are generated from new investor's money. This scam originate from Charles Ponzi in the 1920s who did this kind of fraud in US.

Funny thing is that someone who strongly emphasize the danger of ICO scam are more of the leaders of cryptocurrency market. Vitalik Buterin who founded ethereum warned investor about the danger of ICO project and added that "it is not clear how things will look in a year or two. In the end the market will need to cool down. A lot of projects will fail and people will lose money." Another co-founder of ethereum Joseph Lubin said in the interview with CNBC that "there have been a lot of copycat projects where people copy all the same materials (and) don't intend to deliver any value to the people buying the tokens". Meanwhile Brad Garlinghouse, CEO of Ripple also shared the same view in his CNBC interview by saying that "I think a lot of what's happening in the ICO market is actually fraud, and I think that will (eventually) stop

7.2. Mining pool

As all we know, basically new bitcoin is issued only through coinbase transaction which gives a block reward to miner. Therefore all bitcoin basically owned by miners and accordingly the first beneficiaries from crazy bubble of cryptocurrency definitely are miners. We already learned that over 90% of blocks now are being produced by top 10 miners and the secret of this enormous hashing power comes from ASIC machine and making a networking pool for parallel processing.

Actually the biggest competitiveness is by far the ability to supply cheapest electricity. As enormous electricity power is demanding in hash puzzle, a place to deliver cheaper electricity become the first target of miners. hydroelectric of iceland is one of the most preferred place for miners. Miners are searching for globe a place to deliver a cheaper electricity.

Meanwhile the development of mining ASIC is really dazzling. The ability to provide high end ASIC machine is another critical point of mining profitability. As

ASIC for mining is of no use after 3 to 6 months, a delay in delivering high end ASIC could be a significant impact to profitability.

While this stupid competition of 'Who waste more electricity with cheaper cost?' game continues, the miners and ASIC providers make most of their profit. Funny thing is that all this profit comes from the pocket of ordinary person who are drown into sea of speculative gambling of cryptocurrencies and there are ruthless and knave villains out there encouraging people to drink narcotic crytpo-gamble!
.

7.3 Commercial Cryptocurrency

Ripple is a cryptocurrency that went straight to third place in terms of total asset as of the end of December, 2017. The name might not sound familiar, but its total assets amount to almost 75 billion USD. Ripple homepage explains and promotes its strengths compared to other cryptocurrencies that they can process a transaction in less than 4 seconds on average, while bitcoin takes an hour and ethereum takes more than 2 minutes. Also, it is claimed that 1500 transactions can be processed in a second. However, there is something unique about this company. There is no mining associated with ripple. Ripple doesn't use any words related to blockchain in its whitepaper. It uses term distributed ledger instead. In fact, ripple is hard to be classified as a decentralized system and thus may not be classified as a blockchain.

Unit of ripple is XPR, and all XPRs are owned by the company. According to the company homepage, 100 billion XPRs are to be issued. Half of the issued XPRs will go to the contributors, and the other half will be owned by the company. It is a bit different from other cryptocurrencies. What is more interesting is that ripple is a private company, whereas bitcoin is a voluntary community. If you look at the list of investors of this company, you will find companies like Accenture, Soft Bank Group, Google Ventures, Standard Chartered, Santander, and Seagate.

More and more commercial cryptocurrencies are appearing in the market. The biggest difference between commercial cryptocurrency and traditional bitcoin like cryptocurrency is the owner of the operation. Commercial cryptocurrency is the cryptocurrency developed by private company or group who has control over core operation. In this sense, most of commercial cryptocurrency, albeit not all, are hard to be classified as a blockchain as they almost always violates decentralization for the sake of an improvement in performance.

These commercial cryptocurrencies can further be classified in two completely different purposes One purpose is to create an intrinsic value through technology. It is to develop a service, which digitalized legal tenders cannot provide, and have people pay for and use the service. The other purpose is just for enjoying current bubble turbulence of cryptocurrency by squeezing money out of people's pocket through encouraged speculation. Let's look at each case separately.

7.3.1. Commercial Cryptocurrency with functional value

A cryptocurrency itself has no value as it is just a sequence of bits meaninglessly recorded in computer. It has no 'fiat' nor intrinsic value. However, there is a way for a cryptocurrency to create its own intrinsic value. It is to create a functional intrinsic value. For example, if a cryptocurrency can provide a service that a digitalized legal tender cannot, then people would be willing to pay for that service. At this point, what people pay for the service will become the intrinsic value of cryptocurrency, and it will be a functional intrinsic value based on technology. The value depends on the quality and usefulness of the service and will be a pure intrinsic value regardless of current speculation.

-ç- In this case, the word cryptocurrency is never proper. As it is a service it should use a service name and should never appeal as a cryptocurrency.

Currently, there are some companies that are claiming to have developed a service using commercial cryptocurrencies, but there haven't been any distinguished accomplishments, yet. Anyway, if some service that can offer better conditions or value than current legal tenders in international transactions are to be developed, people would willingly pay for that service. However in that case, it should abandon itself the name 'cryptocurrency' and should use its own specific service name. Then the internal reward system of blockchain should use a term like token or coupon not cryptocurrency as this service is never a coin nor currency. If this service still insists using the name cryptocurrency and let brokers site do broker that to public then again the crazy bubble will form and by the economic reason, the developers themselves will be in great paradox of pursuing bubble than peaching its service value.

After all, if we look at this matter through the eyes of economics only, it would be very difficult for a functional intrinsic value to emerge before cryptocurrency speculation totally vanished. The first step to remove crazy bubble and clearly distinguish blockchain with value from useless blockchain(a blockchain only for cryptocurrency) is to discard the name cryptocurrency and use a different name for blockchain reward system such as token or coupons in order to distinguish its value from that of other speculative cryptocurrencies.

i There will be a confusion of mixed terms again if companies continue to stick to the name cryptocurrency and not take the name token or coupon. It would be impossible to distinguish tokens that pursue functional intrinsic value from cryptocurrencies which only pursue value as a speculative currency. Eventually, another argument surrounding cryptocurrency will form, people will have two extreme claims in which they used the same term to talk to two different objects.

7.3.2. Commercial Cryptocurrency for Speculation

Speculative purpose commercial cryptocurrency are seeking for maximum profit out of crazy bubble from huge speculation. Their purpose is to make themselves look more like legal tenders so that they can maximize speculative profits. However, such cryptocurrencies also pursue various kinds of functionalities. Nevertheless, what they ultimately seek to gain through these functional developments is to make as many profits as possible by creating speculative values of high prices as if it had the right to issue a legal tender.

It is not easy to distinguish between technology oriented tokens and cryptocurrencies for speculative purposes because sometimes both seek to the same target such as maximization of liquidity. What the two seek through the improvement of liquidity may differ from one another, but it is still difficult to distinguish between the two. Both will claim to aspire technological improvement, and cryptocurrencies will use blockchain as a shield to protect themselves. Tokens might mistake cryptocurrencies for their allies and work closely with them.

While many speculative capitals including hedge funds initially used a passive strategy where they mainly use market sweep and sought margin by controlling supply chain, they will now try to maximize their profits by founding their own cryptocurrency issuing companies or directly investing in them. The most ideal destination for these groups is to form an appropriate speculative value of a cryptocurrency whose liquidity is maximized and make profits as if they have the right to issue a legal tender. It would be like having a widow's cruse.

7.3.2.1. Derivatives and bitcoin

A derivative is a product whose value is determined by the change in the value of underlying asset. It buys and sells specific rights and obligations that may be exercised in the future when the conditions are met. Here, an underlying asset is an object of investment and can be anything. Gold and silver as well as stock index, individual index, real estate or even weather could be the object. Popular examples of derivatives include ETF, which is traded conveniently in the market as if it were a stock, and ELW, ELS, and DLS, which are traded over the counter.

What's scary about derivatives is that they don't have restrictions. This means that underlying asset of a derivative can be another derivative. As this complexity increases, the leverage effect of finance increases exponentially, and in some cases, an imaginary wealth of thousands of times the real assets can be easily created.

> Nick Leeson is the very person who let Barings Bank of UK be sold to ING Group of Netherlands for only 1 USD. In 1992, Nick was assigned to the Singapore branch of Barings Bank and had just started doing an arbitrage on SGX NIKKEI 225, which is a derivative based on NIKKEI index. In the beginning, he made good profits and was trusted by the company that the company even gave him a special bonus of 250% of his annual salary. However, nick's boss had no idea of how nick was making profits out of speculative dealings. Nick's boss, who knew little about finance, only thought that nick was a genius who was capable of making huge profits out of even with safe bond trading. But, nick soon began to suffer losses. His losses were initially 2 million pounds, then almost 0.2 billion pounds by the end of 1994. Nick completely concealed his losses with a fake account. Nick was even promoted to head of investment and was still doing investments on his own. Nick was his own supervisor! Later in January 17th, 1995, Kobe earthquake hit Japan, NIKKEI index dropped, and nick's losses were growing out of control. Eventually, his losses amounted to 1.4 billion pounds. When headquarters found out the situation, it was already too late, and the bank was forced to go bankrupt. Barings bank was the bank from which USA borrowed money to buy Louisiana from France and had a long tradition that it was beloved by the royal family and used to be called the Queen's bank. However, for over 230 years old history to collapse did only take couple of years and it was all caused from derivative goods.[P]

In 2017, BOE, a Chicago-based options exchange, and CME, the biggest derivatives exchange of the world, began dealing bitcoin futures. The media began reporting that the regulatory system has finally recognized bitcoin and active investments are to take place. But there is a view that it is a beginning of the test of wolves of Wall Street to see the usability of bitcoin as an underlying asset for their derivatives. The media might be excited about the fact that bitcoin has finally been recognized by the regulatory system, but it is actually not so surprising if you think of all the things which Wall street used as underlying assets for their derivatives like the subprime mortgage. After all, derivatives are just about gambling. They don't care about the long-term stability or value of their underlying assets. Derivatives have maturities. Once they reach their maturities, their underlying assets become meaningless and this is completely different from stock where values go accumulated as time goes by. It is the greed of Wall Street that is willing to use nuclear threat of North Korea as an underlying asset even. Thus, we shouldn't be too quick to conclude that bitcoin has been officially recognized as a currency just because there are derivatives that use bitcoin as their underlying asset.

Peter F. Drucker, who is considered to be the progenitor of modern economics, once said about derivatives, "But these financial instruments are not designed to provide a service to customers. They are designed to make the trader's speculations more profitable and at the same time less risky- surely a violation of the basic laws of risk and unlikely to work. In fact, they are unlikely to work better than the inveterate gambler's equally 'scientific' systems for beating the odds at Monte Carlo or Las Vegas – as a good many traders have already found out."[T]

7.4. Black Money

In September, 2013, FBI shut down an online website called Silk Road and arrested Ross William Ulbricht, who was known as the Dread Pirate Roberts. The remaining gang opened Silk Road 2.0 in November, 2013, but it was also shut down immediately. Later, Ross was charged with 8 different counts and was sentenced to life in prison without parole. This case was particularly given great attention because the website, which was often called the black market of internet, was found to have used bitcoin instead of legal tenders in many aspects such as drug trafficking. Just before the website was shut down, there were over 10,000 items being traded, and about 70% of them were illegal drugs. All transactions, which were estimated at about 40 to 50 million USD, were done in bitcoin every year, Silk Road charged commission on its users for its escrow service and bitcoin-to-USD conversion service.[R]

Hiding proceeds of crimes have always been the criminals' homework because they believe that they will be able to live a happy and comfortable life as long as they can hide their illegal profits well enough even if they get arrested. In 2011, a South Korean man was arrested for hiding 10 million USD worth of his illegal profits from running an illegal gambling website under his garlic field. He just dug farm in front of his house and buried his paper cash in plastic bag, which eventually detected by police and was confiscated. It the man had known about bitcoin back then; he wouldn't have gone to trouble to dig up his own garlic field to hide his money.

Bitcoin is the perfect place to hide any black money. If criminals hide all their money in bitcoin, then there is no way to retrieve any of it. Unless they confess their password for wallets and handed over the device where they saved private key, there is no way to even know how much is in their wallets. Therefore, it would be a far much better choice for criminals to hide their illegal money in bitcoin than hiding it under the ground and trying to avoid police investigation. At least for this purpose, the prime purpose of bitcoin which is to be free from intermediary (and thus to be anonymous in transaction) perfectly match the demand for criminals.

It is important to enhance and maintain regulations on external environments including brokers in order to minimize harboring of criminal proceeds. Harboring of criminal proceeds may only be minimized if every possible method to liquidate bitcoin into legal tenders is checked and watched. However, you may be able to detect harboring of criminal proceeds with all these regulations, but there is still no way to retrieve the money unless the criminal tells you the password to his wallet. Currently, judging from a variety of circumstances, one can reasonably suspect that all this crazy bubble about bitcoin may be the started by black money and then amplified through brokers site which in turn was either invested or founded by these criminal capital themselves.

As long as cryptocurrency is around, love of black money for it will continue.

> *i* FBI announced that the bureau confiscated 30 million USD's worth of bitcoin from Ross. But, as explained before, there is no way that FBI was ever able to confiscate that money. So even a government can't confiscate any money. Therefore, if the bureau really retrieved that money, it was either that Ross told them his password(I don't see this possibility) or the bureau succeeded in hacking Ross's wallet. As explained in *5.1.3.1. Problem of Wallet software itself,* wallet software is relatively easy to hack. Thus, it is most plausible that FBI figured out the password through software hacking or directly breached wallet.

Recently, there are some brokers that are preparing consulting services in which they track down cryptocurrency transaction histories. In Bitcoin system, as discussed earlier, it is possible to follow along specific addresses and look into their contents. Bitcoin addresses are encrypted hash values, so it may be able to check the remaining balance of a specific address but it cannot collect any information about the owner. However, there are still some opportunities to try and specify an individual by tracking the IP address while someone submits a transaction to the bitcoin system. Nevertheless, this kind of attempt is not easy at all. Recently, cryptocurrencies that are virtually impossible to trace have been developed. For example, Dash promotes its characteristic of being impossible to trace as its greatest strength. The following statement is shown on homepage of Dash.

"Protect your financial information. PrivateSend ensures your activity history and balances are private."

7.5 Tax Evasion

In the 1900s, there were only 18 charitable foundations in US. The number grew to 2839 in the 1950s and over 62,000 in 2002. The U.S. constitution states 50% of inheritance tax, but charitable foundations are exempted from tax and don't even have to pay capital earnings tax.[Y]

Those who are rich in US establish charitable foundations with almost no exception. Even George Soros has a foundation called Open Society. In addition, rich people around the world are all art lovers. They trade artworks that are worth millions or even billions of dollars. One of Da Vinci's paintings, which was recently auctioned off, was sold for over 500 billion dollars. There is even an artwork trading place right next to the Geneva Airport, and this building is directly connected to the airport, so artworks of high prices can be delivered immediately and safely as soon as they are sold. Of course there would be no one to naively believe that the rich has tendency to love artwork than ordinary people. All these are related to tax.

If a wealthy father bought 1 billion dollar worth of bitcoin, gave it to his son, and the son sold the bitcoin to the market, then it would be exactly the same as giving 1 billion dollars to his son without paying any taxes. They don't need to be bothered by annoying money laundry or borrowed-name bank account.

Bitcoin is like a gift from god to the wealthy because it allows them to perfectly protect their wealth from taxes. Also, they can even make profits with bitcoin thanks to speculative bubble. So, they will continue to hide their wealth in bitcoin for the moment. Now, they don't have to go to trouble to travel to tax havens and borrow names for secret funds. They also won't have to waste a whole room just to stack gold bars or wads of cash. Bitcoin is secure from robbery and does money laundering for you when you buy it. While these people used to accumulate their wealth through inflations of legal tenders in the past, now they have another joyful option in which they can have an indirect inflation through cryptocurrency or market manipulation.

The poor are more vulnerable to inflation because most of their wealth is in the form of cash. A synonym of inflation would be depreciation of cash. Thus what inflation impacts most is the cash. The rich usually diversify their wealth into many forms such as stock, real estate, and jewelry, so they can easily dodge an inflation, but the poor can't help but face it feebly.[w]

7.6. Brokers which replaced brokers

Bitcoin is a cryptocurrency that used the proof-of-work method in order to eliminate the need for a trusted third party. Satoshi Nakamoto anticipated that if the brokers disappeared, then unnecessary fees will disappear also. Nevertheless, most of bitcoin is being traded through brokers, a brand new brokers which has never been required before and even not necessary today. These bitcoin brokers are literally do broker between buyers and sellers and enjoy most of fee themselves.

Most people are paying 0.1 ~ 0.2% of fees doing transactions through these brokers daily. Contrary to Satoshi Nakamoto's hope, bitcoin actually created even more types and also numbers of brokers. The current bitcoin is completely surrounded by miners who charge 60 ~ 100 times the bank fee and brokers that charge 0.1 ~ 0.2% of transaction amount, a huge amount compared to bank transaction. Financial institutions are gone, but miners and brokers have taken over the seat, and their demanded charges are so expensive. Transaction fees keep increasing, and assets will evaporate as bitcoin transactions continue.

Vacancy of governmental supervision has been breached by brokers and miners. Do you think they are honest and trustworthy? Well, the answer is straight forward. They are there to make money.

Summary

- It is up to each cryptocurrency broker to choose what cryptocurrencies to list, and the number of cryptocurrencies listed by each broker is completely different also. The prices are of course different, too.
- Commercial cryptocurrencies are privately owned, and the development backgrounds and purposes are completely different from those of public cryptocurrency.
- If cryptocurrencies are used as hiding places for illegal criminal proceeds, there is practically no way to stop it. It will be used by criminals continuously.
- It is likely that cryptocurrency will be used by the rich to evade taxes and hide their assets, and there is really no way to stop it.
- Initial purpose of bitcoin was to eliminate any brokers or intermediaries, but professional miners and cryptocurrency brokers have replaced financial institutions and became the brokers. And cryptocurrency brokers are the one which has never been required before and even today there is no need for cryptocurrency brokers. However cryptocurrency brokers rule the world as they make tremendous fortune out of bitcoin speculations and world is manipulated by the rich normally.

8. Bitcoin and Cryptocurrency

So far we analyzed bitcoin in terms of money and discussed about its surroundings, a broker which replaced a broker. Now based on what we have discussed so far, this chapter discusses on the future of bitcoin and blockchain.

8.1. Future of Bitcoin

Bitcoin is the first implementation of blockchain in the form of cryptocurrency. Since it is the first, many defects have been pointed out from its original design to operation. It was already pointed out that bitcoin lacks consideration for regular commercial environment in the first place. Many cryptocurrencies such as ethereum tried to solve various problems of bitcoin, but there is still not one cryptocurrency, which is considered to be more usable than digitalized legal tenders or to have created a whole new value.

This chapter will focus on bitcoin in particular among all cryptocurrencies, because it is the first and prototype for all the other cryptocurrencies.

8.1.1. Stop mining risk

Bitcoin is a system, which relies on mining. Block production is like the heart of bitcoin system. Once the mining stops, no transactions are possible and the system will not be sustained.

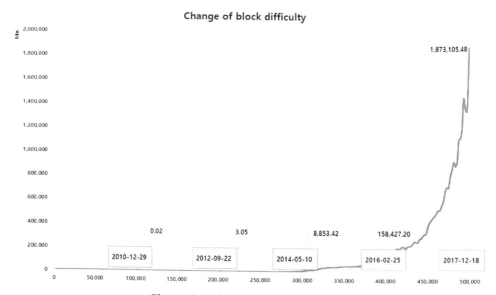

Figure 8-1 Change of block difficulty

Figure 8-1 is a graph, which shows how block difficulty has been changed over time. The difficulty has increased 12.9% on average per every period.[31] Earlier, it was explained that block difficulty must be controlled in order to maintain a constant block creation time regardless of the development of hardware considering that an integration degree of semiconductor doubles every 18 months and a performance of computer doubles too. However, if you look at the graph, the increase in block difficulty has been actually 113.3 times every 18 months instead of double regardless of Moore's Law. This is clearly not a natural increase from hardware development but an artificial increase resulted by putting as many resources as possible each time in competition.

After the adjustment on December 18th, 2017, the difficulty is now almost 2 trillion times harder than that of genesis block. It should have been only 63 times harder if the adjustments strictly followed Moore's Law. Figure 8-1 might have

---

[31] Please recall that difficulty is adjusted per every 2,016 blocks. Thus 1 period is a time it took for previous 2,016 blocks to be generated. Theoretically 1 period should be 2 weeks.

you think that the increase was so dramatic only recently, but that is not true. Block difficulty has always been increasing dramatically.

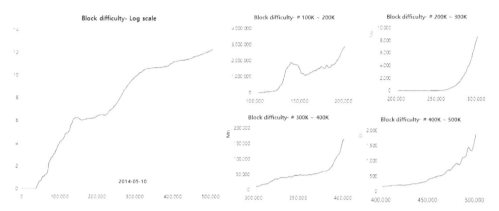

Figure 8-2 Change in log scale(left) and change for every 100,000 blocks(right)

Let's look at Figure 8-2. The graph on the left shows how block difficulty changes in log scale. The graph is almost a straight line. As the log scale graph is almost straight, it means that the difficulty has been increasing exponentially all the way. Actually, if you divide it up by periods of 100,000 blocks for each, you can more clearly see that the difficulty truly increased exponentially during each period.

It is easy to explain why the difficulty increased exponentially in the early days of creating the blocks. The early block difficulty was set less than a typical capacity of hardware. In the first place, mining was not designed for dedicated machines but personal computers. Therefore, it was actually much less than a typical capacity of hardware and the competition wasn't so severe, so it was not a big deal to catch up with the increased difficulty. However, the situation is different now. Let's look at the log scale graph in Figure 8-2 one more time.

Starting from May 10th, 2014, when #300,000 block was created, the increasing trend seems to slow down that the graph turns into a fluent curve. While the competition for mining intensified, the increase margin of block difficulty actually decreased. This may be due to the fact that there left no more room in investing more hardware. From this point, the capacity of miners have been saturated. As a result, the unit production investment costs per block must have increased significantly. Table 8-1 clearly shows the mining capacity saturation.

Block number	Block creation time	Difficulty	Rate of difficulty increase per every 100,000 blocks(times)
1	2009-01-09	1	-
100,000	2010-12-29	14,484.16	14,484
200,000	2012-09-22	2,864,140.51	198
300,000	2015-05-10	8,000,872,135.97	2,793
400,000	2016-02-25	163,491,654,908.96	20.4
500,000	2017-12-18	1,873,105,475,221.61	11.4

Table 8-1 Block Difficulty increase rate per 100,000 blocks

Table 8-1 compares the increase rate of block difficulty for every time 100,000 blocks are built. Although block difficulty multiplied thousands to tens of thousands times for every 100,000 blocks in the early days, it only multiplied 20.4 times when #400,000 block was created and 11.4 times when #500,000 block was created. The competition has intensified by hundreds of times, but the increase rate for block difficulty actually decreased, so it clearly shows that the mining business has reached saturation. In fact, it would be odd if a miner didn't put everything into the competition considering the current crazy price of bitcoin, so we can actually reasonably guess this saturation without such data.

8.1.1.1. Suspension of mining due to external factors

The amount of electricity consumption for bitcoin mining is increasing endlessly as the fierce competition to catch up with the exponentially increased block difficulty continues. Currently, the amount of electricity consumed for mining is out of knowledge. Some argue that the total electricity consumption for bitcoin mining in 2017 was over 30TWh, while other argue that it is not even more than 700MWh. 30TWh is 42,857 times of 700MWh. Since the two numbers are vastly different, it seems like one of the two is clearly untrustworthy(or maybe both). It is difficult to know which number is more accurate, but 30TWh is the same as the half of the total household electricity consumption of South Korea.[A] Considering that South Korea is the 7th or 8th largest electricity producing and consuming country, 30TWh may be an exaggeration.

Anyway, consuming an outrageous amount of electricity for mining won't be able to avoid criticism that it is a waste for another waste. Already, public opinions are forming in many countries that express concern about the waste of electricity that is caused by bitcoin frenzy. Countries that are especially negative towards bitcoin are observing the situation carefully. China has yet to respond to the matter with only passive countermeasures such as shutting down broker websites, but it is also possible that the Chinese government might ban mining itself in the future. Such a terrible waste of electricity can be associated with protection of the environment, so it could be used to justify such assertive measures. As of now, China is directly or indirectly controlling over 90% of the world bitcoin mining capacity. In short, the mining market of the world is dominated by China. Existence of bitcoin may be seriously threatened if China shut down the mining market. Of course they can move to another countries but in that case stable supply of cheap electricity become uncertain.

If a super large mining group that has been dominating the mining market suddenly stops mining due to external factors, there are not so many mining groups or companies that could cope with the current block difficulty. For the time being, the remaining miners might benefit from the disappearance of the bigger miners, but it would be too uncertain to make aggressive investments in order to take over the market and the block difficulty would be too difficult to handle. Also, a game of chicken among small and medium-sized mining groups will continue to it reach a new Nash Equilibrium. Suspension of mining due to external factors is hard to predict, so it will serve as a weakness until institutional regulations are in place.

8.1.1.2. Closure due to profitability – Mathematical Analysis

This section is about analyzing the profitability of bitcoin mining by analyzing it mathematically, so it requires knowledge of basic probability distribution in order to understand the following discussion. Thus, if you find this section difficult to understand, it is perfectly okay to skip this. It won't affect your understanding of the book at all. Let's just remember that the mining profitability relies too much on price of bitcoin against legal tenders, so it is dangerous.

The number of blocks that can be produced daily and the reward that can be gained from creating a block is almost fixed in bitcoin system. The daily production of blocks is fixed at 144 blocks(algorithmically), the block capacity is limited to a maximum of 1MB, so the reward market is not a growing market. It is a fixed market. Therefore, even if you invest more resources, the whole market cannot get any bigger. This game is not about growing the size of the market by investing more. It is rather a typical zero-sum game within a fixed market. Also, mining is a machine labor-intensive business which uses machines rather than a technology-intensive business. The result of the competition is determined by the one who used more electricity to force the machines to work more than anyone else. It is an environment caused by the PoW method which is designed to intentionally force excessive work on hardware. Unit mining cost competition in hardware is meaningless since it is not a technical work. Thus actual unit mining cost is mostly looking for a cheaper electricity.

Meanwhile, if one cuts down mining investment, then the mining success probability directly decreases, and if one expands mining investment then the success probability directly goes up. Mining is an all-or-nothing game. Each time you win a competition, you get 100% of the reward, but if don't, then you will lose all your investment. This kind of closed mining business environment built by bitcoin blockchain is vulnerable even to a slight defect in the design of blockchain ecosystem and could cause a fatal damage to the system. In this chapter, we will analyze in detail what problems are caused by this closed environment of bitcoin blockchain.

i Design defect of bitcoin blockchain is that the unit mining cost ever increases due to bitcoin way of PoW. The hash puzzle used by bitcoin blockchain is an extreme PoW method based on ASIC friendly SHA-256 hash technique, which is easy to be caught up with ASIC machine. Hash puzzle method in bitcoin determines its winner mostly in a deterministic way without any intervention of randomness, so more investment means winning the competition. As a result, it only encourages a rise in unit mining costs.

Let's talk about mining productivity again, which we briefly discussed back in *6.3.7. Temptation to invest in mining*. There were 3 parameters that affect mining productivity: mining reward(B), unit mining cost(m), and probability of success in mining(p). It is estimated that highest ranking mining companies have already invested all available resource capacity they have. Thus, it is unlikely that among the leading companies, one suddenly increases its probability of mining success sharply. Also, due to the labor-intensive characteristic of the mining business, unit mining cost will not varies much. Therefore, it would be safe if we assume that the last parameter 'mining reward in legal tendency' will dominates a profitability. Actually, it is already quite obvious that the most influential factor in the productivity of bitcoin is its price against legal tender considering high fluctuation of the market.

USD-converted mining reward is the total amount of bitcoin acquired by mining successfully multiplied by bitcoin price against USD. Though, the reward given after successfully mining a block consists of a fixed amount of subsidy and a variable amount of fee, as the range of fluctuation for commission isn't big, so we will assume that the reward itself is fixed. Thus, USD-converted mining reward is only proportional to bitcoin price against USD.

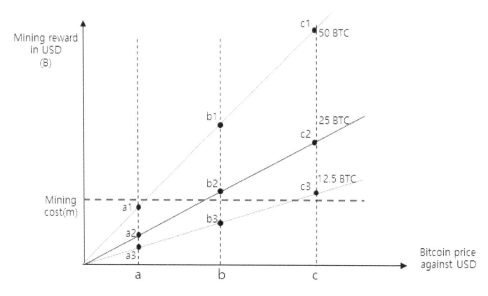

Figure 8-3 Mining reward in relation to bitcoin price against USD

Figure 8-3 shows the mining reward in relation to bitcoin price against USD. The blue line at the top is when the reward is 50 BTC, and the lines in the middle and at the bottom are when the reward is 25 BTC and 12.5 BTC, respectively. The dotted line in red is the mining cost per block. When dollar value of bitcoin is formed at C, the mining reward is always higher than the mining cost. In other words, one can make stable profits since c1 > c2 > c3 > m. However, if value of bitcoin decreases to b, then b1 > b2 > m > b3, so one will suffer a loss if mining reward is only 12.5 BTC. Lastly, if value of bitcoin further decreases then everyone will suffer a loss in any case because m > a1 > a2 > a3.

The problem is that the only way to recover from the decrease in bitcoin dollar value is to expect for a higher productivity which means to increase block creation success probability. After all, there is no other way around except praying for the mining success probability to be increased a little bit!

Then, is it realistic to expect that the mining probability to be increased further and the loss would be recovered? Let's do some calculations. Let's assume that a mining company A creates 25 blocks a day on average. It's quite powerful in that

A accounts for almost 17% of the total hash power. If the average number of blocks created by company A is λ, then the probability mass function, where random variable X represents the number of blocks A can produce in a day, follows Poisson distribution.

$$P(X = x) = \frac{e^{-\lambda}\lambda^x}{x!}$$

Now, assume that value of bitcoin has dropped 50%, and A can't sustain anymore with a daily production of 25 blocks. In order to respond to the decreased mining reward, it was calculated that A needs to produce 33 blocks a day, which is 30% more than the original productivity. Now, what would be probability of A producing 33 blocks without changing any condition. We need to find $P(X \geq 33)$ to answer this question. With $\lambda = 25$, the value of $P(X \geq 33)$ is,

$$P(X \geq 33) = \sum_{x=33}^{\infty} \frac{e^{-25}25^x}{x!} = 1 - \sum_{x=0}^{32} \frac{e^{-25}25^x}{x!} = 0.07145$$

Thus, there is only 7.1% of probability for A to turn a profit. Either the company will have to more eagerly pray for bitcoin price to bounce back again or stop operating.

This risk gets even worse when the price fluctuates rapidly. If bitcoin price sharply rises, mining companies will increase their investments competitively for more margins, so the mining cost to maintain the mining competitiveness will continue to grow. Then, if the price suddenly drops, the daily required production demand will drastically increase due to sharply increased production cost, m. However, as explained earlier, daily production of blocks is fixed at 144 no matter what resources are put in. Figure 8-4 provides a graph of the increase in required daily production demand and the likelihood of maintaining the production of company A.

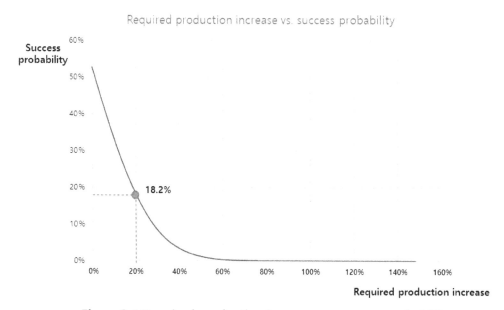

Figure 8-4 Required production increase vs. success probability

Here's how we read the graph. Let's assume the situation where the production needs to increase by 20% in order to recover the loss from the previous example. In other words, you have to produce more than 30 blocks a day. Since the production needs to be increased by 20%, you need to look for 20% on the horizontal axis. If you look at the point on the curve that corresponds to the 20% of the horizontal axis, it is the red dot in Figure 8-4. Now, if you read the value on the vertical axis, that is the success probability. That is, probability of increasing the production by 20% is only 18.2%. Unless the external factors change, there is no way to continue mining.

In fact, it is possible to calculate the theoretically appropriate price of bitcoin if we use this analysis. The principle is very simple. We need to substitute the actual cost expense of mining in USD and calculate bitcoin price against USD inversely for the range in which the mining can maintain a stable profit, then we can have the theoretically appropriate price of bitcoin. However, I want you to not wonder whether it is higher or lower than the current price because the calculated price is meaningless indicator as intrinsic value of bitcoin is zero. This is just an inverse calculation of the balance sheet of miners. However on the other hand, this value is of utmost importance in that bitcoin price below this level could mean a complete destruction of entire bitcoin ecosystem as miners would stop working. Again, intrinsic value of bitcoin is 0.

8.1.2. The fee strikes back

We have briefly discussed about bitcoin transaction fee in *3.2.4. Transaction Fee*. In the early days, transactions could be done without fees, but the minimum fee is now 1000 sat, and the processing time decreases in proportion to transaction fee. Also, the average of randomly sampled transaction fee was 30 USD. Now, let's analyze the correlation between transaction fee and transaction processing time by examining randomly selected transactions.

Table 8-2 compares transaction fees and processing times of 5 randomly selected transactions in #500,000 block.

Transaction Fee (BTC)	In USD	Processing Time
0.00001704	0.3408	7221 min
0.00017463	3.4926	11,412 min
0.001	20	69 min
0.0035	70	191 min

Table 8-2 Transaction fee and its processing Time

The first transaction in Table 8-2 paid 0.00001704 BTC or 1704 sat in fee. This is close to the minimum fee of 1000 sat. But, do you see how long it took to process this transaction? It took 7221 minutes or 5 days. The second transaction is even worse. It paid 3.5 USD which is more than 10 times the previous fee, but the processing time increased to 11,412 minutes or 8 days. It's like sending the money on Monday and waiting for it to be finalized until next Tuesday. As you pay 20 USD in the third transaction, the processing time finally reduced to 69 minutes. 20 USD is almost the amount you pay for an international transfer. Let's look at the last item. It took 191 minutes to be processed even though the fee was 70 USD.

Imagine you have to pay over 70 USD to transfer money through your bank and wait for over 3 hours while watching a rolling wait cursor. Most of you would call up the bank and complain about the waiting time. The current bitcoin is inappropriate to be used as a currency. In addition, you can't do micropayments. Payments of less than 20 or 30 USD will be spent on transaction fee, so it is practically useless.

The processing times in Table 8-2 could be slightly different from actual processing times. In fact, bitcoin system does not record the submitted times of transactions. After all, there isn't really a way to measure a processing time. The so-called processing times above are calculated by measuring the difference between the time a transaction arrived to a local computer memory pool and the time it was actually recorded on a block. These times may not be exactly the same as the actual processing times but are not so different from them.

As shown in Table 8-2, the processing time of a bitcoin transaction relies on its transaction fee, and it encourages the continuous increase of the fee. Transaction fee of bitcoin is expected to increase consistently for the following reasons.

- Absolute bottleneck
- Interests of brokers
- Replenishment of block reward

8.1.2.1. Absolute Bottleneck

The number of bitcoin users is increasing rapidly. The exact number is unknown, but the number of people who have downloaded bitcoin wallets are well over 15 million. Currently, the maximum number of transactions that can be processed within a day is about 300,000. That is only about 3.5 transactions per second. The basic cause of such a limitation is that the block size is limited to a maximum of 1MB. Also, I explained that a hard fork such as Segwit 2X is necessary in order to fix this problem, but there isn't enough mutual consensus for that.

However, the problem is that the number of transactions a block can hold and the number of blocks that can be produced in a day won't change despite a rapid growth of bitcoin transactions. Due to this bottleneck problem, the processing of transaction is consistently slowing down, and the transaction fee is increasing as people consistently have to pay more to shorten their processing times.

The bottleneck makes miners more likely to prefer higher transaction fees. Because there are full of transactions waiting to be chosen, there is no reason for them to process transactions with lower fees. They only need to process those transactions with low fees when there is some room left. As a result, the miners' preference for high transaction fees caused by the absolute bottleneck phenomenon and users' voluntary paying of higher transaction fees eventually form a vicious cycle and continue to encourage the increase of transaction fee.

8.1.2.2. Interests of Brokers

Of more than 300,000 transactions that are processed daily, there are very few or no transactions in which people actually used bitcoin to buy products. Most transactions are just exchanges between legal tenders and cryptocurrencies or between cryptocurrencies. Therefore, most transactions are done by brokers on behalf of individuals, and decision of transaction fees are commonly done by the brokers as well. For brokers, it brings them more profits to increase the turnover rate through faster processing than reducing the customers' transaction fees. Most users who trade through brokers don't have a clear understanding of transaction fee and don't care much about the concept of blockchain. Thus, they do not and cannot know how much they are being charged in transaction fee by the brokers. As a result, brokers are very open to pay more for a quicker process. Thus, the continuous increase in transaction fee is even more encouraged.

Meanwhile, if you buy bitcoin through a broker, your bitcoin will most likely remain in the broker's virtual wallet until you actually withdraw it and put it in your own wallet. To move it from the broker's wallet to your wallet, brokers usually charge around 0.0015 ~ 0.003 BTC, which is almost 60 USD. Brokers explain the reason for this huge charge as a bitcoin transaction fees. However, 0.003 BTC is unnecessarily expensive as long as your need is not urgent according to Table 8-2.

> *i* Bitcoin wallets calculate recommended transaction fees for their users. If you pay super express fee from Table 3-2, that is 0.00556052 BTC per KB. In general, roughly 0.2K bytes(20% of 1K) are enough for a single in and single out transaction. Therefore, 0.001112(=0.00556052 * 20%) BTC would be enough. Also, if you are not rushed and are willing to wait for a day, then just 0.000324 BTC would be enough. 0.000324 is 6.4 USD but, brokers charge fixed rate of 60 USD. You are charged around 10 times the sufficient fee for just transferring your bitcoin that was held by the brokers to your wallet.

Let's take a look at the following figure.

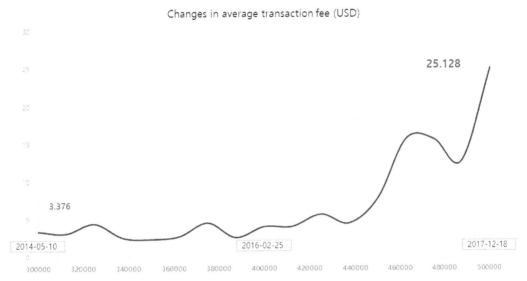

Figure 8-5 is a graph that illustrates the change in average transaction fee since May 10th, 2014, when # 300,000 block was created, until December 18th, 2017, when # 500,000 block was created. The transaction fee used to remain at around 3 USD, but it began to increase sharply in 2017. This trend continued and the average transaction fee has increased by 7.4 times, and it is still increasing. One might have to pay 30 bucks as transaction fee in order to get a 5 bucks cup of coffee or be held at the coffee shop for a week until the transaction is processed after paying just 3 dollars in fee. I have no idea about logic behind the claim of those who argue that bitcoin will become currency of future. It seems there is still long way to go for bitcoin to be something similar to a currency.

8.1.2.3. Replenishment of block reward

So far, it looks like the brokers control the transaction fees. This is because almost all transactions are directly processed by the brokers and the fees are determined by the brokers too. Of course, it is actually the miners that secretly encourage the increase in transaction fee, but still, it is the brokers which are mainly instigating the transaction fee fluctuations.

However, things might be different in the future. It is uncertain that the miners will still be satisfied with the current level of transaction fees in the future. Earlier, transaction fee was disregarded when calculating the mining profitability because the percentage of it in a mining reward is relatively small. As of now, the block reward is 12.5 BTC and the transaction fee is between 3 and 4 BTC. So, it is only about 20 to 25%. However, when the further reduction of reward by half is realized on July 6th, 2020, as scheduled, and the reward reduces to 6.25 BTC, then things will be greatly different. First, the percentage of transaction fee in a block reward will increase up to 30 ~ 40%, so the miners will push for transaction fee raise. There can be many ways to do so. One way is to deliberately process transactions slowly. In order to fix the bottleneck problem, the only solution is to pay more in transaction fee. Also, miners could try to build a new transaction fee system favorable to them and modify the system as a whole by attempting a soft fork or hard fork.

After all, it is possible that the miners who have been passively watching the transaction fee increase in the background may begin to induce the transaction fee competition. There are already over 1400 different cryptocurrencies which miners can target. If not July 6th, 2020, in July 3rd, 2024, in extreme cases, miners may stop mining bitcoin or move to another cryptocurrencies. If this happens, bitcoin ecosystem will collapse.

8.1.3. Bitcoin – Failed Experiment

Bitcoin experiment is failing. Due to the extreme application of PoW, the mining power has already been monopolized by few groups, and it already lost its identity as a decentralized system. With transaction fees that are 100 times more expensive than that of banks and annihilation of micropayments, bitcoin has gone total opposite directions from what Satoshi Nakamoto had peached for in the beginning.

Now, the cryptocurrency world are like pandemonium surrounded by greedy scammers and speculators. Speculators are exploiting people's money by controlling supply to the market and criminals are easily laundering and hiding their black money. Meanwhile, the rich are enjoying their tax evasions and benefit from margins. This result was definitely not conceived by Satoshi Nakamoto, being a naïve engineer. Once again, intrinsic value of bitcoin is 0.

> *i* When blockchain was used for cryptocurrency, one of basic property of blockchain mutated and became a fatal function of cryptocurrency. This mutation acts as the black hole of black money. As this deadly additional function itself is a basic property of blockchain, cryptocurrencies using blockchain would never serve for sound financial transaction from the beginning. What is this fatal function? I want you to think about it. The answer will be explained in *8.2. Future of Cryptocurrency.*

Bitcoin will continue to function as the shelter of black money. But, compare to recently developed cryptocurrencies, it's comparatively inadequate even for that purpose. The value one might get from using bitcoin instead of a legal tender will be nothing more than satisfying the curiosity. It is incapable of immediate processing, costs more fees, and its price fluctuates. Unfortunately, there is nothing that bitcoin has advantages in commerce activities. Satoshi Nakamoto's poor choice of blockchain application brought a new kind of financial chaos. There isn't even a simple cure to this problem. As it was the first experiment, a flexible structure which could reflect the improvements properly while the experiment was continued was definitely needed, but the limitations of a decentralized system such as difficulty of system maintenance and design limitations hindered the reflection of these improvements.

Bitcoin system does not have a centralized control system. Bitcoin system upgrade is not an update of a certain server but every participants in the system have to upgrade to a newer software. It is impossible for all of the voluntarily participating individuals to act in perfect order. Hard fork is inevitable, but various interests are intertwined, so it is also out of the discussion currently. There may be 'currency' in its name, but bitcoin has failed to prove its potential as a currency, and the failure of the experiment is practically clear.

8.2. Future of Cryptocurrency

The concept of cryptocurrency was already established in 1983 and was actually realized in the name of Digicash in 1995. Then, how is Digicash which was realized in 1995, fundamentally different from bitcoin that was born in 2009? The biggest difference between the two is that Digicash used a centralized system while bitcoin used a decentralized system. This concept of decentralization has given birth to a very fatal additional function as it was used by cryptocurrency, and that is the absolute anonymity. Absolute anonymity can only be achieved by a decentralized cryptocurrency, and a cryptocurrency based on a centralized system can never have it. This absolute anonymity is the mutation and is the very answer to the question from the previous section! This anonymity is completely opposite to the transparency of finance and has caused many problems. As discussed earlier in Chapter 7, dark sides of cryptocurrencies are all examples of abuse of this absolute anonymity. The current speculation surrounding cryptocurrencies is also using the anonymity. Also, the reason that there is no way to stop the market manipulation is from this absolute anonymity.

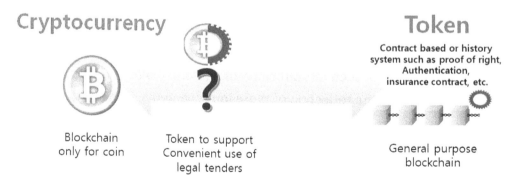

Figure 8-6 Cryptocurrency vs. Token

Figure 8-6 shows two extremely different uses of blockchain. The left end is a type of blockchain that only exists for cryptocurrency. It doesn't do anything other than functioning as a cryptocurrency, and the cryptocurrency only exists to serve as a currency. Many people are incapable of distinguishing between blockchain and cryptocurrency because of the blockchain only for cryptocurrency. Bitcoin, the first blockchain in the world, was also created for the purpose of currency only. Even experts sometimes make a wrong claim that cryptocurrency cannot be separated from blockchain because it is part of blockchain because they don't understand the difference between tokens of general purpose blockchain and blockchain only for currency. Currently, all the speculations are due to the anonymity created by blockchain that only exists for cryptocurrencies, and most of the 1400 cryptocurrencies are developed to serve only as a currency. Blockchain cryptocurrencies have yet to prove its positive side. Rather, they are causing problems due to the absolute anonymity created by themselves. In this point of view, we can say that blockchain for cryptocurrency only is not a future technology but a technology for dark world.

Meanwhile, the right end of the figure shows general purpose blockchain, which uses the term such as token or coupon instead of cryptocurrency and token only exists as a component of ecosystem to support stable operation of blockchain. The Blockchain on the right side of the figure exists to achieve a wide range of purposes. Its uses are endless. For example, it can be used in proof of title, history management, electronic coupon, real estate contract, real estate registration, birth registration, copyright management and insurance contract, etc. The role of token is to give the member of a collaborative community compensations for their voluntary efforts. This token can be used to exchange for a previously promised legal tender or equivalents. Also, these tokens may not even exists depending on the method of implementation. Therefore, even though cryptocurrency blockchain and general purpose blockchain may use the same blockchain technology, their definitions of transactions and purposes are completely different. For cryptocurrency blockchain, transactions are strictly about money transactions. For general purpose blockchain, the definition of transactions is variable by circumstances.

If there are only these two extreme cases of blockchain, then it would rather be easy to distinguish between cryptocurrency blockchain and general purpose blockchain. So it will be easy to discard a cryptocurrency. However, the fence sitters are always the problem. These are the type of blockchain that is illustrated in the middle of Figure 8-6 and has the characteristics of both types of blockchain. These blockchain are hard to be categorized as one type for certain, so people argue with each other while looking at the same object. These kinds of blockchain emphasize the technology of general purpose blockchain on the surface but are hard to be distinguished from cryptocurrencies. Tokens discussed in *7.3.1. Commercial Cryptocurrency of Functional Value* are example of this type, but they will stick to the term cryptocurrency instead of token for they prefer the speculative bubble value for now from the economic point of view. Nevertheless, when each country starts to take stances on cryptocurrency to expel them, then these gray coin will color their face to true tokens.

Cryptocurrencies cannot be eliminated completely. They can be developed at any time since the development platform that is distributed for free is so convenient that anyone could easily develop a cryptocurrency. However, it is possible to suppress the vitalization of it. Regardless of what added values a cryptocurrency might have, it is not so meaningful unless it can overcome the huge side effect caused by the anonymity. At least, the side effects of blockchain cryptocurrencies have made us question the necessity of their existence so far.

It has been 47 years since gold was kicked by dollar bills. Just like dollars were able to kick gold out of the scene by Thomas Gresham's law[32], cryptocurrencies could expel fiat money. If the anonymity of cryptocurrencies become more generalized, then the value from financial transparency will diminish, and there could be a great financial confusion.

---

[32] Thomas Gresham is famous English finance administrator in 16th century. He is famous for his saying that "bad money will drive good money out of circulation"

Many people mistakenly believe that cryptocurrency is money that is completely independent of country or any other forces. Capitalists can buy cryptocurrencies at any time using legal tenders and even create them on their own. As long as cryptocurrency is traded in legal tenders, it can never be an independent currency. Just because the issue is independent, it does not mean that it can have economic independence. Already bitcoin and over 1,400 cryptocurrencies have been taken over by the evil scammer and capitalists and are being used as another tool of greed. It has been 47 years since the US dollar has kicked gold out of the scene. There are many economists who have doubts as to whether the system of debt money can sustain for long. There may be an entirely different currency system. However, an economic system cannot be changed by just science and technology alone. A well designed economic system with the support of science and technology can bring real change.

Many countries still didn't put any clear regulation on cryptocurrencies. Meanwhile, more and more scammers are starting to lure general public into crypto-gambling. According to Peter Drucker, the reason for being of government is by far 'governing'. Government is there for effective and fundamental decision making for a given problem. If it is just 'doing' like any other authorities then it has no value. This supreme organization should be separated from 'doing' authorities and its only mission should be a decision making.[E]

Summary

- Bitcoin has the risk of suspension of mining due to an increase in block difficulty.
- Bitcoin transaction fees continue to rise for the following three reasons, up to 100 times the average banking fee.
  - Absolute bottleneck

- Interests of brokers
- Replenishment of block reward
- Experiment of bitcoin as a currency has failed, and the speculative scammers are surrounding it.
- The purpose of the cryptocurrency blockchain exists only for cryptocurrency and is completely different from the token of general purpose blockchain.

9. Future of a blockchain

9.1. New era of blockchain initiated by bitcoin

Set the discussion on usefulness of a bitcoin aside, the new disruptive technology initiated by bitcoin is quite a something. Many programmers engaged in development of blockchain which resulted in over 1,400 cryptocurrencies in the market.

Bitcoin was the first to show the potential usefulness of decentralized system while ethereum was the first general purpose blockchain by implementing smart contract capabilities using turing-complete script language. Thus before ethereum, the functionality of blockchain is quite limited and mostly serve for recording simple information such as simple financial transaction. Using ethereum, people now can define any programs which execute itself to its final status so that consistent auto execution of contract of any types finally become possible. This surely deserved to be called as an innovation.

Later technological evolvement in blockchain system is quite amazing. Decentralized application platform is now so much well organized that anyone can freely access source code then tailor to their fit with ease. Firstly, bitcoin blockchain proved possibility of blockchain based payment system, then smart contract concept now opened a door to a real general purpose use of a blockchain which includes record, contract, authentication, or even as a transparent storage. This usage is not limited to commercial purpose. Many governmental usage also could be possible.

i In fact the biggest threat to big financial institution or government body is not an outside hacker but a malicious insider. This voluntary or forced malicious insider can change information any time. However, nobody can change blockchain data once it is written!

Sometimes there are person who tries to further classify blockchain claiming that blockchain which uses different consensus mechanism from PoW such as 'proof-of-stake' is a big innovation. They even call it a 3rd generation blockchain. However in technical point of view, this kind of an assertion could be a bit nonsense. Different consensus mechanisms many times target different problem domain and also with different assumptions, thus might not even possibly be compared.

Blockchain concept itself needs an entire book to discuss and thus the purpose of this section is just to draw very core of blockchain which applies commonly to every blockchain initiations.

9.2. Bitcoin – start of a dream, revealed limitation

The core concept of a bitcoin blockchain which is the first and prototype of all blockchain can be summarized by following 4 basic rules and 2 assumptions.

[Basic rules]
1. It is designed that if a node complies with a given rules then only truth can be written on the block.
2. If some node violates a given rule, then that cheat could be detected quickly and with ease.
3. If some node tries to hide violation, it takes prohibitively expensive cost to perform
4. When two different truth conflicts, rule is to follow the one with more efforts invested in making the truth.

[Basic assumptions]
1. System is an ecosystem mainly sustained by voluntary labor forces offered by participants.

2. Within ecosystem, sum of all virtuous powers always outnumbers those of malicious one. This does not mean that there are more honest persons in the world but does mean that doing virtuous acting is economically much more profitable than acting maliciously by design. Thus no specific motivation to act maliciously.

Basic concept of bitcoin blockchain	Adopted technology and rule in bitcoin system
1) It is designed that if a node complies with a given rules then only truth can be written on the block	Integrity of a bitcoin application design itself.
2) If some node violates a given rule, then that cheat could be detected quickly and with ease.	SHA-256 secure hash
3) If some node tries to hide violation, it takes prohibitively expensive cost to perform	PoW with SHA-256
4) When two different truth conflicts, rule is to follow the one with more efforts invested in making the truth.	Decentralized consensus algorithm which chooses the heaviest blockchain data.

Table 9.1. Elements of bitcoin blockchain concept and its application implementation

Table 9.1 shows 4 elements of a bitcoin blockchain and technologies adopted for bitcoin application. Rule 1 and 2 which regulate fundamental integrity of bitcoin system were well designed and working fine. However rule 3 and 4 raises lots of issues and questions as time goes by. Especially the PoW mechanism implemented with ASIC friendly SHA256 for irreversible property drives massive waste of unnecessary energy and also causes system to be dominated and thus monopolized by nodes with massive hardware. This is one of the critical design defect of bitcoin which eventually endangers sustainability of a system.

The hash puzzle implemented in bitcoin blockchain uses extreme way which has almost no randomness so that winner is determined only in deterministic way.

This is all-or-nothing game and thus this chicken game drives participants to put every resources on has until completely crushes the other. On top of this SHA-256 hash algorithm adopted for bitcoin is so AISC friendly and thus polarization of mining power could have been predicted from the beginning. At least, these 2 minimal points addressed, ASIC friendly hash and full deterministic way of selecting PoW winner, should be considerably modified. From the same context, many questions and doubt on PoW method are around. Someone argues that proper adjustment to PoW will do the job while others claim that PoW itself is not suitable for blockchain.

Meanwhile several new ideas such as 'Proof-of-Stake(PoS)' is quite actively in discussion. However, strictly speaking the problem domain for PoW and PoS is not quite the same. There could be many different proposals and ideas coming but actually still not a single idea completely outperforms the others. All the ideas has pros and cons and as shortly mentioned earlier, some idea even deals with different problem domain by imposing several new assumptions to anonymous decentralized system.

The rule 4 together with rule 3 which orders to follow heaviest blockchain data extremely polarize hash power to force each individual give up the race itself. This property completely contradicts basic concept of P2P networks which basically states that every nodes should be equal in its rights and responsibilities within the network. However it is clear that all these questions raised by bitcoin system drives new evolution of blockchain.

Meanwhile current mechanism of mining motivation surely can be criticized as one of the worst design of incentive engineering. The only reason for investing tremendous energy and hardware for mining in bitcoin system is the profitability of so called "coin" and the value of coin is coming only from people's lunatic gamble on coin. Thus depending on this lunatic behavior, the entire ecosystem could collapse in a minute. Once miners stop mining, then system dies. Blockchain ecosystem is sustainable only when someone provides voluntary labor and that voluntary labor is sustainable only when it is being properly and stably paid either by money or by some other motivation! So in a strict sense, bitcoin system has never been complete because it never provided any concrete solution for this incentive mechanism. We will discuss more detail later in coming section.

9.2.1. Standardization and compatibility of blockchain

Standardization and compatibility always become important issue for newly introduced technology. What has been done to standardize blockchain for last 9 years? To make long story short there is no such activity. In fact, actually the blockchain itself is still an incomplete subject and thus standardization is out of question.

As shortly mentioned above, the implementation of blockchain varies a lot depending on purpose and its operating environment. On top of which a blockchain is a complete ecosystem, not a single technology components. So even in the future, it should be a combination of standardized packages rather than whole turn-key based solution. Let alone its standardization, even a standardized or unified definition is not easy. Depending on view, blockchain definition could be completely different and thus in some strict criteria many blockchains in the market are actually not a blockchain.

However it is clear that as ethereum platform forms a vast community, many developers follow the way ethereum does. This will create a common guideline among followers and eventually to form a de facto standard for a certain group. Ethereum wants to monopoly term DApp, which an abbreviation of decentralized application, and it seems like they want the term DApp only refers to some smart contracts running on ethereum Mainnet. However it is in a great doubt that ethereum network and their smart contract is enough to accommodate actual industrial needs. In fact that platform is too limited in many aspects.

In next section we will analyze common concepts used for every blockchain and explain it as an ecosystem. Through this, you will understand what to consider to design well defined blockchain that serves your purpose.

9.3. Implementing a blockchain: Composing new ecosystem

Making a decentralized application with blockchain is to construct new infra ecosystem. Bitcoin system itself is a complete ecosystem. In ecosystem, virtuous cycle of voluntary labor and incentive is formed to sustain its system. Thus the proper design of ecosystem between labor and incentive is most critical part which should balance by itself. Otherwise that ecosystem will eventually dies and will vanish. Bitcoin is an experimental currency and its payment system. That experiment suggested lots of improvement points and important consideration points for proper ecosystem design. In this section we will discuss on general blockchain properties regarding its components, and requirements.

Elements of general blockchain	Design of a bitcoin blockchain	Description	Role
Proper incentive to participants (Incentive Engineering)	Paying self-issued cryptocurrency (bitcoin)	Proper incentive to motivate stable voluntary labor from participants	Sustainability of an ecosystem and efficiency of system maintenance policy
Role of participants	Basically all nodes are equal (selectively as a full node or SPV node from one's own choice) transaction processing by	Define roles of each nodes. Role could be the same or be classified according to the levels of work.	Security, Efficiency, Integrity and maintenance policy of a system.

	making a block and validation of a transaction.	Even, role could be voluntary or be ordered depending on design.	
Decentralize d consensus rule	The heaviest blockchain. That is, the blockchain that required the biggest energy requirements for producing.	Define rule by which every nodes can identically synchronize its data status at all times (How to break a tie)	Integrity and efficiency of an ecosystem
Irreversibility validation rule	Finding nonce for hash puzzle for PoW	Define method to implement irreversible transaction record. Unlimited ways can be applied together with decentralized consensus mechanism. (How to select a leader to write a ledger)	Efficiency and integrity of an ecosystem
Define transaction	Define bitcoin transfer as a transaction.	Define mission and objective of a blockchain.	Define functionalities of ecosystem. Reason for being existence

			and mission.
Maintenance	Still no (official) hard fork. Soft fork only	Method to reflect changes of system. Debug, Fetch, Upgrade, new rules , etc.	Way of evolving of ecosystem.

Table 9.2. Elements of a blockchain ecosystem and design of ecosystem

Table 9.2 shows elements which comprise blockchain ecosystem and what to consider to sophisticatedly define blockchain. If you are engaged in blockchain project now or may will be then the first thing you should do is to check each elements in the table against your plan, role, efficiency, etc.

9.3.1. Proper incentive to participants

It's really surprising that only few discusses on importance of incentive engineering in blockchain ecosystem. As a matter of fact, incentive system in blockchain is the heart of an ecosystem and without proper incentive scheme, blockchain cannot survive. This incentive is tightly linked to the mission and objective of a blockchain.

In general, blockchain ecosystem is supposed to be composed of voluntary participants.[33] It could be composed solely of voluntary anonymous participant like bitcoin system, but it also could be preselected set of participants with predetermined qualification conditions. Nodes contribute to system using their own resources. On due course, they have to spend time, efforts, hardware, electricity and direct/indirect costs. Therefore without proper compensation on this cost, the motivation to support system tremendously decreases. Thus for stable and sustainable operation of blockchain, proper incentive scheme is of utmost importance.

---

[33] There could be various implementation versions.

In case of bitcoin, the incentive to miners is self-issued coin which has no intrinsic value at all. This is a bit nonsense. The only reason that miners suffer to put enormous energy currently is lunatic bubble price of bitcoin in the market, which will eventually disappear soon due to technical defect in design and economic reason. In this sense, bitcoin system is incomplete and cannot be sustainable.

In some cases, blockchain without incentive scheme is also possible. In this case, the participants are normally not an anonymous but a group with common objectives and mission. Also in this case, PoW will be very light because as we can identify participants and thus there is very little needs for utmost solution required to protect attacks from arbitrary malicious nodes.

Bitcoin system is composed of completely voluntary nodes and gives self-issuing coin to miners and this is almost identical to every sequel (or sometimes called altcoins) coins. This is simply putting the cart before the horse. Blockchain is only needed when it could serve for a certain purpose and then compensation is paid to participants who contributed to the system. However in blockchain cryptocurrency the only purpose of blockchain is for cryptocurrency itself which has no other mission or purpose. Thus unless cryptocurrency itself has some value, the blockchain for cryptocurrency is useless. I already mentioned that blockchain based cryptocurrency is useless and good for only malicious use in anonymity. In this sense blockchain which has some clear and specific functionality other than cryptocurrency itself should completely stop using the term cryptocurrency but start using different term such as token or coupon. Meanwhile the token given to participants as a compensation would be exchanged with legal tenders or its equivalents. In this sense, all the source of compensation should come from profits gained from blockchain service or cost saving by converting centralized system to decentralized system. In this aspect of blockchain utilization, it is more convenient for big company (which has various sources for incentives) to develop blockchain rather than small startups. In the near future, when commercial blockchain is started to be adopted in financial institute then the incentive system which directly pays legal tenders also appear.

Incentive scheme is a heart of a system that supplies nutrient. When the scheme is improper, it's like body with unhealthy heart. Sometimes incentive system is also linked to upgrade policy. When incentive system is flexible then it has little burden to system upgrade including hard fork.

"Incentive system should be stable in value and needs to be predictable."

9.3.2. Role of participants.

Basically participants of blockchain shares some role. It shares some part of role of centralized server. Ultimate blockchain may be the one where every nodes are equal in right and responsibility. However starting from bitcoin system, what we noticed is that equality of all nodes are not necessarily ideal or desirable. Bitcoin is two tier system such as full-node and SPV nodes. Actually it is not easy for every nodes to take a burden of copying all the data themselves at all times. Depending on application area and especially for commercial purpose blockchain, there probably could be many different layers of nodes. Each layer has its own role and responsibility, then will be compensated differently of course.

Roles of nodes are also linked to security and integrity of a system. However as the role of each nodes becomes diverse, it loses its strong points of decentralized system. For example, if one specific set of nodes has a certain important role, then the target of hackers will become clearer. Many PoS and DPos algorithms assume some specific role from certain nodes in a deterministic ways. In this case if these nodes are compromised by hackers then entire system would be endangered.

9.3.3. Decentralized consensus rule.

Basically blockchain data is distributed, replicated and stored in every nodes. This way of distribution is the key nature which incapacitates hacker's attack as well as the physical safety from natural disaster such as fire and earthquake. However this distributed data needs to be synchronized consistently.

Decentralized rule can be summarized as a continuous cycle of selection of leader and then validation of leader's record.

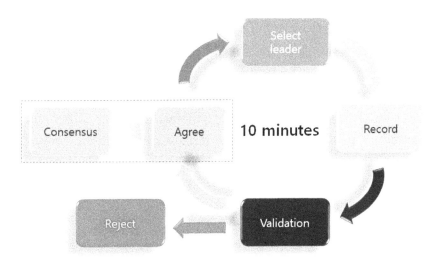

Figure 9-1 Decentralized consensus cycle in bitcoin blockchain

Figure 9-1 shows cycle of decentralized consensus. Very beginning is to select a leader according to a given rule, which is to select a node that will record the truth at a given round. In case of bitcoin the rule to select a leader who solves hash puzzle first. In this sense in both centralized and decentralized system, someone who writes a truth at a given moment is always one. This is a secret that even in decentralized system, system effectively have only one truth at a time. The difference is that in centralized system, the leader, and thus a writer, is predetermined and never changes whereas in decentralized system, the reader is changing every round according to a given rule.

In centralized system, we just simply trust writer and there is no process of validation. However, in decentralized system, we cannot trust anyone and thus there is a process of validation. Validation is a process where every nodes checks validity of current record written by newly selected leader at a given round. The result of validation is either to reject or to agree on the record. When every nodes agree on the record then finally consensus in made and this is how every nodes

263

synchronize common single truth at each round. This round repeats every 10 minutes as new block generates in every 10 minutes.

Meanwhile, decentralized consensus rule also has to define how to select a single truth out of multiple truths when they are conflicting. This does not just mean to check the validity of status. The validity of truth is very basic and even all nodes always tell only truth, there still could be a conflict of status due to network latency and this temporal inconsistency cannot be avoided. So decentralized consensus rule should define 2 things actually. The first is to define how to validate integrity of a given blockchain data status, and the second is, more importantly, to define how to break tie when there are more than 2 blockchain data status where each blockchain data itself are perfect in their integrity.

What bitcoin system adopted is to follow the blockchain data which is heavier than any other blockchain data. The weight of blockchain is directly linked to hash puzzle difficulty used for PoW. If all the blocks have the same difficulty, the heaviest blockchain data simply becomes the longest blockchain data.

PoW based rule basically could be an ideal mechanism for absolute anonymous system because cheating always requires lots of energy and therefore a gain from cheat should be bigger than the energy invested. Ironically this very characteristics of PoW is the biggest threat to sustainability of bitcoin system because it also requires same amount of cost for virtuous activity.

Many people claim that new mechanism such as PoS is the future direction of decentralized consensus rule. However in technical point of view, this claim is wrong. The problem domain of PoW and PoS is not necessarily the same. For example, in PoS, we could have prior information who might be the next block maker, which is not the case of PoW. What is important here is that we don't need to be obsessed by solution for extremely anonymous environment but we should not be confused with solutions for different conditions either.

Decentralized consensus rule is directly linked to integrity and efficiency of blockchain ecosystem and many various new ideas are being discussed. This is the very core of blockchain as this ensures the consistency of status among nodes.

"Decentralized consensus rule is the core part of blockchain which secures integrity of ecosystem. The proper design is directly linked to integrity and efficiency of blockchain."

9.3.4. Irreversibility validation rule

Irreversibility validation rule defines a mechanism to prevent change of content once it is written. Typical way of prohibiting modification is PoW. Actually in extreme anonymous environment, PoW is one of the best way to block fraud because the harder to cheat something, the lesser the attackers attempt to do.

What irreversibility validation rule does is basically to make modification extremely difficult. The way bitcoin blockchain implemented is to make modifier recalculate PoW of every blocks after modification point, which is almost impossible because he or she not only needs to recalculate the PoW but also has to be the first one to solve the puzzle and thus to make a longer chain of all.

The characteristics of SHA-256 that is only computation intensive and very ASIC friendly drives miners to put more ASIC machines to defeat opponents. With this, difficulty control system of bitcoin which blindly checks average speed of mining, forms a complete malicious cycle of extreme polarization of mining powers. In this sense, lack of randomization in selecting winner can be thought of as one of the biggest defect in design of bitcoin PoW. It is definite that some modification to bitcoin PoW and its difficulty control system is required and accordingly many different ideas are being discussed. Some minor tuning to bitcoin rule is Z-cash or bitcoin gold where they implemented a different hash algorithm called EquiHash rather than SHA-256. The characteristics of EquiHash is that it is quite a memory intensive which hinders miner to put ASIC for this puzzle. As using ASIC to this memory intensive hash puzzle is not cost effective, it breaks a bit malicious cycle of mining polarization in bitcoin system.

Meanwhile, the biggest difference between PoW and PoS is as follows. In case of PoW, at each round of competition, the condition to be a leader is (theoretically) identical to every nodes while it is not in case of PoS. Nodes in PoS system accumulates different contribution points(so called stakes) to system and has different privilege in competition. Ultimate case of PoS could be the one where node with the most coins will be a leader(of course this ultimate rule will not be practical in real world implementation but is easy to explain a rule, though). Many readers already could see the intrinsic problem of PoS itself. As a condition for competition is not the same to each nodes, it can be abused in many ways and thus it is (theoretically) more difficult to put an integrity than PoW in ultimate anonymous environment unless we trust them. Thus basically PoS could even be interpreted that it brought blockchain system from proof based domain to trust based domain again.

However, may be more important question would be, "Do we really need a solution that works in an ultimate anonymous condition?" In commercial environment, the ultimate anonymity may not be the case. We can control and put a minimal constraints to the system and then the problem become much easier. Thus you have to consider operating environment of blockchain when you design a new system. You should realize that how various and different implementation of blockchain could be possible depending on purpose and operating environment.

"Irreversibility validation rule is linked to integrity and efficiency of a blockchain ecosystem. This rule has direct relation to decentralized consensus rule."

9.3.5. Define transaction

Defining a transaction means to define an application area and purpose of blockchain. Transaction defines mission and reason for being of that blockchain ecosystem. Too broad definition will make rule complicated and decrease efficiency. If its definition is too narrow then it may result in incomplete functionality and thus generates a dependency to other blockchain or even to some centralized system for further processing.

All in all, the proper definition of functionality scope is the critical to efficiency and stability of a system. Actually the most important consideration at this point is that one must check the pros and cons comparison with centralized system. Still centralized system is more suitable in most of the cases. So before you start blockchain project you need to check following points.

1. Is there significant advantage in overall investment and maintenance cost?
2. Is there a significant importance in irreversibility of a record?
3. Is there clear improvement in security?

There must be at least 1 "Yes" to above 3 questions. Otherwise you definitely don't need decentralized system. Currently so many people blindly start to develop blockchain system without considering what are advantages over centralized system.

Unlike bitcoin blockchain where you should code yourself for new purpose, in ethereum platform many new types of contract could be added easily. Ethereum manages its status using the concept of account. So called 'Externally Owned Account'(EOA) is almost identical with bitcoin transaction whereas 'contract account' in etherum, you can put your own code written in script. Once your contract account which has some program code in it is posted to some block of ethereum, you can call that contract anytime by sending a message using EOA. In this way, without modifying a source code itself you can create another functionality within ethereum platform. However what basically ethereum smart contract does is simply to result in 32bit pair of key and value. Thus still quite limited in its usage. If you are thinking of complex and big project, you have no choice but to design your own blockchain from the beginning and has to construct your blockchain network yourself.

"Defining a transaction is to define a purpose and mission of blockchain and must be started with a question that 'Do we really need blockchain system?'"

9.3.6. Maintenance

One of the biggest disadvantage of using decentralized system is its complexity of maintenance. In case of centralized system, scheduled upgrade is quite straightforward. All we have to do is to set a specific date for upgrade and reflect changes in a systematic ways. This way, reported bugs fix and new function addition can be efficiently done. However in case of decentralized system, software upgrade means upgrade of core client program of participants. As this cannot be forced, upgrade of client program of an each participant is solely up to at their own will. Thus there always can be a rule inconsistency between participants who already upgraded their core clients and who didn't. In practice, it is almost impossible that all participants have the same version of software at all times. Changes of rule normally involve conflicts of interests and thus make someone to resist upgrade on purpose.

These changes always create a soft fork or hard fork depending on changes as I explained in chapter 3. Thus maintenance policy has to consider all aspects such as incentive scheme, decentralized consensus rule, irreversibility validation rule as well as transaction definition. Thus even though one can briefly summarize that minimizing conflict of interest is the key of proper design, the actual design to minimize conflict of interest is really difficult and sophisticated job. As one ultimate example, depending on the environment, upgrade can be forced just like the centralized system. In that case, every connection should upgrade current software to the latest version forcibly and only those who agree on this policy can join the network.

"Key of maintenance policy is to minimize conflict of interest and this involves all aspects of ecosystem"

9.3.7. Other considerations

So far, we checked points to consider to define blockchain ecosystem. Once ecosystem is defined, normally it forms a closed system and operates on its own. However there are cases where different blockchain ecosystem cooperates to achieve common and bigger mission. In this case the communication protocol between different ecosystem also become important. This communication is not limited to between different blockchain system but also could be between blockchain system and centralized system. Up to now, there is minimal work on this kind of communication protocol.

In the future, each blockchain might be specialized to its modularized needs and cooperates each other to achieve a diverse goals. This way is much more stable and flexible than one big giant ecosystem which has all the capabilities in it.

"Cooperation between blockchain system and also with centralized system needs to be considered. Thus define a functionality as an open ecosystem is also need to be considered"

9.4. Complete definition for blockchain

In *2.1. Defining terminology – Blockchain and Bitcoin*, we defined blockchain as follows.

"Blockchain is the base technology of a decentralized ledger which can be safely used in an anonymous system."

However this definition is a bit biased and said the complete definition will be made at the end of this book. As we discussed all 6 components necessary to design blockchain, now is the perfect time to properly define blockchain to its very nature.

"Blockchain is an ecosystem which solves decentralized consensus problem based on irreversibility validation rule in decentralized system"

There are couple of difficult words in definition but all are already explained. In a nutshell, blockchain is a leader election system and set of validation rules which contribute to an eventual consistency of a decentralized system. To achieve this, all jobs are done by voluntary participants to whom the incentive is paid for their efforts.

Summary

Bitcoin blockchain can be summarized with 4 basic rules and 2 basic assumptions.
[Basic rules]
1. It is designed that if a node complies with a given rules then only truth can be written on the block.
2. If some node violates a given rule, then that cheat could be detected quickly and with ease.
3. If some node tries to hide violation, it takes prohibitively expensive cost to perform
4. When two different truth conflicts, rule is to follow the one with more efforts invested in making the truth.

[Basic assumptions]
1. System is an ecosystem mainly sustained by voluntary labor forces offered by participants.
2. Within ecosystem, sum of all virtuous powers always outnumbers those of malicious one. This does not mean that there are more honest persons in the world but does mean that doing virtuous acting is economically much more profitable than acting maliciously by design. Thus no specific motivation to act maliciously.

Building a blockchain can be compared to compose new infra ecosystem and needs to consider following points.

- Proper incentive to participants (Incentive Engineering)
- Role of participants
- Decentralized consensus rule
- Irreversibility validation rule
- Define transaction
- Maintenance policy

Complete definition of blockchain is as follows.

"Blockchain is an ecosystem which solves decentralized consensus problem based on irreversibility validation rule in decentralized system"

| Closing |

Bitcoin is not a legal tender nor will be. The same is true of all other cryptocurrencies. Technology alone cannot change economy system. True evolution is achieved when technology is used for well planned economy system.

In 1972, assume Alex and Brian who were paid equally. However, Alex was paid 1 ounce of gold whereas Brian was paid with 43USD. At least in 1972, the value which Alex and Brian possessed were the same. However if we calculate their values in 2017 again, the difference is more than 30 times. Alex's gold is 30 times more valuable than Brian's paper dollar! Brian has to achieve 7.66% in yearly complex interest rate or 64.8% in yearly simple rate for more than 45 years to catchup Alex's gold. Of course such a miracle is impossible and ordinary person (which Brian represents) were deprived of their income to someone. What happened? This is so called inflation. Many economist blames fiat money system to be responsible for this loss. Despite the heavier labor efforts, the wealth gap deepens every day because of the inflation.

Since Japan started to print paper Yen, US followed to print enormous amount of paper dollar from 2008 under the nice name called 'quantitative easing'. Through this, world is in delusion of economical abundance, which is a very short and temporal and soon the fierce wave of inflation will rampage again to remove economic bubble built by paper money. This will directly impact ordinary people and we don't know how much painful it might be. Quantitative easing is still on going process and US is just slowing down its speed. This created deep distrust on current monetary system and triggered the demand for new and fair system.

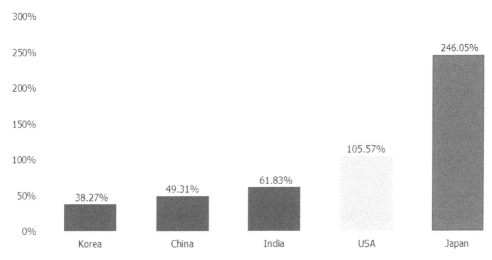

Figure A. General government gross debt % of GDP, 2017, IMF

Figure A shows government gross debt percentage of GDP in 2017. Japan already reached 240% and US is around 108%. This is quite different from that of China, Korea and India, where the ratio has been stable or in reasonable amount of changes over the last decade. Bitcoin which came in the middle of this turmoil is like a sea water to thirsty person adrift on the sea. To the person who doesn't want to be pooled by paper money prank by major powers, bitcoin looked like a mysterious living water. Now, more and more people realized that actually it was a salt water dressed like living water. Satoshi Nakamoto is not an economist but a computer scientist. In other words, he never developed cryptocurrency to cure the problem of fiat money. He just chose cryptocurrency to test his new technology. All this bubble and illusion were built by the scam of other greedy mankind afterwards. Greedy capitalist and scammer swallowed technology and then vomit all this disgusting puke. They abuse technology called blockchain to instigate a person to put money on the table. This is quite useful and graceful trick compared to old dirty scams such as inflation or others in terms of payback period and return rate. At the very heart of this bubble, there is a brokers who enjoy fee from crazy and massive trade of lunatic speculators.

Many media quotes Vitalik buterin and other cryptocurrency developers when it comes to economical meaning of cryptocurrencies. It is quite true that there are few experts who could explain about this prospect. However all cryptocurrency developers are just technician and never an economy experts. Dumping biased opinion of stakeholders without well balanced and comprehensive analysis will deepen the misunderstanding of ordinary people.

Actually there is one critical logical contradiction behind voice of independence of money. All those cryptocurrency advocators shout for independence of money by challenging 'nominal money'. However notion of 'nominal money' has no relation at all with 'legal tender'. Legal tender could be nominal fiat money as of today or could be gold standard as was in the 1960s. Thus what might be problem is nominal system, not legal tender system. In short, these crypto sophist's assertion can be summarized as following. "There is problem in nominal money and thus legal tender system should be removed "

Unless the distrust towards fiat money resolves, the thirst and desire will never disappear. However as explained several times, cryptocurrency with absolute anonymity is far from the solution and should never be allowed. This cannot be justified in any cases. It may have couple of advantages but the adverse effect from anonymity is too big to allow. Greedy capitalist and criminal who desperately needs shelter of black money will try their best to prolong and strengthen the power of cryptocurrencies. They will use all their power which includes political power also. I'm now writing a separate book for the scam of current financial system and hope to publish soon.

Meanwhile, blockchain has still long way to prove its real value. It has potential of transparency, safety, cost efficiency, and collaborative sharing economy. For example, huge financial company and government institute is quite well prepared to outside hackers. However fraud from insider is still a big problem. Insider can always have a chance to cheat on the system either voluntary for personal interest or from being forced by a person above. But a truth written in blockchain can never be removed. Once it is written, it is there as it was forever. In this sense a casual idea to adopt blockchain system for transparency of used car history such as mileage and accident record is quite interesting.

One final comment though is that many people advocate blockchain by saying that it will remove a necessity of third party and thus will remove unnecessary fee. This is truly quite amazing feature of blockchain. However removing third party always has counter effects also. There are areas or points where we desperately needs mediator. This is especially true in financial transaction and areas where criminal can abuse a vacancy of mediator. Simply saying, for me, I'll never use Air B&B if it is operating in full anonymity. It is as dangerous as you are in the middle of criminal den. On top of that, removing trust third party fee doesn't necessarily mean a reduction of fee as it can incur another unexpected fee.

We have to see the technology but without illusion.

Hope this book helps you better understand blockchain.

Appendix 1 – Structure of Block

Size of block – 4 Bytes

In the first 4 bytes of a block is an integer that represents the size of the entire block. In bitcoin blockchain data, a size block is limited to 1 MB You will know the validity of block in term of size simply looking at this this integer.

Block Header – 80 Bytes

The next 80 bytes are the block header and contain the summarized information of all the data in a block. Since block header is important, let's take a look into details of it first and then back to rest of block elements.

The following 6 information are in a block header.
- Version Information – 4 Bytes
- Previous block header hash – 32 Bytes
- Merkle tree root – 32 Bytes
- Time stamp – 4 Bytes
- Target difficulty bits – 4 Bytes
- Nonce – 4 Bytes

Block Header – Version information – 4 Bytes

The version information of a block represents the version of bitcoin system at the time of block creation. Version information is like legal revision information in real life. As laws get revised, rule of bitcoin blockchain may be changing. Decentralized consensus or block validity checking rules can be changed at any time as well. Therefore, version information is very important since it tells you what rules were applied to check the validity of the block as it was created.

Compared to centralized system, decentralized system is quite inefficient when it comes to maintenance and upgrading of a system. A centralized system can complete the job by replacing the software of the central server at a scheduled time all at once. Also, it can establish a certain schedule plan, anticipate an end date, and even anticipate expected influences of the update. However, in a case of decentralized system, a change in the system can only occur when every single member of the network voluntarily updates their software. Since there is no central server, all functions rely on the members of the network who have volunteered to join it, establishing a sophisticated schedule is impossible in the first place. Imagine, is it ever possible for tens of millions of voluntarily participants of a network to update their software all at once at a fixed time? Therefore, when scheduling a maintenance of a decentralized system software, you have to design it while keeping this fact in mind. A decentralized system can be categorized into two types according to how its software is revised: soft fork and hard fork.

i   A decentralized system sometime uses a software with a timer attached in order to have the similar effect as having everyone update their software at the same time. The software already has the new rules applied, but they are inactivated. So, when the scheduled time comes or certain conditions are met, they will activate all at the same time. Though limited, it can have a similar effect to a planned upgrade.

Block Header – Previous Block Hash – 32 Bytes

Every block has a unique number that helps identify itself. Earlier, it was said that a block can be compared to a certain page of a ledger. Every page of a ledger has a page number so that transactions can be searched for. This is similar to when we search for specific contents using indices and page numbers while reading a book. Likewise, each block has a unique number dedicated to it. This unique number is in the form of hash value which is 32 bytes long instead of a serial number.

Hash value of a previous block is used to make the hash value of the current block as well. Therefore, if one hash value is changed, then all the hash values after it would be changed, so it is easy to detect any changes.

Block Header – Merkle Tree Root – 32 Bytes

In a merkle tree root, a summarized information of all of 2000 ~ 3000 transactions is condensed and stored. Even the slightest change in a single transaction will cause the merkle tree root value to be changed. Therefore, it is designed in such a way that with only 32 bytes, a change in more than 2000 ~ 3000 transactions can be detected right away. This was explained in detail in *4.3.1. Merkle Tree.*

Block Header – Time Stamp – 4 Bytes

Time stamp is a 4 byte value that records the creation time of a block. In chapter 1, the creation time of genesis block and the # 500,000 block could be known all because of reading this field. Actually, this value on genesis block reads like 1231006505. This encrypted code looking value is in fact a time recorded in Unix time notation. Unix time notation sets 00:00:00, Jan 1st, 1970 as 0, and counts how many seconds have passed since then. Thus, 1231006505 on genesis block means that 1,231,006,505 seconds have passed since 00:00:00, Jan 1st, 1970. It is 18:15:05, Jan 3rd, 2009 in regular time notation.

All Blockchain data are stored separately on personal computers. Therefore, block creation times recorded in this field is actually recorded according to the local times, and these times may be slightly different from the accurate block creation times because the time on the local computer could be different from the actual time. For this reason, bitcoin system verifies the time recorded on a block by comparing it to the previous 11 blocks and currently connected peers. As a result, block creation time may have 1 ~ 2 hours of error from the actual block creation time.[c]

Do you remember the millennium bug incident in 2000? In old computer systems, only 2 digits were given for years, so 1999 would have to be written as 99. So, the bug was a kind of error by overflow that the next notation, 00, was recognized as 1900 instead of 2000. Unix time uses signed 32 bits, so the same problem will occur on Jan 29th, 2038 by overflow. After that time, the numbers go negative, so they are before Jan 1st, 1970. However, Unix time used by bitcoin system is unsigned. Thus, it can use one more bit, which was originally the sign bit. After all, extra 231 seconds are available, so it would be safe from overflow for another 68.1 years. Overflow of bitcoin system would happen in 2106, not 2038

Block Header – Target Difficulty Bit

Target difficulty bit records the difficulty information for generating a block. The reason why the word 'bit' is attached at the end is that the value itself is not the target difficulty. The target difficulty is a value recording conditions for finding the nonce which is the correct answer of a hash puzzle. The target difficulty is a very large number of 32 bytes in length, so it is compressed to 4 bytes using exponential notation to save memory. *Appendix 4 – Block's Difficulty* discusses how a 32-byte value can be restored from this 4 byte value and what target difficulty is in detail.

Block Header – Nonce – 4 Bytes

Nonce is the answer to a hash puzzle. When verifying the validity of a block, this nonce value is checked to see if it is the right answer. What hash puzzle really is and how to find a nonce is explained in *4.1.5. Nonce and block hash puzzle* in great detail.

Total number of transactions in a block – 1 ~ 9 bytes

So far we have looked through block header, now let's come back and see remaining components of a block. Earlier, it was said that a block typically stores 2000 ~ 3000 transactions. Thus, because the number of transactions is always variable, it is necessary to record how many transactions are in a block. This field, which is the third component of a block, stores an integer that is the total number of transactions in the block. However, in order to save memory, it uses 1 through 9 bytes according to actual number of transactions. It may look complicated, but it's necessary for saving memory.

The rules of using data variably is as follows. If the first byte is smaller than 0xFD(253 in decimal), then only one byte is used and itself is the number of transactions. In this case, 8 bytes have been saved in total. If the first byte is greater than or equal to 0xFD, then the following rules have to followed to use the remaining bytes. If the first byte is 0xFD, then the following 2 bytes represent the number of transactions. 3 bytes including the first byte were used. If the first byte is 0xFE, then the following 4 bytes, and if it's 0xFF, then the remaining 8 bytes represent the number of transactions. Table 1-1 summarizes the rules.

Value of first Byte	Number of the following bytes which represent the number of transactions	Total number of bytes used
< 0xFD	0	1
FD	2	3
FE	4	5
FF	8	9

Table 1-1 First byte value and transaction number bytes

All transactions in a block – Variable size

In this part, all of the actual transaction data are stored. 2,000 ~ 3,000 transactions are arranged in a row, and all the transactions are stored in a state of being connected in a line through a serialization process. The 32 bytes hash value constructed from the information of all transactions is stored here in the merkle tree root as described in 4.3.1. So if any minor changes occur here, we can immediately detect that through the merkle tree root value

Appendix 2 – Concepts of Hash Puzzle

The process of finding the correct answer to a hash puzzle is explained using pseudo code.

1. Set n = 0
2. Substitute the desired value given by bitcoin system in the Target variable. Target = get_target_value_from_system()
3. Compute f(n). f(n) is a hash function, which can verify PoW of bitcoin.
4. If f(n) <= Target, go to 6. If not, go to 5.
5. Increment n by 1 and go back to 3
6. n is the nonce value you are looking for. Report that n is the nonce and exit the program.

Let's take a look at each step.

Steps 1 and 2 are initialization steps where you initialize variable n and Target. n will store the nonce. Target is to be received from bitcoin core application. As explained earlier, bitcoin system adjusts the difficulty periodically, so the target value has to come from the system every time.

In step 3, a hash function, f(n), is computed. The correct answer mean an integer n which happens to result in hash value smaller than or equal to Target. That n become the nonce.

In 4, we check if f(n) is smaller than or equal to Target. If so, then we have the nonce. In this case, we go straight to step 6 and exit the program after reporting that n is the nonce and block has been completed. However, if f(n) is greater than Target, then you have to go to step 5 and increment n by 1. Then, you repeat the whole process again after going back to step 3.

Previously, it was explained that PoW needs to have an asymmetry property, so it would take a lot of effort and resources to do it, but it should be as simple as possible to verify the PoW. In the previous procedure, the procedure for verifying the PoW is to compare the value of f (n) with the Target. On the other hand, the procedure that requires PoW is to repeat the procedures 3 and 5 repeatedly. That is, it repeatedly calculates f (n) while incrementing n one by one.

Therefore, to design the previous procedure to meet the original purpose of the PoW, step 4 should be as simple as possible and steps 3 and 5 should be repeated as many as possible. The hash puzzle of bitcoin system is built on this very principle. The f (n) value in procedure (4) can be calculated in an instant, but it is designed to require a great deal of repetition for step (3) and (5) to find the nonce. In the case of # 450,000 block, it was necessary to repeat more than 2.97 billion times to find the right answer. It is a design that perfectly matches the asymmetric property of PoW.

I explained earlier that the size of the block header is fixed and its size is 80 bytes. Note that in this 80 bytes, there were 4 bytes to write the nonce, which was the last field in the block header. The nonce of the # 450000 block was 2,972,550,269. If it is expressed in hexadecimal, it becomes 0xb12d847d. Now, if you actually look into the block header of the # 450000 block directly, it is 80 bytes hexadecimal number as follows.

00000020daf37bb5b5d98651b1c65cdd1c34ce79ab5b48f0354a4c02000000000
0000000251952424d22534025140c2aabbda76b9bd60d103f49516408bd577df5
8c50ff9122895847cc0218*7d842db1*

Let's take a closer look at the last four bytes in *italic*. The value is 7d842db1. Compare this number with the nonce of the # 450000 block, 0xb12d847d, which was just calculated in hexadecimal. Have you found a relation? Let's look at the following figure.

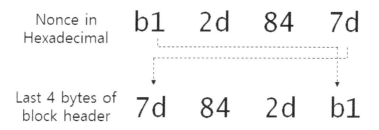

Figure 2-1 Nonce and the last 4 bytes of block header

Figure 2-1 shows the relationship between the nonce and the last 4 bytes of the block header. Yes. It is the same as the hexadecimal number of the nonce backwards in bytes. In other words, it was actually the nonce. It is like when you read a book, you do not read it from left to right, but from right to left in Arab countries. This inversion is referred to as the least end or little endian. Using this method, the high digits are placed on the right rather than on the left, so we use the word little - endian.

Now, if f (n) described above is described more precisely, it can be expressed as the following figure.

Figure 2-2 Detailed conceptual diagram of hash puzzle

Figure 2-2 is a conceptual diagram that explains f (n) described above in more detail. The role of the function f (n) is to calculate 80 bytes of block header using a hash function. In this case, increasing the value of n by 1 means calculating the hash value by changing the last four bytes of the block header(letters in the dotted box in Figure 2-2). Do you remember that the block header field also had a previous block hash value of 32 bytes? The previous block of # 450,000 blocks is of course # 449,999 block. If you actually look at the hash value of the # 449,999 block, its value in hexadecimal format is as follows:

0x00000000000000000024c4a35f0485bab79ce341cdd5cc6b15186d9b5b57bf3da

Some readers might have already noticed it, but this value is also in the 80 bytes of the block header we saw previously. Of course, it's inversed in little-endian way.

$$f(n) = Hash\left(\begin{matrix} \text{0x00000020}\underline{\text{daf37bb5b5d98651b}} \\ \underline{\text{1c65cdd1c34ce79ab5b48f0354a}} \\ \underline{\text{4c02000000000000000002519524}} \\ \text{24d22534025140c2aabbda76b9b} \\ \text{d60d103f49516408bd577df58c5} \\ \text{0ff9122895847cc0218}\textit{7d842db1} \end{matrix} \right)$$

Figure 2-3 Hash puzzle detailed conceptual diagram 2

Figure 2-3 shows the previous block hash value and the nonce part in the block header. In the figure, the part indicated by characters with under line is the previous block hash value, and the part indicated by italic characters is the previously described nonce value. If we actually calculate f (n), what is the result of the calculation? Is it an integer? If f (n) is computed, the result is an integer value of 32 bytes, which is always a fixed length, and the value is the hash value of this block! That is, the hash value of # 450,000 block is the hash value obtained through this process. How a hash value is actually calculated is explained in *4.1. Hash function*

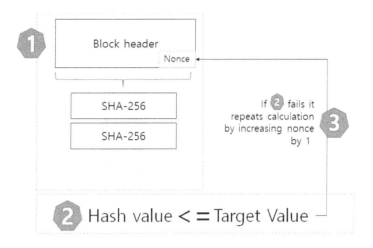

Figure 2-4 Finding Nonce

Figure 2-4 summarizes the process of finding a hash puzzle. In ①, double SHA-256 hash value of the block header is obtained. In ②, this value is compared with the block target value. If the value is larger than the block target value, the nonce is incremented by one in step ③, and then step ① is repeated. If it is smaller than or equal to the block target value in step ②, the nonce is found. So, the block is complete. This is completely in line with the procedure we looked at with the pseudo code in the previous section. The dotted box at the bottom of the block header in ① is the part in italic characters in Figure 2-2.

As we have seen, to obtain the hash value of a particular block, you have to keep changing the nonce to check if it meets the condition (= the hash value is less than or equal to the target value). To obtain the hash value of the current block, the hash value of the previous block must be known. Therefore, there is no way to calculate the block hash value in advance. This is because the hash value of the previous block must exist before the block hash value can be calculated. There may be a reader that is thinking "why don't we partially calculate hash value in advance except previous block hash?", but there is no such way. Due to the nature of the hash function, there is no way to calculate it partially beforehand.

It is very important that the hash value cannot be calculated in advance. That is why every time there is a winner of a block, all the other defeated nodes have to discard all their work and start to compete from the beginning. If someone creates a new block in the middle of a hard work, the value in the hash function that has been worked on suddenly becomes the previous of previous block hash value, not the previous block hash value. Therefore, even if the nonce is found, it is invalid. Finally, for a new operation, you should just read the hash value of the newly created block, set it to the previous block hash value in the block header, and start the operation again.

Appendix 3 – Bitcoin Address

Bitcoin uses bitcoin address for transaction. Bitcoin address serves as a kind of account number. A bitcoin address contains a lot of information, and the most important of which is the information associated with the public key you learned in asymmetric cryptography. A bitcoin address contains the cryptographic hash value of the public key of the person receiving the bitcoin. If the person paying the bitcoin uses the public key hash value contained in the bitcoin address for that transaction to lock it, the corresponding bitcoin can only be used by the person with the matching private key.

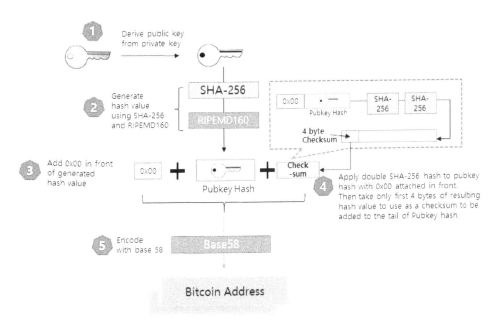

Figure 3-1 Creation of Bitcoin Address

Figure 3-1 shows the process of generating a bitcoin address. This address was automatically generated by wallet for you. The picture itself seems quite complicated. This is because there are many steps. However, each step uses a method that we already know and is not at a level that you cannot understand. However, RIPEMD 160 in ② and Base 58 in ⑤ are introduced for the first time. However, as you can guess that SHA-256 generates a 256-bit hash value, while not knowing the internal operation principle of SHA-256, RIPEMD160 is a kind of hash function, and it can be guessed that the output would be 160 bits. RIPEMD 160 is a type of hash function and its output is 160 bits. RIPEMD160 is a hash function made by the academia compared to SHA, which was led by the US National Security Agency. Because of this, RIPEMD160 is not much used compared to SHA-2. Its performance is known to be similar to that of SHA-1. RIPEMD has 128, 160, 256, and 320 bit versions of the algorithms, which are labeled RIPEMD-128, RIPEMD-160, RIPEMD-256, and RIPEMD-320, respectively.

Let's look at the figure again. In ①, the bitcoin wallet first generates a private key and derives a public key to be paired with it. The generated public key value becomes a 256-bit hash value through SHA-256 in ②, and the value changes to a 160-bit hash value through RIPEMD 160 hash function immediately. The 160-bit or 20-byte hash value is incremented by one byte before through ③, and after ④, the remaining four bytes are added, and everything changes to a 25-byte value. The byte added in the front in ③ is just 0. That is, simply 0x00 in hexadecimal. The four bytes added in ④ are a check sum. The rule for making checksums in ④ is simple. As shown in the box at ④, add 0x00 to the front of the public key hash value generated in ②, and apply SHA-256 hash twice consecutively. Take only the first four bytes of the generated 256-bit hash value and discard the rest. These four bytes become the checksum and get appended to the end of the public key hash value.

⑤ is the process of encoding with base 58Check. Since base 58 is encoding, not hash, please don't guess that it will generate 58 bits. Base 58 replaces an arbitrary number with a combination of familiar numbers and alphabets. It is mainly used to convert binary file types into a combination of numbers or alphabets, which was often used to attach arbitrary binary files to e-mails in the past when e-mail was not able to process binary files. Base 58 is similar to the somewhat coarse hash function we made earlier.

0	1	2	3	4	5	6	7	8	9	10	11	12	13	14	15	16	18	19	20
1	2	3	4	5	6	7	8	9	A	B	C	D	E	F	G	H	J	K	M

21	22	23	24	25	26	27	28	29	30	31	32	33	34	35	36	37	38	39	40
N	P	Q	R	S	T	U	V	W	X	Y	Z	a	b	c	d	e	f	g	h

41	42	43	44	45	46	47	48	49	50	51	52	53	54	55	56	57
i	j	k	m	n	o	p	q	r	s	t	u	v	w	x	y	z

Figure 3-2 Bitcoin base 58 mapping

Figure 3-2 shows the base 58 mapping of bitcoin. Numbers 0 through 57 correspond to numbers and alphabets. How you encode the input value with base 58 is easy, if you think of it as a base 58 calculation. First divide the input value by 58, and then map the remainder (from 0 to 57) to the base 58 table. The quotient is again divided by 58 and the remainder is mapped again. Repeat until there is no more quotient so that all input values are converted into base 58. This is similar to expressing a given number in 58-decimal notation.

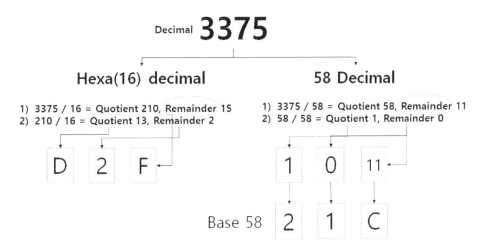

Figure 3-3 How to convert decimal 3375 to hexadecimal and 58-decimal, respectively.

Figure 3-3 shows how to convert decimal 3375 to hexadecimal and base 58, respectively. As 10 to 15 are mapped to A to F in hexadecimal, base 58 similarly

289

maps from 10 to 57 to corresponding alphabet and numbers. That is, once you have expressed it in base 58, you can rewrite it according to the base 58 table. One process that needs to be taken care of is when there are consecutive leading zeros. For example, decimals 03375, 003375, and 000003375 are all 3375, and the leading consecutive zeros have no meaning in algebra, but all must be taken into consideration in case of encoding as each digit occupies a certain position. Thus, 003375 and 3375 show the same result with a 58-decimal conversion calculation, but the result is different for base 58 encoding. In this case, you can use the method of separating the leading consecutive zeros and the remainder to convert the leading zeros to all 1s in byte units, and the remainder to combine the two numbers using the original exponentiation. Due to process ③ in Figure 3-1, at least 1 byte of 0 is always present in the bitcoin address at the front. As mentioned earlier, the leading zeros do not affect division algebra even if they exist. Therefore, when creating a bitcoin address, if there are leading zeros in ⑤, it should all be separated and converted to 1's in byte unit and just put them in front of address. Figure 3-4 illustrates this method with a picture.

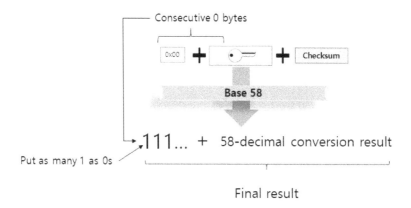

Figure 3-4 Taking care of the leading 0s in base 58

Because of this property of base 58, bitcoin addresses always have the following two characteristics:

- Bitcoin addresses always begin with 1. In step ③ of Figure 3-1, we added 1 byte 0 at the beginning, because 0 is mapped to 1, as shown in the table above.
- The number of divisions can vary depending on number and as a result, the length of a bitcoin address is variable. In other words, the length of the address is not fixed but varies up to 34 characters.

In the past, base 64 was generally used, then base 58 was designed without those couple of letters that look alike: 0, O, I, and l. Because of this, base 64 has an official mapping table, but in the case of base 58, it may vary slightly from application to application. Therefore, the base 58 mentioned here is bitcoin base 58, and the mapping order may be different from the base 58 used in other applications.

More details on Bitcoin address can be found on BitcoinWiki. (https://en.bitcoin.it/wiki/Technical_background_of_version_1_Bitcoin_address es)

Appendix 4 – Block difficulty adjustment

It was previously explained that, the target value is 32 bytes, but it was stored in 4 bytes in order to save storage. So the field name is not target difficulty but target difficulty bits. This section describes how to calculate a complete 32-byte target value from the 4 byte target difficulty bits.

First, let's randomly select any block, for example, block 431,201, and then read the target difficulty bit value written in this block. The target difficulty bit in this block has a value of 0x1804de5e.

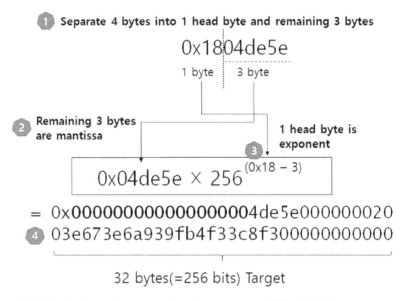

Figure 4-1 Calculation of target value from target difficulty bit

Figure 4-1 shows the process of generating the target value from the target difficulty bits. In ①, the 4-byte target difficulty bit value is split into the first 1 byte and the remaining 3 bytes respectively. In this case, the last 3 bytes serve as a mantissa and the first 1 byte serves as an exponent. In ②, the last 3 bytes are placed in the mantissa. On the other hand, ③ shows that the first byte is placed in the exponent part. By calculating the target value using the formula in the figure, we can get the 32-byte target value as ④.

Earlier it was said that the difficulty is automatically adjusted every time 2016 blocks are generated. This difficulty has continued to increase since genesis block was created. Generally, if we set the difficulty of genesis block to 1 then we can compare relative difficulty of the adjusted one. Now, let's compare how much the difficulty of block 431,201 has increased compared to the difficulty of genesis block. First, let's calculate the target value of genesis block in the same way. If we look at the block header of genesis block, the target difficulty bit is 0x1d00ffff. Now let's calculate 32-byte target value from this target bits using the same method we have applied just before.

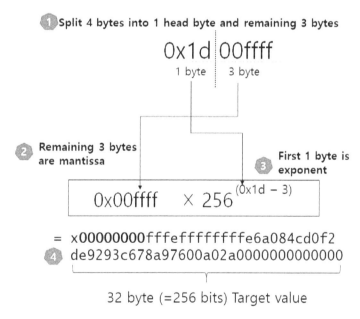

Figure 4-2 Calculation of Genesis Block's Target Value

Figure 4-2 shows the process of calculating the block target value from the target difficulty bits of genesis block using the same rules. There are only eight consecutive 0s in the result of ④! Even at a glance, its difficulty seems so much easier than that of block 431,201. Now if we divide ④ of Figure 4-2, which is the target value of genesis block, by ④ in Figure 4-1, we can get the difficulty level of block 431201 in the multiple of genesis block difficulty. The value is 225,832,872,179.45914. In other words, the difficulty of block 431,201 is 225,832,328,179 times more difficult than genesis block.

Appendix 5 – Transaction Script

Bitcoin transactions are described in a script language. A script language is a simplified programming language, and it can be thought of as a sequence of tasks that the computer must perform. You can think of JavaScript language. Normally, bitcoin transactions are represented through the JSON format, and in this section we will also look at the contents of generic transactions using this format.

> JSON stands for JavaScript Object Notation. It is a data exchange format that is easy to read and is easy to analyze and create, making it a commonly used language as part of the JavaScript language. It is completely independent of all programming languages, but has borrowed a lot of notations from the C language, such as C or C ++. It is also the most commonly used data format for asynchronous communication between browser and server.

Figure 5-1 shows a typical transaction shown in JSON format. The transaction consists of an input part ① that collects UTXO and income part of bitcoin, and an output part ② which is a part that spends it.

```
{
    "txid": "324fb0facb6f90491b9de83013863807544f6f71c0614edb90a1edd6e938deb0",
    "hash": "324fb0facb6f90491b9de83013863807544f6f71c0614edb90a1edd6e938deb0",
    "version": 1,
    "size": 374,
    "vsize": 374,
    "locktime": 0,
    "vin": [
      {
        "txid": "190e17101c295fb72fecbb4c951c66ed12bde057a4acb5b482a08677c0f9c1cc",
        "vout": 1,
        "scriptSig": {
          "asm":
"3045022100eb72a9ca47cffe9744353d4a38b460fbdbc15a81025f4b4f6bd5ffcfec56356102201a82d2273c938894809bc949176da393e4b09c11265dae
6ba195ca3754e147fb[ALL] 03b18e31a12cc65a9a19fb4e73e44ac4af42f1efe2dc44dc97f2d0afd3f1749ef5",
          "hex":
"483045022100eb72a9ca47cffe9744353d4a38b460fbdbc15a81025f4b4f6bd5ffcfec56356102201a82d2273c938894808bc949176da393e4b09c11265d
ae6ba195ca3754e147fb012103b18e31a12cc65a9a19fb4e73e44ac4af42f1efe2dc44dc97f2d0afd3f1749ef5"
        },
        "sequence": 4294967295
      },
      {
        "txid": "2da4ba7e9313489d0d229ffbeadec64cfba2eea448d89b151d9e7e953737d4de",
        "vout": 1,
        "scriptSig": {
          "asm":
"3045022100f065dd89940261a88031560d74428b98b5aac612fa58fbe4d7a71cbea518158702203d018b3dd95513e20b1800e107bee69c92307ea9e790ce8
b2db7086c8b0f24d0e[ALL] 03b18e31a12cc65a9a19fb4e73e44ac4af42f1efe2dc44dc97f2d0afd3f1749ef5",
          "hex":
"483045022100f065dd89940261a88031560d74428b98b5aac612fa58fbe4d7a71cbea518158702203d018b3dd95513e20b1800e107bee69c92307ea9e790b
e5b2db7086c8b0f24d0e012103b18e31a12cc65a9a19fb4e73e44ac4af42f1efe2dc44dc97f2d0afd3f1749ef5"
        },
        "sequence": 4294967295
      }
    ],
    "vout": [
      {
        "value": 0.04000000,
        "n": 0,
        "scriptPubKey": {
          "asm": "OP_DUP OP_HASH160 51025d6d2ef8a3ed522e0b2cfe9b8a393b4fc540 OP_EQUALVERIFY OP_CHECKSIG",
          "hex": "76a91451025d6d2ef8a3ed522e0b2cfe9b8a393b4fc54088ac",
          "reqSigs": 1,
          "type": "pubkeyhash",
          "addresses": [
            "18PLZrkEhCrkDAuBk4ZKovsFJUgAzCSVLb"
          ]
        }
      },
      {
        "value": 0.00877108,
        "n": 1,
        "scriptPubKey": {
          "asm": "OP_DUP OP_HASH160 d3f0c771e2ea4612f992710d227fe058e09713e8 OP_EQUALVERIFY OP_CHECKSIG",
          "hex": "76a914d3f0c771e2ea4612f992710d227fe058e09713e88ac",
          "reqSigs": 1,
```

Figure 5-1 Transaction in JSON Format

If you look the transactions represented in JSON format, most of them are hexadecimal numbers, but in ②, there are also some other parts that look like commands such as OP_DUP. Now, let's look at the input part, ①, and the output part, ②, one by one.

Input

Figure 5-2 shows an enlarged view of the input portion of Figure 5-1.

```
"vin": [
    {
①      "txid": "190e17101c295fb72fecbb4c951c66ed12bde057a4acb5b482a08677c0f9c1cc",
        "vout": 1,
        "scriptSig": {
            "asm":  "3045022100eb72a9ca47cffe9744353d4a38b460fbdbc15a81025f4b4f6bd5ff
                     cfec56356102201a82d2273c938894808bc949176da393e4b09c11265dae6ba1
                     95ca3754e147fb01  03b18e31a12cc65a9a19fb4e73e44ac4af42f1efe2d
②                   c44dc97f2d0afd3f1749ef5",
            "hex":  "483045022100eb72a9ca47cffe9744353d4a38b460fbdbc15a81025f4b4f6bd5
                     ffcfec56356102201a82d2273c938894808bc949176da393e4b09c11265dae6b
                     a195ca3754e147fb012103b18e31a12cc65a9a19fb4e73e44ac4af42f1efe2dc
                     44dc97f2d0afd3f1749ef5"
        },
③      "sequence": 4294967295
    },
    {
        "txid": "2da4ba7e9313489d0d2296fbeadec64cfba2eea448d89b151d9e7e953737d4de",
        "vout": 1,
④      "scriptSig": {
            "asm":

                        • • •
```

Figure 5-2 Input part of a transaction

The top of ① indicates the part where this input is coming from. Please recall that an input is always from someone's output unless it is a coinbase transaction. The 32 byte hash value in txid can be guessed to be the second entry of the output, since the source of this input is the transaction number and vout is 1. This index of input and output always starts from 0, so 1 is the second item. However, no matter what you look at, there is no information on BTC balance of this input. This can be known only by backtracking the output transaction.

Let's track this transaction by actually using the ID 190e17101c295fb72fecbb4c951c66ed12bde057a4acb5b482a08677c0f9c1cc recorded in ①. Figure 5-3 shows the transaction that has been traced directly using this ID. First, if you look at ① in Figure 5-3, you can see that this transaction exactly matches the ID of the transaction in Figure 5-2. If you look at the second item in the output section of this transaction, you can find the part with 0.01683108 bitcoin. This is the output that was the source of the input. Since both the input and output indices start at 0, we can see that 1 is the second item and n: 1. We have now confirmed that the amount of input, after tracing, is 0.01683108 BTC.

```
{
    "txid": "190e17101c295fb72fecbb4c951c66ed12bde057a4acb5b482a08677c0f9c1cc",
 ❶ "hash": "190e17101c295fb72fecbb4c951c66ed12bde057a4acb5b482a08677c0f9c1cc",
    "version": 1,

                          ...

    "vout": [
        {
            "value": 0.02222000,
            "n": 0,
            "scriptPubKey": {
                "asm": "OP_DUP OP_HASH160 4222ccb4c6e61f7dfad676a4caec8eeb98c7ce1a OP_EQUALVERIFY OP_CHECKSIG",
                "hex": "76a9144222ccb4c6e61f7dfad676a4caec8eeb98c7ce1a88ac",
                "reqSigs": 1,
                "type": "pubkeyhash",
                "addresses": [
                    "172hHajw61JJh6CRPEzH1j88Pcg4Vh5nAq"
                ]
            }
        },
 ❷      {
            "value": 0.01683108,
            "n": 1,
            "scriptPubKey": {
                "asm": "OP_DUP OP_HASH160 d3f0c771e2ea4612f992710d227fe058e09713e8 OP_EQUALVERIFY OP_CHECKSIG",
                "hex": "76a914d3f0c771e2ea4612f992710d227fe058e09713e888ac",
                "reqSigs": 1,
                "type": "pubkeyhash",
                "addresses": [
                    "1LKe26oiEmpjybYTxDDLxSspQgZ3EcppiD"
                ]
            }
        }
    ]
}
```

Output

Figure 5-3 Transaction 190e17101c295fb72fecbb4c951c66ed12bde057a4acb5b482a08677c0f9c1cc

Let's go back to Figure 5-2 and take a closer look at the second box, item ②. In item ②, there is a part marked asm and hex in the lower part of ScriptSig. We do not know what exactly it is, but it seems like there are two entries under ScriptSig. The role of these two values in ScriptSig will be discussed in detail when I explain the execution part of the script later. Here, it is OK for us just understand that item ② contains information that can prove ownership of this UTXO. That is, in item ②, there is a script which describes how to unlock the lock with the encryption key, and it can open the lock device described in PTPKH.

Item ③ is called sequence but it is not used for now. It is an item that has never been used, actually. When designing the initial bitcoin system, there were some special functions built into transaction. A timer was put on transaction and it prevented it from processing the transaction during that time. If you want to change the transaction within that time, you can create a new transaction at any time and write in a larger sequence value, which is designed to ignore previous transactions with lower sequence values. However, this function was never used.

④ is another input. Since there may be an arbitrary number of inputs, this part is repeated as many times as the number. There is also no information on the input of ④ on how many BTC it is. Again, you should trace the transaction as before. If you actually trace back the transaction, you can see that the amount is 0.03204000 Bitcoin.

Output

Let's look at the output section from now on. Figure 5-4 is an enlargement of ② of the previous figure 5-1. In ① of figure 5-4, this output was to spend 0.04 BTC and from n: 0, we know that it is the first expenditure item.

```
        "vout": [
        {
①       "value": 0.04000000,
        "n": 0,
        "scriptPubKey": {
②       "asm": "OP_DUP OP_HASH160 51025d6d2ef8a3ed522e0b2cfe9b8a393b4fc540 OP_EQUALVERIFY OP_CHECKSIG",
        "hex": "76a91451025d6d2ef8a3ed522e0b2cfe9b8a393b4fc54088ac",
        "reqSigs": 1,
        "type": "pubkeyhash",
③       "addresses": [
        "18PLZrkEhCrkDAuBk4ZKovsFJUgAzCSVLb"
        ]
        },
        {
④       "value": 0.00677108,
        "n": 1,
        "scriptPubKey": {
                        • • •
```

Figure 5-4 Output Part of a Transaction

In the previous section where we examined input part, the amount was not specified anywhere, but in output part the amount is clearly specified. Someone who has received this bitcoin will not have the amount in input part, and thus would track back to this place to look up balance as if we did trace back the transaction to check the amount of the input. Remember that item ② is the lock part described in PTPKH, and the person who can unlock it is the person with the corresponding private key and public key. If you look closely at the "asm" part of ②, you will see something like OP_DUP OP_HASH160, unlike the input that was filled with hexadecimals. This is the script code that specifies how to unlock the lock. To unlock it, you need to make sure that the final result is TRUE through the execution of the script. If true, the lock can be unlocked by proving that it is the owner, and if the last result is FALSE, the lock cannot be released. Item ③ is the bitcoin address of the person to receive this output. The bitcoin address mentioned above contains the public key hash value of the recipient of the money. Another output is recorded in item ④. Like the input, there can be any number of outputs and they are repeated as many as that number. In both output and input, the index is zero-based. So the second output is written as n: 1.

Execution/Running of Script

Now let's take a closer look at how to run the commands in the script we saw just before. To put it briefly, the input section contains the public key and private key information for unlocking the script. The output section is locked so that you can run the script in the output section to open the lock only when the value is TRUE.

Figure 5-5 Locking of UTXO

Figure 5-5 shows only the part of the output where the script was located. This script part is composed of 5 items, ①, ②, ④, and ⑤ are all script commands, and ③ is a public key hash value that changes according to the recipient. If we denote variable as <>, the above items can be rewritten as follows.

300

OP_DUP OP_HASH160 <PubKeyHash> OP_EQUALVERIFY OP_CHECKSIG

The public key hash value has been replaced with the variable <PubKeyHash>. This variable is assigned the public key hash value of the recipient. Public key hash is described more in detail in *Appendix 3 - Bitcoin Address*.

①

```
"asm":  "3045022100eb72a9ca47cffe9744353d4a38b460fbdbc15a81025f4b4f6bd5ff
        fec56356102201a82d2273c938894808bc949176da393e4b09c11265dae6ba195
        ca3754e147fb01  03b18e31a12cc65a9a19fb4e73e44ac4af42f1efe2dc44d
        c97f2d0afd3f1749ef5"
```
②

Figure 5-6 Information on unlocking the UTXO

Figure 5-6 shows a closer look at the ScriptSig part of the previous section. The picture is divided into two parts. The long number starting with 30450221 and ending with 01 is the item ①, and the part in ② is next item. Items ① and ② are information of private key and public key for proving ownership of UTXO, respectively, and this is also a variable that changes according to the person. Therefore, if we use the variable notation <> here again, we can express ① as <Sig> and ② as <PubKey>. ① <Sig> is the signature part signed with the private key and ② <PubKey> is the public key part.

Figure 5-6 can now be simplified as follows.

<Sig> <PubKey>

i The private key of the bitcoin is a value signed by asymmetric encryption method called ECDSA and then encoded by the DER(Distinguished Encoding Rules). In Figure 5-6, there are parts marked with bold and large fonts, all of which have special meanings. The leading 30450221 has codes of 0x30, 0x45, 0x02, and 0x21 respectively. This part of the bitcoin transaction input is most likely to start with 30450221. 0x30 indicates the starting point of DER. 0x45 indicates the length, which means that it has a length of 69 bytes since it is hexadecimal 0x45 = 69. 0x02 means that the following numbers are integers. 0x21 means the length of the whole integer, which means that the 33 bytes integer is obtained because 0x21 = 33. In the second line, the bold and large text 0220 is also a code of 0x02 and 0x20. Likewise, since it is 0x02, the integer starts and its length means 0x20 = 32 bytes. The bold and large text 0x01 on the third line means SIGHASH_ALL, which means that this signature applies to all inputs and outputs. Sometimes, [01] is displayed instead of 01. Actually, ① in Figure 5-1 is labeled [ALL] instead of 01.[K]

Now, before you get to know the script in earnest, you need to know about stack based languages. The script language used for bitcoin transaction is based on Forth, a stack based language developed by Charles Moore in 1970. To understand this script, you have to understand the data structure of the stack. If you understand the concept of a stack, then the script is very simple to understand, and until you understand the concept of the stack, it can be somewhat difficult to understand because of the order of operations. Let's look briefly at the concept of the stack, and then continue with the script for the bit coin transaction.

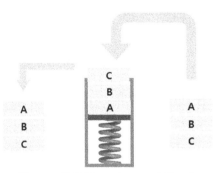

Figure 5-7 Structure of Stack

Stack means stacking up. As shown in Figure 5-7, the first data entered is the bottom and the last data is the top. When you take out the data, the most recent entry is at the top, so the first entry is at the bottom and the last entry is at the bottom. As shown in the figure, A, B, and C are stored in the order of storage, but when they come out, the order of C, B, and A is reversed. Due to this nature of the stack, this structure is also referred to as last-in-first-out (LIFO) or first-in-last-out (FILO).

Now that we know the basic nature of the stack, let's look at stack operations. The formula we are familiar with is infix notation. In the infix notation operator is placed between the operands to be operated such as the addition or subtraction operators. 3 + 2, 2 - 4, or 4+3-2 and so on.

However, in computer computation it is often more convenient to use so-called postfix notation. In postfix notation operator is placed after the operands, and not between. That is, if the above example is expressed in the postfix method, it would become 32+, 24-, 43 + 2-. Now I'll explain how this post fix operation actually work with following figure.

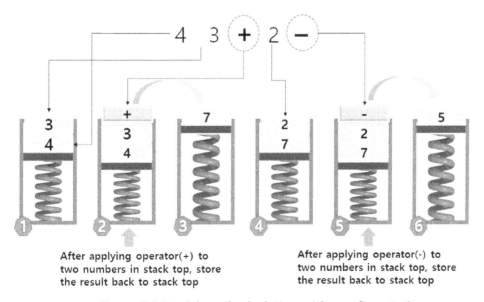

After applying operator(+) to two numbers in stack top, store the result back to stack top

After applying operator(-) to two numbers in stack top, store the result back to stack top

Figure 5-8 Stack based calculation with postfix notation

Figure 5-8 shows the stack based operation method in postfix notation. The principle is simple, if you meet a number, just stacks on top. Then, when you meet operator then operator is applied to number(s) at the top defined by the operator (two in case of + or -), and the result is restored back to the top.

Let's look at ①. 4 and 3 are numbers, so we just stack them to top. Since the + operator in ② and the + operator is defined as adding two numbers, the result calculated by applying + operator to top two numbers 3 and 4 are stored at the top of the stack, which is 7 in ③. In ④, 2 is a number, so we just stack it to top again and then if we see the operator - in ⑤, apply the - operator to the top two numbers 2 and 7 and finally the result 5 is stored at the top.

Like infix, the order of operators and numbers is also very important in postfix. If we specify 43 + 2- as 432 + -, we get a completely different result.

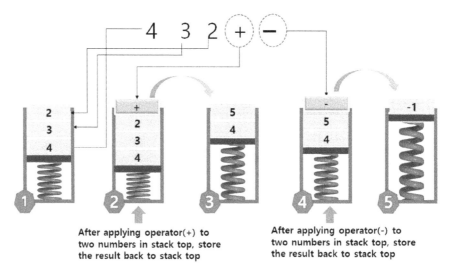

After applying operator(+) to two numbers in stack top, store the result back to stack top

After applying operator(-) to two numbers in stack top, store the result back to stack top

Figure 5-9 Change of result when the order is changed

Figure 5-9 shows the process in which the calculation result changes when the order of operation notation changes. One thing to note is that in previous example, all operators use two operands but depending on the definition of operator it could be zero or any numbers.

If we denote 4 3 + 2 - in actual bitcoin script it can expressed as follows.

4 3 OP_ADD 2 OP_SUB

It is basically the same as the postfix notation except that OP_ADD is used instead of + and OP_SUB is used instead. This operation is written using the actual bitcoin script. So if you actually write this operation in a Bitcoin transaction, the system will get a result of 5 through the calculation.

Now that we have a look at the stack and stack based operations, let's look at the lock and key scripts again.

1 <Sig> <PubKey>

2 <OP_DUP OP_HASH160 <PubkeyHash> OP_EQUALVERIFY OP_CHECKSIG

Figure 5-10 Key and Locking – Unlock script and lock script

In Figure 5-10, ① is a key script containing information that can unlock the UTXO with the script in the input part, and ② is a lock script that locks the UTXO to prevent anyone from accessing it. Because of this, ① is usually called Unlock Script (or ScripSigs) and ② is called Lock Script (or ScriptPub). Now if the result of apply ① to ② is TRUE, then it will open the lock. The definitions of all the operations used in this script are shown in Table 5-1.

Operator	Operand	Explanation

OP_DUP	x	Copy x
OP_HASH160	x	RIPEMD-160(SHA-256(x))
OP_EQUAL	x, y	True if x and y are the same. If not, False.
OP_VERIFY	x	Remove the top item of stack. Then if the top item was False, transactions is invalid. It if was True, nothing happens.
OP_EQUALVERIFY		Execute OP_EQUAL and OP_VERIFY in order
OP_CHECKSIG	<Sig> <PubKey>	Check if <PubKey> and <Sig> are derived from private key. If True, then put True in stack. If False, then put False in stack.

Table 5-1 Operators and their meanings

💡 More detailed explanation on all the operators used by Bitcoin should referred to (https://en.bitcoin.it/wiki/Script)

Now that you've learned the stack based language and the definition of the operator, let's actually open the lock. The script for opening the lock with the key is to connect ① and ② and write as follows.

<Sig> <PubKey> OP_DUP OP_HASH160 <PubkeyHash> OP_EQUALVERIFY OP_CHECKSIG

Figure 5-11 illustrates the above script with a picture. Now let's try to run the script one by one, following the picture. Here, it is assumed that the actual owner is processing the operation.

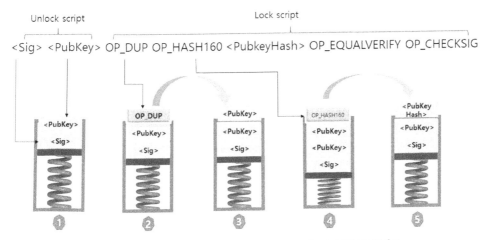

Figure 5-11 Executing script to unlock UTXO (1/2)

* Step ①: <Sig> and <PubKey> are not an operator, so they are stacked on top.

* Step ②: OP_DUP is an operator and the definition is "to copy value at the top of the stack ".

* Step ③: As a result of OP_DUP, <PubKey> is cloned and stacked at the top.

* Step ④: OP_HASH160 is also an operator, which does 'to hash the value at top of the stack with SHA-256, and then hash the result with RIPEMD-160'. This is exactly the same procedure as we saw in bitcoin address.

* Step ⑤: <PubKeyHash> was created as a result of executing the operation instruction of ④ and result is stacked at top.

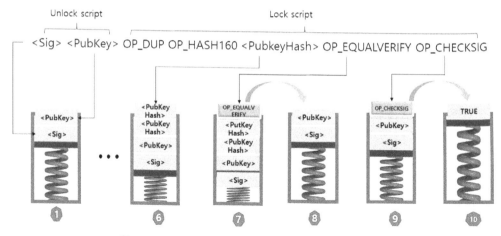

Figure 5-11 Executing script to unlock UTXO (2/2)

* Step ⑥: ⑥ is not an operator but a number <PubKeyHash>, so it is stacked on top.

* Step ⑦: OP_EQUALVERIFY is a compound operation instruction. This is combination of OP_EQUAL and OP_VERIFY, first OP_EUAL is applied and then OP_VERIFY is applied. The definition of OP_EQUAL is that if the two topmost figures are the same, then the TRUE value is stacked on top, or if it is different, the FALSE value is stacked on top. OP_VERIFY is defined as 'if the topmost value of the stack is FALSE, it indicates that the transaction is invalid and deletes the top value. If the top value of the stack is TRUE, only the top value is removed and nothing happens. Thus, we first compare the top of the stack, <PubKeyHash>, with the second, <PubKeyHash>, and return TRUE because these two values are equal. Since this value is successively TRUE through OP_VERIFY, it simply removes this value and nothing happens.

* Step ⑧: ⑧ is the result of ⑦, and after removing the uppermost value, TURE, <PubKey> which is below now become the top.

* Step ⑨: OP_CHECKSIG is an operation command. The definition of OP_CHECKSIG is to make sure that <PubKey> is derived from the private key of <Sig>, and TRUE is stacked on top if it is correct, and FALSE is stacked on top if it is not. As a result of this command, <PubKey> returns TRUE because it is derived from the private key of <Sig>.

308

* Step ⑩: As a result of ⑨, the final value is TRUE, and as a result, it is proved that the owner of this output is correct.

Step ⑦ is a procedure for checking the public key hash value first, and step ⑨ is a procedure for checking whether the private key and the public key match. Therefore, if you do not have the corresponding private key, you will not be able to go through step ⑨ and fail to release the lock. Only the person with the proper private key can go through all the steps and release the lock completely.

Implementing transactions in scripts has several advantages. There is no need to modify an existing program, even if you change the way to verify that a transaction is valid, or if you add several alternate rules. If there is a change in the rule, only the script needs to be newly written, so the rule for verifying the validity of the transaction can be operated very flexibly. The part that is described in the script for verification is called the transaction puzzle. This transaction puzzle must be resolved before it proves the ownership.

Reference

A. 'Korea electronics statistics' ,KEPKO, 2016

B [Consensus Rules Changes] bitcoin.

https://bitcoin.org/en/developer-guide#consensus-rule-changes

C [Block timestamp] bitcoinwiki.

https://en.bitcoin.it/wiki/Block_timestamp

D 'Isaac Newton was a genius, but even he lost millions in the stock market', Business
Insider, Elena Holodny, 2017

http://www.businessinsider.com/isaac-newton-lost-a-fortune-on-englands-hotteststock-
2016-1

E 『The Age of Discontinuity』, Routledge, Peter Drucker, 1992

F 'Federal Reserve Board issues final rule regarding dividend payments on Reserve Bank
capital stock', Board of Governors of the FRS, 2016

https://www.federalreserve.gov/newsevents/pressreleases/bcreg20161123a.htm

G 『The Island of Stone Money: UAP of The Carolines』, Cornell University Library, William
Henry Furness, 2009

H 'Global Financial Stability Report October 2017', IMF, 2017

I 'The Byzantine Generals Problem', ACM Transactions on Programming Languages and
Systems, Vol.4 No.3, Leslie Lamport, Robert Shostak, Marshall Pease, 1982

J 'Bitcoin: A Peer-to-Peer Electronics Cash System', Nakamoto Satoshi, 2008

K [Elliptic-curve cryptography] Wikipedia.

https://en.wikipedia.org/wiki/Elliptic-curve_cryptography

L [Initial coin offering] Wikipedia.

https://en.wikipedia.org/wiki/Initial_coin_offering

M [Merkle tree] Wikipedia.

https://en.wikipedia.org/wiki/Merkle_tree

N [Proof-of-work System] Wikipedia.

https://en.wikipedia.org/wiki/Proof-of-work_system#cite_note-DwoNao1992-1

O [Cryptography] Wikipedia.

https://en.wikipedia.org/wiki/Cryptography

P [Nick Leeson] Wikipedia.

https://en.wikipedia.org/wiki/Nick_Leeson

Q [Zimbabwean dollar] Wikipedia.
https://en.wikipedia.org/wiki/Zimbabwean_dollar

R [SilkRoad] Wikipedia.
https://en.wikipedia.org/wiki/Silk_Road_(marketplace)

S 「The intelligent investor」, HarperBusiness, Benjamin graham, 2016

T 「The essential drucker」, HarperBusiness, Peter F. Drucker, 2001

U 「The death of money」, Portfolio, James Rickards, 2015

V 「The new case for gold」, Portfolio, James Rickards, 2016

W 「Inflation - Die ersten zweitausend Jahre」,, Hanno Beck, Urban Bacher, Marco Herrmann, 2017

X [SegWit] Wikipedia.https://en.wikipedia.org/wiki/SegWit

Y 「Currency War」, CITIC Press Corporation , song hong bin, 2008

Z 「Exchange rate war」, Wang yang, 2011

a 'Uncomfortable truth behind stock trading turnover rate', Hanwha security, 2013

www.ingramcontent.com/pod-product-compliance
Lightning Source LLC
Chambersburg PA
CBHW062108050326
40690CB00016B/3253